CARING CULTURES

CARING CULTURES
HOW CONGREGATIONS RESPOND TO THE SICK

Susan J. Dunlap

BAYLOR UNIVERSITY PRESS

Cover Design by Nicole Weaver, Zeal Design
Cover art based on *Peace Wall* by Jane Golden and Peter
Pagast, ©1998 City of Philadelphia Mural Arts Program.
Mural photo by Jack Ramsdale. Used by permission.

Library of Congress Cataloging-in-Publication Data

Dunlap, Susan J., 1956-
  Caring cultures : how congregations respond to the sick /
Susan J. Dunlap.
      p. cm.
  Includes bibliographical references and index.
  ISBN 978-1-932792-87-4 (pbk. : alk. paper)
  1. Church work with the sick--North Carolina--Durham.
2. Church work with the sick--North Carolina. 3. Care of
the sick--North Carolina--Durham. 4. Care of the sick--North
Carolina. 5. Care of the sick--Religious aspects--Christianity.
6. Religious gatherings--Christianity. I. Title.

  BV4460.D86 2009
  259'.409756563--dc22
                                        2009003947

Printed in the United States of America on acid-free paper with
a minimum of 30% pcw recycled content.

This book is dedicated to
my parents,
Harold and Jean

TABLE OF CONTENTS

ACKNOWLEDGMENTS

$\mathcal{M}$uch gratitude is due the Louisville Institute for funding this research and writing project through a General Grant.

I also want to thank the people who read parts of the manuscript and offered excellent advice: Homer Ashby, Mary McClintock Fulkerson, Susan Hazlett, Leonard Hummel, Kate Joyce, Judy Pidcock, and Rob Parker. Teresa Berger, Tracy Mancini, Darryl Owens, Denise Thorpe, and William C. Turner were invaluable consultants along the way.

To the pastors whom I interviewed, I give my deepest thanks. For their willingness to open themselves and their congregations to me and my tape recorder, I am grateful. I wish I could recognize them all by name.

Enormous gratitude goes to the care givers and care receivers whom I interviewed, who allowed me to record their words of passion, pain, and faith, which are the heart of this book.

Thanks to Kent, Terri, Samuel, Luke, and Ruth for the support and delight that nourished me, and thanks to Paul for feeding me in so many ways, during the years that I was writing this book. Finally, thanks to Anna and Prasad whose love sustains me and daily brightens my life.

This book is dedicated to my parents, Harold E. Dunlap and M. Jean Dunlap, whose abounding nurture and encouragement has supported this research and writing project, as they have my whole life.

Prologue

Setting the Stage

The Churches' Context in the City of Durham

*T*hey say Durham's flourishing was sparked only a half mile from my house at the site of a major Civil War surrender. While the generals negotiated the surrender in the Bennett farm house, Confederate and Union troops shared smokes outside. The negotiations lasted nine days. When the Northerners went home, they brought word of the excellent Durham tobacco, and the market for Durham's main product grew. Upon his release from a Union prisoner of war camp, Washington Duke was one of those who saw that there was money to be made in the tobacco business in Durham. He and his family profited greatly from these growing sales, and grew their business to be the largest tobacco producer in Durham. Ten years after the generals gathered, "Durham's Station" had grown from 150 to 2000, and twenty-five years later its population was thirty times greater (Wise, 65).

For decades Durham was known as the City of Tobacco, home of the Bull Durham brand, which the Dukes eventually owned. Tobacco processing and textile mills made up the bulk of Durham's economy. Textile mills were essential for making the bags used to ship the tons of tobacco manufactured in

Durham. In the 1880s the Dukes began to manufacture cigarettes in addition to loose tobacco. They created the American Tobacco Company, then the largest cigarette manufacturing company in the world. When the Supreme Court ordered its breakup in 1911 under antitrust laws, the emerging corporations included a smaller American Tobacco Company, Liggett and Meyers, Brown and Williamson, and R.J. Reynolds. Not only did the extraordinary wealth of these corporations drive the economy of their host cities, including Durham, but the philanthropy of their owners literally built major institutions in central North Carolina.

Washington Duke made it possible to move the small Trinity College to Durham in 1892. Three years later a partner of the Dukes, George Watts, built the first hospital, for whites only. Washington's son, James B. Duke, donated $40 million in 1924 to create the Duke Endowment, with a provision that roughly one-third of the proceeds would go to Trinity College in Durham, which was then renamed Duke University, in honor of his father.

The university grew, especially its Medical Center, and attracted others in biomedical research and business. In 1959 Durham created a special tax zone for what would become Research Triangle Park, 7000 acres devoted largely to biomedical and other scientific research, located within minutes' drive of the three major universities in Durham, Chapel Hill, and Raleigh. Durham is now the City of Medicine, having changed the name in 1983. According to the official site of the Durham Convention and Visitors Bureau,

> This identity is built on its outstanding hospitals and major national and international healthcare companies. It is built on the city's cutting-edge research companies, its specialty clinical services and its nationally recognized medical teaching facilities.
>
> Durham has become synonymous with medicine. Nearly one in four people in Durham work in a health-related field, making medicine the city's leading industry. The City of Medicine has more than 300 medical and health-related companies and medical practices with a combined payroll that exceeds $1.5 billion annually.

This is Durham history from the perspective of those with social and economic power: the tobacco barons and the institutions that their philanthropy built. At the same time in Durham, African Americans were creating a parallel community with its own institutions, businesses, and leading figures. Immediately after the Civil War, former slaves, "those who worked in the menial drudgery of the plantation, the ones who worked in the 'big house,'" and "yeomen farmers whose ancestors were born free" (Jones, 2001, 13) moved to Durham, provided labor for its tobacco and textile industry, and built a world on the other side of the railroad tracks they called Hayti ("hay-tie"). Durham's oldest and most prosperous African American churches were started in brush arbors in the late 1860s, only a few years after freedom. If African American women worked as domestics in white Durham, and the men worked in its factories and mills, they spent their money in the African American part of town. Churches, businesses, and schools thrived.

Black Durham also benefited from Duke largesse. The Dukes contributed heavily toward the construction in 1900 of Lincoln Hospital in Hayti, "with grateful appreciation and loving remembrance of the fidelity and faithfulness of the Negro slaves to the Mothers and Daughters of the Confederacy, during the Civil War."[1] A window in the prestigious St. Joseph's AME church sanctuary bears a prominent picture of "our friend" Washington Duke.[2] By the 1920s, only sixty years after emancipation, African Americans had built a community with a hospital, newspaper, undertaker, bank, movie theater, black-owned manufacturing establishments, and college, and with North Carolina Mutual, "The World's Largest Negro Life Insurance Company" (Jones 57). Spacious, three-story Greek revival and Victorian homes lined the streets in prosperous areas. At his visit in 1910, Booker T. Washington called Durham "a Mecca for Negroes" and sent a researcher to study this "example of his philosophy of self-help" (Jones, 57). In the space of one lifetime, African Americans created from virtually nothing an eye-

[1] The plaque in the foyer of Lincoln Hospital (Jones, 37).
[2] St. Joseph's AME has moved to a new location. This sanctuary is now the site of the Hayti Heritage Center.

catching center of black life, labeled "the city of Negro Enterprise" in an Indianapolis newspaper (*Indianapolis Star,* November 10, 1910; quoted in Jones, 57).

This flush of enterprise, creativity, and industry happened under the pall of white racism whose most violent manifestation was the Ku Klux Klan. Lynchings were not unknown in the area where Durham was developing. Like other Southern towns, Durham had its Jim Crow years. The arbitrary means of control and the humiliating assertion of white power even in the most trivial of commercial interactions did not escape Durham. "And I remember when they wouldn't sell you a Coke. You could buy a Pepsi, but you could not buy Coke. If you'd go in a store and ask for Coke, they would reach in there and give you Pepsi. They only sold Coke to white folks," remembers Theresa Lyons of Durham during segregation (Chafe et al., 2001, 26). Nor did Durham escape more pernicious forms of white supremacy. Ms. Lyons also speaks of a school principal who believed his status would grant him certain freedoms, such as the freedom to buy meat at the local grocery store. He was beaten for his attempt (26).

Blacks and whites slept at different hotels, played on different sports teams, worshipped at different churches, lived in different neighborhoods, and ate in different restaurants. When African Americans bought ice cream at the Royal Ice Cream Company, they entered by the back door and stayed in the "colored" section. One Sunday afternoon, though, in June of 1957, Methodist Pastor Douglas E. Moore and several others sat down at the counter in the "white area" (Jones, 162; Wise, 131; Branch, 260). They asked for ice cream, and they were asked to leave. They were eventually arrested. It was not until three years later that the sit-in at Woolworth's forty miles down the highway in Greensboro shook America. The Civil Rights movement began its sit-in era in earnest and Durham was a part of it, having its own sit-in only one week later at its own Woolworth's. In 1960, Martin Luther King Jr. paid a visit to White Rock Baptist Church in support of Durham's sit-in actions, where he first issued the call to "fill up the jails!"

Hayti began its demise in the late 1950s, and during the 1960s Durham's black community was fractured further by urban renewal. Major homes and businesses were razed in favor of a freeway connecting downtown and Duke University to the new Research Triangle Park. Today a jail and a baseball park, the home of the Durham Bulls, sit on large parts of the site of the formerly bustling Hayti.

In the meantime, Durham's transition from tobacco to a biomedically and technologically based economy brought extraordinary growth. Called the "No. 1 area for economic growth in the past 25 years," Durham has experienced not only growth in the economy but also in quality of life, commended by such disparate magazines as *The Utne Reader* and *Redbook* magazine.

All of the growth has meant construction—construction of research facilities, hospital buildings, office parks, shopping malls, roads, sewage and water lines, and housing developments. Furthermore, as the population and economy has increased so has the need for low-skill service workers such as janitorial staff, restaurant workers, and landscaping laborers. These needs for construction workers and service workers have been partially met with a dramatic influx of Hispanic workers, mostly from Mexico. The Latino population increased seven-fold from 1990 to 2000. From 1980 to 1990, Durham's Latino population increased from 2,000 to 2,500. During the following decade, the population increased from 2,500 to 16,000. *Tiendas,* small grocery stores, dot the commercial areas; Mexican produce and Hispanic Catholic devotional candles are sold at the local Kroger; Spanish TV and radio stations are on the air; and casual observation reveals that almost all workers at construction sites are Hispanic. The state of North Carolina is no stranger to Latino workers, but most of them have been agricultural workers in rural areas, out of sight of urban Durham. Schools, social services, health care providers, banks, businesses, and the judicial system have scrambled to hire bilingual staff to accommodate the rapidly growing population. Two-thirds of the Hispanics in North Carolina were not born in the US, and practically none of this subgroup are U.S. citizens (NC Division of Social Services).

In this Southern town that tobacco built, the population is 190,000: roughly 10 percent Latino, 40 percent African American, and 40 percent Euroamerican (10% other). The racial lines that used to be drawn on a bipolar, black-white axis are in flux, and the analysis of power along racial lines has become more complicated, including the power to obtain quality health care. If 40 percent of all Americans lack health insurance, in Durham that number drops to 17 percent, and is even lower for African Americans in Durham (14%). Latinos, on the other hand, are 80 percent uninsured (Durham Health Partners). Like most cities in the U.S., access to such social goods as health care is affected by race and ethnicity, though in Durham the lines are drawn differently.

If you were to soar over the city of Durham today, you would see remnants of the industry that built it: the old tobacco warehouses and textile mills with their lovely brickwork. Some of them are now upscale shopping centers, office buildings, and condominiums. You would also see robust signs of the industry that sustains it now: Duke University Medical Center, with a hospital, clinics, medical school, nursing school, and enormous buildings dedicated to medical research.

Also from above, you would see evidence of the almost 400 churches. There are the numbered churches, mostly "Firsts," and of course the Saints, from James to Titus. Durham has the Mounts: Bethel, Calvary, Carmel, Gilead, Hermon, Moriah, Olive, Sinai, Vernon, and Zion. You would see churches with names like More Than Conquerors, Highways and Hedges, Seedtime and Harvest. There are also splashy names full of promise: Sunrise, New Horizon, New Destiny. One would wonder about the practices of The New Aggressive Church of Deliverance, and feel some curiosity about the one named The World's Greatest Church.

These churches, with their various names, from mainstream to marginal, are dedicated to serving God in Jesus Christ. They preach their understanding of the gospel, educate their children, marry those in love, and bury their dead. Somewhere along the way, as churches have done since Jesus' day, and as the Hebrews did before that, they also care for those who become sick in the interval between birth and death.

This book takes a closer look at how three of these churches care for the sick: Downtown Mainstream Protestant, founded only six years after the surrender at Bennett Place; an African American Pentecostal Holiness Church located a few blocks away from civil rights leader Rev. Douglas Moore's church; and the Hispanic subcongregation of an enormous Roman Catholic church. These three churches represent the varied ethnicities of Durham, as well as different classes and incomes, and each of them, in its own way, serves those in ill health. All three attempt to follow faithfully the one whose heart was moved to compassion to serve the sick, the weak, the poor, and the marginalized, in this complex town in central North Carolina.

INTRODUCTION

I've got some of the light in me,
You've got some of the light in you,
And a little bit of light from everyone
Is enough to see you through.[1]

The Latina woman pointed to a small porcelain statue of baby Jesus wearing the white clothes of a doctor. On his chest was a small patch that read "Niño Dr. Jesus." She smiled and said, twice, "Here is the doctor of the house." Her husband sat in a wheelchair paralyzed from a fall.

The Anglo man with advancing prostate cancer asked for "a hand." He had been offered a laying on of hands by church leaders, but instead he asked church members to send him cut-outs of their hands so that he might have a tangible sign of support. He received paper hands; felt hands; quilted hands; colored, painted, and scribbled hands. He spoke of them often until he died.

A Euroamerican woman in treatment for breast cancer received a soft, pink blanket signed by members of her care team. She felt "surrounded by names and prayers" as she drew it close around her.

1

Another Latina woman, when taking medicine, always said, "I was prescribed this medicine for my pain. In the name of Jesus, may it be for my health."

An African American woman told one of the most moving stories. She had grown up in the projects and used to sell cocaine. Eventually she became a nurse and returned to church. Then her two-week-old son was diagnosed with sickle cell anemia. She told me, "When I first heard of his diagnosis, I was devastated. I cried. I felt guilty. I was angry with God. I got depressed. I knew it was a God awful disease." Hearing her story was like traveling through two worlds simultaneously: a medical world and a church world. She told of taking her son to the doctor, and she told of the red patch her pastor gave her to pin on his diapers, which he wore constantly until he was three years old. She spoke of sitting in the emergency room waiting for medical care and of leaning over his body, praying and anointing him with oil. She told of hospital stays, and she told of curling up next to him in the hospital bed and saying, "In the name of Jesus, I plead the blood of Jesus, I bind every evil attack, I curse every attack of the enemy, and I believe God for your healing in the name of Jesus." She told of a change in herself, from depression and guilt to ministering in God's name to other parents of sick children, from anger with God to believing that only God has kept her son well, from devastation to discipleship. She spoke of acts of extraordinary support from her church: nights spent with her in the emergency room, meals, money, flowers, balloons, fruit baskets, and abundant prayer. I realized that the two worlds of medicine and faith were seamlessly merged for her.

While Durham is officially "The City of Medicine" with its internationally acclaimed Duke University Medical Center, there is another level of response to illness in this city: that of its people of faith. Dr. Jesus, a collection of hands, a pink blanket, a prayer over a pill, and a red prayer cloth all capture the great variety of responses to ill health in these churches.

Helen Keller said, "Although the world is full of suffering, it is also full of the overcoming of it." She captures a truth critical for people living with illness: there is suffering, but there are also countless times when it is overcome. She does not deny suffering, nor does she suggest that with intense effort it will go away or that with correct techniques applied it will end. But it does happen that, and we have evidence of it in actual lives, people live in ways so that they overcome their suffering. It is redeemed. It is transformed. It is rendered sacred by God Almighty.

Congregations are repositories of wisdom about how suffering can be overcome. They are bearers of wisdom from sacred texts, founding forebears, and living saints who not only speak words of wisdom but also embody them in their lives. Somewhat transcending these saints and texts is the dynamic organism of the congregation, whose interconnections and habits and truths form a living entity itself.

It is my firm conviction that congregations have much wisdom to share with one another. As congregations from different traditions enter into the places of suffering together, and hear stories, beliefs, and accounts of responding to suffering, the wisdom residing in each congregation will be enhanced. This is not a vision of merging wisdoms. Nor is it a vision of pasting a new practice onto the old. Rather, it is a vision in which each congregation's wisdom is enlarged; it sees a little more of God and where and how God is present; it learns a little more about forms of praying, caring, thinking, advocating, serving, and teaching that expand its ability to receive the grace of God.

In Mumbai, India, the main train station was built in a Gothic-style architecture, yet somehow not quite. The western beholder stares at it, at once seeing familiar western Gothic forms, but knowing that they have been subtly transformed by another coherent and beautiful style. For example, in a row of familiar Gothic arches, the lines of some of them have been stretched and reshaped to form a clearly Indian-shaped arch. The effect of this modification of forms is to produce something new that is mostly familiar and yet different, and certainly strikingly beautiful.[2] It is my vision that congregations retain their established identity, but that, here and there, some activities will assume a different style, will be transformed by the wisdom of other congregations, and find their wisdom and faithfulness enlarged.

As congregations from different traditions encounter one another, and as they share stories of suffering and stories of its overcoming, each will be changed, their wisdom and habits of caring transformed by what they have found in one another. Each retains its distinctiveness but is nevertheless enhanced in ministry, with its repository of wisdom enlarged.

For one particular stream of churches, mainstream American Protestantism, transforming encounters with others may be necessary in order to survive. Not only are membership numbers declining steadily, but in many cases vitality is waning. It is my conviction that, unless mainstream American Protestant congregations break out of largely white, largely middle- and upper-middle-class sensibilities and embrace forms of vitality from other traditions, we will starve ourselves spiritually and continue to face encroaching atrophy. The reach of our strengths, such as our intellectual rigor, our commitment to social justice, and our suspicion of efforts to identify the created world with the divine, is at risk of shrinking to smaller and smaller realms.

We will be renewed by access to practices that affirm areas that we have ignored or belittled: emotion and embodied life. Our worship and piety are often sorely lacking in acknowledgment of both feelings and bodies. We typically fail to worship God with the fullness of feeling and embodied selves. Furthermore, our iconoclastic, Protestant roots have cut us off from affirmation of the aesthetic and iconic. We are slow to affirm forms of beauty and the created world that bespeak and mediate God. The nurture of personal devotional practices is uncommon, even nonexistent, in many congregations. Our willingness to risk naming how and where the Spirit of God is at work in body, soul, psyche, family, and society is waning. Again, the hesitation to identify the finite world with God, or to be overly confident about one's knowledge of the mind of God, is one of the strengths of Protestantism. However, this hesitation has perhaps been overdone, and it is to our detriment. The arguments of this book are slanted toward the branch of the Church universal that I call home, mainstream American Protestantism, because I fear for its future.

Through historically and culturally thick descriptions of a particular practice as it is displayed in three different congregations, it is my hope that this book will convince the reader to enter into lasting relationships with individuals and congregations of a variety of traditions, and be changed by them. As the children's song says, we each have only some of the light, and when we share it, we find enough to see us through the trials of human life. Our grasp of the mystery of God and God's ways with humanity is strengthened when we encounter one another's readings of scripture, traditions of prayer, received historical texts, and oral traditions of both worship and practical advice for living.

This book introduces three congregations and their responses to ill health in their midst. It is not about an ideal church or a church typical of a particular tradition. Nor is it about a stripped-down, least common denominator, generic church. These churches are not distinguished by being exemplary of "best practices," nor are they necessarily representative of what many churches do. They are simply three congregations of different cultural, racial, and theological heritages in the same town. Healing Waters Church is an African American congregation in the Apostolic Holiness tradition. First Downtown Church is a Euroamerican mainstream Protestant church. Our Lady of Durham is a Roman Catholic church, in which I study the large Latino subcongregation.

THE STUDY OF CONGREGATIONS

The study of congregations, one's own or one very different from it, is exhilarating. Congregations are extraordinary constellations of individuals, texts, histories, conflicts, reconciliations, loves, losses. They are full of memories of baptisms and funerals, weddings celebrated, and divorces mourned. They include such particularities and oddities as prayer and protest, devotional pamphlets and American flags, vacation bible schools and spaghetti suppers, processions and pageants, shouts of joy and pain, prayers of lament and praise, sermons great and small, funds collected and funds dispersed, protests personal and political, strollers and walkers, pita bread and grape juice, coffee and donuts, individuals and clans, electric organ and violin, drum and trumpet, glue and crayons, copy machines and pencil sharpeners, sin and redemption, death and resurrection. The inseparability of the gritty and human with the sublime and heavenly inspires this investigation of particular congregations—the fusing of the creaturely and flawed with eternal and perfect love, the indivisibility of the pita bread and grape juice from the body and blood of Jesus Christ. That we should ever meet the redeeming power of God in the humble stuff of congregations is witness to the extraordinary nature of both: the creator of the universe and all that dwells therein who chooses to transform them through radically historical human associations, and the fragile and sinful congregation as a place where the power of God is loosed. It is hardly believable; it strains the imagination. Yet this is what we claim. We make this claim on the basis of reason and sacred text, but mostly because, time and again, so many have been bathed in redemption through God's reach in and through congregations.

The diversity of America is played out in the diversity of our churches. Sunday morning worship can be the sight of silence in Quaker meeting or shouts of ecstasy in a Pentecostal service. Musical instruments range from pipe organ to tambourine. Prayers can be spontaneous and emotional or codified and aesthetically crafted, and are often a combination of both. Clothing can be ethnically specific or generically retail. Teaching can focus on the Bible, the saints, or eastern styles of meditation. Multiple adjectives describe churches: Presbyterian and Lutheran, liberal and conservative, Romanian Catholic and Swedish Pietist, Korean speaking and Swahili speaking, evangelical and progressive, African American and Hispanic, traditional and contemporary, megachurch and storefront church, rural and urban. Churches are radically historical and deeply rooted in particular contexts, whether these contexts are geographically defined or defined by class, interest, theological conviction, ethnicity, or language. The diversity of churches and congregational lives testifies to the countless ways the love of God is incarnate.

Concern for congregations is a direction in which the field of Pastoral Theology is moving. John Patton has described the move in our field from a "clinical-pastoral" paradigm to a "communal-contextual" one. "[This concern] is new in that it emphasizes the caring community and the various contexts for care rather than focusing on pastoral care as the work of the ordained pastor" (Patton, 5). If the former focuses on the individual pastor's interaction with an individual care receiver, drawing heavily on psychological categories, the latter shifts the focus to the cultural and ecclesial context, explicating congregational practices and social power structures. Patton even calls upon the caregiver to act as "mini-ethnographer" in order to enhance the quality of their care (43). An entire issue of the *Journal of Pastoral Theology* (Summer 1992) was devoted to exploring the fruitful intersection of congregational studies with pastoral theology. Mary Moschella's *Living Devotions* includes an ethnographic study of Mary Star of the Sea Church, an Italian Catholic congregation in Southern California (2008). Moschella's work also includes a novel approach in her *Ethography as a Pastoral Practice*. Practical Theology, a closely related discipline, has also moved in the direction of studying congregations. Congregational studies is an intrinsic part of Don Browning's method of practical theology. John Swinton and Harriet Mowat also explore a particular congregation in *Practical Theology and Qualitative Research* (2006). Finally, Mary McClintock Fulkerson takes the study of congregations to Systematic Theology in her groundbreaking *Places of Redemption* (2007).

THE CONGREGATIONALLY PRODUCED BODY

One particular way to approach the study of congregations is to attempt to discern the congregationally produced body, to raise the question of what sort of body it "produces," or, what is its "lived body." The usefulness of this category is based on the assumption that the body is the bearer of extraordinary aspects of human life.

It is the site of beauty in dance and art. It is the site of power honed by discipline in sports and pleasure intensified by love. It is the site of physical and spiritual communion between mother and nursing child as the one gives of her body for the other's growth, nurture, and survival itself. Yet the body is also the site of degradation, humiliation, mutilation, and pain. We can name poverty's bodily disfigurements and deformations, physical pain in illness, torture as a tool of raw political power, and control through the humiliation of rape.[3] Furthermore, in a tragic and ironic way, the forces of white supremacy and patriarchy can render invisible the bluntly, irreducibly material body.[4] Yet the body is more than simply the site of the good and the bad. It is also the site of transformation, of redemption. The bodies of those crossing the bridge in Selma in 1965 contributed to the success of the civil rights movement. In the 1980s, as a ministry of accompaniment, participants in Witness for Peace lent their bodies protected by U.S. power to the bodies of Nicaraguans marked for death by death squads. Many who work with infectious diseases risk their bodies in acts of care and cure for the suffering. Is not Christ's body on the cross the ultimate form of redemptive, bodily solidarity with others? This book is partly fueled by the awareness of the human body as the site of not only intense beauty and pain, but also redemptive solidarity.

The matter of the body is particularly relevant to the field of Pastoral Theology because so many of the issues we address implicate the body: the sick body, the dying body, the addicted body, the abused body, the depressed body, the aging body, and so forth. Therefore the matter of embodied beauty, pain, and redemption, and how they are enabled or hindered by social context, is intrinsic to our work. With the recognition that the body is socially constructed, we can no longer view the body as a brute, mute, physiological fact, separate from the communities and societies where it dwells. Social, cultural, and economic contexts mold and shape bodies in at least two ways. First, the actual physical body is subject to the socioeconomic context. For example, if you are poor in parts of the world, you are more likely to have a malnourished body; if you live in the United States, the odds are you have an overweight body. Second, social context affects our *experience* of our bodies: our interpretation of what pain, sexual desire, hunger, and touch mean, for example. Physical pain can mean I am a hero if I am wounded in battle, or it can mean humiliation if I am mugged in the street. Sexual desire can be celebrated as an expression of a God-given impulse to connect, or it can be a source of shame and self-hatred. Pastoral touch can be interpreted as invasive and threatening or comforting and caring. Social context has the power to enhance embodied beauty, pain, and redemptive solidarity, or it can subvert them, and this is a matter of central concern to Pastoral Theology.

The study of congregations and the body as an intellectual category converges in this book on how churches care for the sick. This is a book about three congregations' responses to the body when its fragility comes to the fore in times of illness. During illness a congregation is faced with the body and its vulnerability, and each congregation has developed ways of thinking about the body, habits of responding to it, and understandings of God's response to the body's pain or peril. In order to capture these very specific features of a congregation's relation to the sick body, I will describe congregations as sites of matrices of *beliefs* and *practices*. My way of accessing the myriad particularities and details of a particular congregation is to refer to beliefs and practices.

CONGREGATIONS AS SITES OF BELIEFS AND PRACTICES

Beliefs, which are connected (in some way) to a past preserved in texts, rituals, and symbols, are also connected to present-day *practices*, such as caring, teaching, preaching, serving, worshipping, discerning, and praying. Present-day beliefs in congregations are codified in a rich variety of forms: selections and construals of scripture with its profusion of genres of literature, creeds, confessions of faith, hymnody, liturgy, devotional material, educational texts, and rich banks of orally transmitted material. This collection of material inscribed in text and memory is lived out in varieties of ways in congregational practices. In other words, beliefs carry with them attendant rituals and habits that give them their specific content, and practices acquire their impact as they are linked to beliefs. Beliefs and practices are linked inextricably as each gives the other its particular force or meaning, and so for that reason, I refer to particular belief-practices. Ideally, of course, we would be able to use only the rich word "practices," a term that has been so widely claimed by philosophers, theologians, and social scientists and given multiple definitions, all of which define practice as much larger than simply "typical actions," all of which recognize the discursive, ideational content of practices. However, because we are so accustomed to a belief/behavior dualism, many of us still have a strong tendency to place "practice" in the category of behavior, and ignore its meaning or convictional context. Therefore, though the word "practice" should be able to stand alone, I will refer to "belief-practice" as a way of reinforcing the unity of "typical actions" and "convictions" I am discussing.

What Serene Jones said of doctrine can also be said of belief-practice matrices. She writes that doctrine can be understood with two images: "lived imaginative landscape" and "drama" (Jones, 74). As *landscape*, doctrines (or, for our purposes, belief-practices) create "imaginative spaces that we occupy—we inhabit them and learn to negotiate the complexities of our living through them," including our illnesses. They "demarcate the interpretive fields through which we view the world and ourselves and are not merely 'truth claims' whose objective factuality demands our assent" (74). As *drama*, doctrines (and belief-practices) also function as "ruled patterns of performance" that "craft the character not only of individuals but of entire communities as well." Doctrines (and belief-practices) are the "script" for "ruled patterns of thought and behavior," including the script and ruled patterns for illness (75).

These landscapes, dramas, and belief-practices are not static, unchanging entities that form passive individuals and communities into who they are. The idioms of a religion are not just "inherited," but they are also "improvised, found, and constructed" by creative agents (Orsi, 173). There is a mutually creative activity between congregations and the belief-practices that characterize them. Congregations and their belief-practices construct varying landscapes and dramas out of the material at hand, and it is the purpose of this book to spell out the predominant belief-practices relating to illness in three churches.

However, I am not only interested in *describing* these beliefs and practices; I am also interested in how they *function*. I am interested in the difference it makes to belong to *this* rather than *that* congregation. How is it different to be a sick person in this church rather than that one? What is the illness experience as it is created, shaped, formed by the congregation's peculiar beliefs and practices? What is opened up, shut down, revealed, concealed, released, restricted, enabled, disabled by the various beliefs and practices in these congregations? How do these beliefs and practices function? At the heart of these questions is the question of whether these beliefs and practices, as human constructs, function in community to point beyond themselves to promote trust in God, the one who is beyond all human constructs, or whether they promote the idolatrous search for salvation in the finite.

A congregation's beliefs and practices regarding illness are, finally, a congregation's treatment of finitude. The central issue, or problem, of illness is the issue of finite human existence. I do not speak of finitude as simply mortality, the inevitability of death, the fact that at some point in the future we will all die. Rather, illness is a face-to-face confrontation with the fact that, every day we are alive, we are limited, fragile, vulnerable. Illness confronts us with the reality of our finite bodies and our limited control over their well-being and the well-being of the bodies of those we desperately love. As such, illness can be the occasion for an anxious turn to a piece of the finite world to save them. Therefore a congregation's response to illness reflects a church's negotiation of finitude. A church's response to the anxiety raised by the advent of a season of illness is a sign of their response to human finitude. The final question of this study is whether the beliefs and practices of these congregations encourage trust in God in the context of illness or foster idolatrous trust in pieces of the finite world.

While the unit of study in this book is the congregation, congregations are always situated in larger webs of power, and one's position in that web will affect one's illness. Another way to say this is churches are not composed of generic human beings, and one is never simply a sick generic person. Rather, one is a sick woman, a sick African American, a sick old person, a sick white person, a sick man, a sick Latina, a sick lesbian. While illness may be a lonely, isolating experience, it will always be experienced, negotiated, and strategized within the context of larger power matrices. Karla Holloway writes of "black death" and how African Americans "die a color-coded death" (Holloway, 3). In a similar way, the sick endure "color-coded" illness, or a gendered illness, or Hispanic, gay, female, old, straight, young, or white illness. One becomes ill from a position in the power maps of the world, and these maps do not skirt congregations. Any treatment of illness within a congregation will take into account race, gender, sexuality, and all of the other grids used to assign social power. These power grids are intrinsic to congregational landscapes and dramas, and congregations can resist, promote, or remain silent regarding them. Therefore, a congregation's belief-practices will always be in some sort of relation to these larger power matrices, and this study of them will include a discussion of how they subvert, reinforce, or leave untouched social power structures. How is this belief-laden behavior a response to this congregation's experience of deprivations or privileges in the larger culture? How does this behavior function as resistance to the larger culture? How is it a way of securing power in the larger culture? Finally, how do these belief-practices enable survival, humanizing, and flourishing for the sick, or not?

OVERVIEW OF THE BOOK

Effective pastoral caregiving will take into account Arthur Kleinman's "visible exoskeleton of powerfully peculiar meanings that the patient must deal with" (22) and David Morris' "collective social discourses and codes" (8). Although there has been much important work on how individuals cull meanings from their internal and external sources to construct (consciously or unconsciously) their own peculiar illness meanings, that inner, psychological process is not the focus of this book. This book is devoted to describing congregations as *repositories of meanings* from which individuals consciously or unconsciously gather illness meanings or interpretations. The focus is on congregations as archives of beliefs and practices that shape individual illness meanings or interpretations. Rather than focus on the very interesting process of how the *individual creates* illness meanings, I will describe the *congregation as sources* of those meanings. The unit of study, then, is not the individual, but the congregation.

I devote two chapters to each of the three congregations. One covers the history of the tradition in which the church stands, the place of its particular demographic "slot" in American history, and a general description of the congregational culture. With that larger context established, the next chapter describes and evaluates particular belief-practices of each church.

These three churches were chosen to represent each of the three predominent ethnic groups in my town: African American, Euroamerican, and Hispanic. They also represent very different worship styles: Spirit centered, Word centered, and Eucharist centered. They are not meant to be representative of an ideal type, such as a "typical black church." They were not selected "scientifically," as in a randomized survey. Their inclusion in this book was based more on my personal contacts than anything else. But they do represent three communal-cultural bodies that developed in the same civic-geographic entity. Although I would like to say they were formed from the same basic cultural "soup," or raw material, that would not be true. This town's history of segregation by race and class means that there are different cultural "soups" that coexist but whose mixing is limted. Therefore each congregation's history of formation took place in the same town, but in very different cultures. This is not to say that they are not connected in some way, for example, that the actions of the privileged do not affect the lives of the underprivileged. But it is to say that this town is characterized by a history of deep divide between the communal lives of its various subcultures, and its institutions develop along cultural trajectories that interact only on a limited basis.

I begin with the African American Apostolic Holiness Church. This congregation's primary response to the sick body is healing. Since illness is the devil's doing, not God's, a key element in healing is banishing the devil from the body of the sick. The healers in this church use a variety of materials toward that end, such as oil, herbs, prayer cloths, and water. Then I move to a predominantly Euroamerican downtown Presbyterian church whose primary identity is that of having chosen to stay in the city when other churches were moving to the suburbs. The primary response to the sick is a strong community of support. The emphasis is on following Jesus' example by caring for the sick with acts of kindness and support. Finally the third congregation is the Hispanic subgroup within a large Roman Catholic church. Here the primary response to the sick body is weekly visitation of every person of Hispanic origin in the local hospital. Since most of the Hispanics in this church are from Mexico, there is a strong devotion to the Virgin of Guadalupe. When she appeared in sixteenth-century Mexico, her words included reassurances for those who are sick: "Do not fear that sickness, or any other anguish or sickness. Am I not your mother?" Clearly, responding to the sick is a part of core religious symbols as well as religious practice.

My portraits and analyses of each congregation are based on interviews and participant observation in each church. My relationships with these three churches are uneven: I have followed the Hispanic community for a year or so and the African American congregation for five years, and I have participated as a member in the Euroamerican church for ten years. Therefore I make no attempt to compare the churches along any standardized axes, nor do I attempt to make any neutral evaluations. The portraits are simply what I say they are—a record of my empathetic and appreciative encounter with three communities.

These portraits can serve several purposes. Hospital chaplains can be conscienticized to the spiritual and ecclesial reality in which the hospital patient lives. Hospitals have a way of homogenizing patients, of erasing cultural and ethnic identities in a way that implies that a particular illness will be experienced in the same way by each patient. It is my hope that this book will raise awareness that illness experience is deeply connected to the cultural and religious landscape in which a person lives and that the hospital chaplain will pay attention to culture as an integral part of care. Second, it is my hope that this book will serve as a reminder that all of us need one another because we all have partial truths. Each congregation I describe has something to teach and something to learn from the others. Finally, I have a profound hope that this work will contribute in some way to revitalizing the often floundering mainline denominations. By looking at forms of vitality in other traditions, by articulating God-mediating practices in other churches, and lifting up what we do well in the mainline congregations, my hope is that this stream of Christian witness will be replenished.

HEALING WATERS CHURCH

FINDING HEALING WATERS

*A*rriving for Sunday morning worship, I drove into the gravel parking lot next to Healing Waters Church, made of blond brick, sitting close to busy North Alston Avenue. It was a clean rectangular shape, with a modest steeple and a front door flanked neatly by greenery. A lively elementary school stood across the street. The neighborhood was marked by gang graffiti, one-story bungalows in need of paint, boarded-up buildings, and rundown apartment buildings whose names were rendered odd by missing letters. An emaciated elderly man was selling newspapers on the corner in the blistering heat. African Americans and Latinos sat on their respective front porches, assembled on crumbling parking lots, and walked in and out of the convenience store with bars on the windows.

Inside the church's small vestibule were framed newspaper articles about Pastor Hanford[5] and his family: his wife Evangelist Hanford and their adult children, all six of them, who are well known for their gospel singing. Pastor Hanford founded this independent church in 1982, and eventually two others, earning him the title of Bishop. As I moved into the sanctuary I saw that it held new pews, hardwood flooring, and, in the front, new carpeting and traditional sanctuary furniture. It appeared it would hold about 150 worshippers when full. The church's fresh, orderly interior stood in sharp contrast to the decay in the neighborhood.

There were only a few people present, some milling about, some preparing the sanctuary for the service, and some singing and praying quietly. It was clear that we were in a space set apart for worship: its purpose marked by the colors of the stained glass windows, the paraments on the central pulpit and communion table, the framed "church covenant," and the complex array of musical equipment: an electric organ, electric piano, a set of drums, bongo drums, a bass electric guitar, and five-foot-high speakers. Yet there was a quickening of the sense of the sacred as people started arriving. The sanctuary changed over time from the realm of the mundane to the realm of the sacred *by the bodily presence of the worshippers.* The physical presence of the worshippers, the robes of the leaders, the white dresses of the Mothers, and all their worshipful gestures and voices created sacred space out of everyday space. This quickening, this transformation of space, was in contrast to the relatively static space of my Presbyterian church sanctuary, which seems to stay a hushed repository of the holy more than a living, changing space.

As the service progressed, the sounds that created the sanctuary as a holy space grew more animated: praying, singing, moaning, shouting voices, clapping, tambourines, the array of drums and electronic musical instruments, joined together in song, praise, and prayer. The musical style was variously traditional gospel, contemporary gospel, and something akin to jazz.

All of this, and the pastor had not yet arrived.

After about twenty or thirty minutes, the worship leaders began an enthusiastic build up for his entrance. They spoke with great reverence for him. It was clear that their respect and affection ran deep, that he was a person worthy of honor, and that his arrival was a significant event. I expected a big man, a towering figure, to sweep down the aisle in black robes, full of power and authority. When the moment came for him to enter, I turned around to face the door, and down the aisle came an old man in a black clerical robe, pushed in a wheelchair. I quickly realized he was a quadruple amputee. They rolled him to the front, and, at the time for the sermon, he was picked up like a baby and put on a high stool behind the pulpit. He spoke with great authority and vigor, and he waved his shortened arms to emphasize his points. I was stunned. All I could think of was Paul's words, "God's power made perfect in weakness."

The interplay between the pastor's weak and, in the world's eyes, stigmatized body and his spiritual power and communal authority bespoke the mystery of the power of the cross. Somehow, in and through his broken body, this congregation was being made whole. His power was not diminished by his cropped limbs; rather, it was magnified.

The moments of greatest intensity would begin with the deep sound of someone dancing on the wooden floor. "Shouting" had begun. Heads would turn to find the origin. It could be heard with both the ear as well as something deeper in the body, around where the heart beats. Most often it was in the transitions, after the choir sang, after a minister prayed, after an announcement. The organist, who may have been playing some mellow "filler" music, immediately picked up the rhythm with a high-pitched sound, somewhere between a trumpet and a siren, and the drummer came in. A quick scan of the sanctuary revealed where someone was offering up praise with her whole body and soul as she danced like Miriam with her tambourine and her sisters, like David before the Tabernacle of the Lord, and it was always a woman. She might have been old or young, thin or fat, a long-time Mother or a visitor. But she danced until she was finished. And for that moment, the worship of the people of God was lead by her inner impulse to praise her God to the fullest. Our full attention was on her voice and her body in her moment of expression of her innermost world.

At one point, a woman was immersed in shouting with her eyes closed, her body loosed in free expression, and five or six women rose from their seats in various places in the sanctuary, unbidden. They silently moved toward the woman, linked arms, and surrounded her with a protective circle. They gave her the freedom to dig deep and soar high as she gave thanks to God in corporeal abandon. When she crumbled to the floor, the ushers dressed in white brought a pillow and a "modesty sheet" to cover her legs. By this time others had joined her in expressions of praise to their God. Feet and legs were pounding the floor and faces were marked by tears, grimaces, frowns, concentration, or defiance. And the whole congregation was united in a moment of jubilant praise to the God who makes all things new.

While I had nothing but deep appreciation for what was happening around me, I also felt uncomfortable. I wondered what the other worshippers thought about me—more specifically, how they felt about the presence of my white body, marked by the world as superior and deserving of privilege. I was convinced they were thinking, "What is *she* doing here?" I felt conspicuous, as though my white skin glared like a bare, buzzing fluorescent bulb. Furthermore, after worship began in earnest, I felt worse than an irritant—I felt like an intruder into something very, very intimate that I had no right to watch. It felt like being present as an observer during something as lovely, personal, and intense as a couple embraced in love.

I left the service deeply grateful to the congregation for their hospitality. I also felt grateful to the friend who had first invited me to Healing Waters, a woman I had met at a preschool picnic, and to the pastor, for her warm welcome. I also felt like apologizing to the other departing worshippers for bothering them.

The feeling of discomfort and apology has diminished significantly as a measure of mutual trust has grown between me and the people of Healing Waters. In addition, as my knowledge of individuals and congregational life grew, I was able to move beyond some of my earlier romanticizing of the church and into a realistic respect and affection for the people and practices I found there.

While this is a book that focuses on the practices of caring for the sick, circumscribed descriptions of caring behaviors, or accounts of caring acts cropped from congregational context, are not adequate. Behaviors, actions, and words associated with care for the sick can only be understood in the larger context of the congregation as a whole, particularly its worship practices. And in order to understand any congregation, it is necessary to understand it and its history. The history of this congregation can be understood as the product of converging historical streams.

CONVERGING HISTORICAL STREAMS

Healing Waters Church was founded in 1982 by Pastor Robert Hanford when he broke away from another small church also in the Apostolic Holiness tradition. The membership is now roughly 250, and most people attribute its growth to the warm and welcoming tone set by the founding pastor and to a deep respect for his spiritual authority. He died just after I began to attend Healing Waters. The current pastor is his wife of many years. In her seventies, she presides over morning worship most Sundays. When the text refers to Pastor Hanford, I am referring to her, not to her husband.

How did Healing Waters Church come to be? It did not spring full-blown from the head of the founding pastor, so what historical streams made it? These questions are important not because historical origins reveal the true essence of a community, but because past phenomena reverberate in the present. Furthermore, the past becomes the stuff out of which the present is constructed and deconstructed, with which survival strategies are enacted. Anthropologists tell us that cultures are not static deposits of beliefs, behaviors, and mores, but rather are constantly in flux, hybrids of multiple discourses that function to enable survival in the larger world. People are always actively constructing culture toward the end of overcoming hardship and even thriving. Cultures are more performances in service of survival than inert, unchanging codes of belief and behavior. In order to understand Healing Waters, therefore, we need to understand some of the stuff out of which they are constructing, or performing, church. I have described, to some degree, the present sources of cultural building blocks in my description of the town of Durham. Here I will describe sources from the past in a discussion of three of the most important historical streams out of which this church constructs, writes, and performs its culture: slavery, the Sanctified Church, and Pentecostalism.

Slavery

It is said that the black church in the present cannot be understood without exploring its origins in slavery.[6]

> Black people in the United States differ from all other modern people owing to the unprecedented levels of unregulated and unrestrained violence directed against them. No other people have been taught systematically to hate themselves—psychic violence—reinforced by the powers of state and civic coercion— physical violence—for the primary purpose of controlling their minds and exploiting their labor for nearly four hundred years. The unique combination of American terrorism—Jim Crow and lynching—as well as American barbarism—slave trade and slave labor—bears witness to the distinctive American assault on black humanity. (West, xiii)

In the context of this "distinctive American assault on black humanity," the black church has preached the good news of God in Jesus Christ for centuries. In response to the question Jeremiah raised in the midst of the torment of his people, "Is there no balm in Gilead?" enslaved African Americans miraculously affirmed in song and sermons that, yes, there *is* a balm in Gilead.[7] If ever there were a testimony to God's transforming power, it is that God's people of African origin in America were able to survive singing songs of praise.

Similar to Cornel West, Anthony Pinn refers to the destructive American drive to render black bodies objects. This "thingification" was effected by slave auctions and lynchings, which, in turn, engender a sense of terror and dread among African Americans (Pinn, 48, 72). This terror is the context of both African American religious life and its emancipatory efforts. Referring to the black church as "houses of prayer in a hostile land" (81ff.), Pinn asserts that the "Black Church, when at its best, has developed forms of praxis geared toward addressing the terror and dread of objectification through the nurturing of sociopolitically and economically vital and vibrant Americans, who exercise all the rights and responsibilities endemic to full citizenship" (88). He rejects categorizing the black church as *either* concerned with this worldly emancipation *or* with otherworldly salvation. "[W]hile some churches approached transformation through sociopolitical and economic activism, churches holding to an otherworldly perspective addressed it more passively through a preoccupation with the spiritual condition of the black community. For the latter, the underlying rationale is simple: spiritual growth entails a closeness to God that must imply the full humanity of the practitioner" (89). Pinn reminds us that, while Healing Waters Church would clearly be understood as "holding to an otherworldly perspective," it performs the liberatory function of affirming the full humanity of its members, their worthiness before the greatest power in the universe, and justice as their due.

The first slaves of African origin initially arrived in the New World in the early decades of the seventeenth century. They were the first of approximately 400,000 more human beings to be brought to America, whose descendents eventually numbered 3.9 million. It was not until the end of the eighteenth century, during the revolutionary era, that slaves first began to convert to Christianity in large numbers. Before that, missionary efforts were weak, and slaveholders were either indifferent to their slaves' religious life or reluctant to give them the tools to claim their full humanity.

During the Second Great Awakening (1770–1815) (Baer, 5) launched by Presbyterian, Methodist, and Baptist evangelicals, revivals swept through the land, and black slaves were introduced to Christianity in significant numbers for the first time (Raboteau, 1986, 539). Eventually, relatively independent black Methodist and Baptist churches were formed in the North. In the South, though, black slaves attended white churches, and some had their own prayer services with some white oversight. The Episcopal Diocese of the Confederate States of America published its own teaching tool entitled *Catechism, To Be Taught Orally to Those Who Cannot Read; Designed Especially for the Instruction of the Slaves.*[8] One part reads: "Q. How are you to show your love to your master and mistress and to your parents? A. I am never to lie to them, to steal from them, nor speak bad words about them; but always to do as they bid me." Clearly religion was intended to be a pacifying influence. Yet some risked meeting in secret to interpret and tell the stories of the Bible, pray, and freely worship their God according to the movements of their own bodies, souls, and minds. "[A]t the core of the slaves' religion was a private place, represented by the cabin room, the overturned pot, the prayin' ground, and the 'hush harbor.' This place the slave kept his own" (Raboteau, 1978, 219).

Slavery was the context of the emergence of the "shout." According to Albert Raboteau, during the intensity of the revival, both black and white people would be overcome with the Spirit as they "wept, shouted, sang, jerked, danced, and fainted in response to the powerful pleas of the revival preachers" (1986, 545). Here, again according to Raboteau, "slaves discovered a Christian analogue to African spirit possession" (545). He argues that clapping replaced African drumming, spirituals replaced songs to African gods, and the counterclockwise circle dance closely resembled "possession dances" in Africa (545).

Slaves cared not only for one another's souls but also for one another's bodies when they became ill. While health care professionals did care for sick slaves on occasion, it was for the purpose of restoring a slave's "soundness" as a source of labor and object to be put up for sale (Fett, 20). Slaves cared for one another out of a radically different conception of health, one that emphasized relatedness to others both living and dead (4). Care was provided by kin, which was not necessarily the nuclear family or even blood relatives. Because slavery systematically destroyed nuclear family units, family was defined as including aunts, uncles, cousins, half-brothers, and sisters, as well as nonblood "relatives" who were considered as close as family. When care for the sick was required, it was the extended slave "family" that provided it. In addition, there was "an elaborate system of health care, magic, divination, herbalism, and witch craft widespread among African American slaves" (Baer, 233). These practices met and mingled with Christian practices, which traced illness to God's will, the works of the devil, or personal sin (Baer, 233).

Are the joyous dances of praise traces of Africa at Healing Waters Church? Are the bay leaves that one of the healers uses remnants of a time when herbs were all that slaves had to offer sick and battered bodies? Is the broad network of care within the congregation an heir to slaves' communal response to nuclear families fractured by the sale of black bodies? I believe that it can be argued that at least some of the vitality and creativity of Healing Waters Church has to do with its roots in the black church's redemptive response to the suffering of slavery. Using Pinn's words, Healing Waters can be seen as a "house of prayer in a hostile land," rooted in a creative response to the ravages of a racist world. Let it not be concluded, however, that all of its creativity and vitality are a response to white racism. This congregation, like other African American churches, engages in forms of cultural production that bear no relation to the actions of white people. Its generativity and novelty are its own, neither secondary to nor dependent on an oppressive context.[9]

The Sanctified Church

After slavery, Methodist and Baptist denominations looked down on the folk healing methods of care and on some of the "excesses" of shouting. These practices continued, however, in the "Sanctified Churches." One scholar defines the Sanctified Church today as "an African American Christian reform movement that seeks to bring its standards of worship, personal morality, and social concern into conformity with a biblical hermeneutic of holiness and spiritual empowerment" (Sanders, 5). These churches were usually independent of white-controlled denominations.

Cheryl Townsend Gilkes has emphasized the importance of the Sanctified Church to women as well as the importance of women to the Sanctified Church. The church gave dignity to black women, "providing the positive moral support for their role within their families and their communities" (Gilkes, 29). Sanctified Churches provided places for women's leadership, sometimes as ordained clergy, or more frequently as leaders in highly organized and effective women's organizations. Women evangelists preached revivals and were able to found ("dig out") new churches (29). If women were denied formal leadership positions, in many Sanctified Churches they were "teachers," which meant at times that they were the leader of a church without a pastor. While Baptists and Method-ists were narrowing the role of women in their churches, the largest of the Sanctified Churches, Church of God in Christ, experienced the greatest growth. "Women convinced that God had called them to have a voice in preaching or teaching the gospel 'went over' in to the Sanctified Church in order to exercise their gifts" (31).

The Sanctified Church benefited greatly from this influx. "Sim-ply, black women built and maintained the churches" (Gilkes, 31). Gilkes points out the predominance of women in the composition of congregations. "Church memberships can be over 90 percent female. If one looks beyond the pulpit, it is possible to view the Sanctified Church as a women's movement" (33). Not only has the Sanctified Church provided a place for women to flourish inside the church doors, but many women who call the Sanctified Church home have been active in addressing multiple social problems such as inadequate health care, poor schools, and the needs of the elderly through their work in various women's clubs and organizations. Healing Waters Church's embrace of the founding father's wife as pastor stands in the tradition of earlier Sanctified Churches. Pastor Hanford is clearly the central authority figure in the church, and, of the six ministers of the church, only one is a man. On any Sunday, approximately three quarters of the worshippers are women.

The history of women's leadership in the church, traditions of ecstatic worship, and folk healing methods place Healing Waters as heir to the more marginal traditions within African American churches in America. If black congregations that are members of predominantly white denominations, or mostly black denomina-tions that are offshoots of white denominations, have more subdued worship, are less open to women's leadership, and look down on folk healing methods, then Healing Waters Church stands squarely in the tradition of the Sanctified Church.

Pentecostalism

It was an African American holiness preacher in the sanctified tra-dition, William J. Seymour, who, in 1906 in California, launched the only indigenous American religious movement. Seymour had studied with Charles F. Parham in Houston, Texas, at a school spun off from the Parham's Bible school in Topeka, Kansas. Parham had recently arrived at the novel theological assertion that "speaking in tongues *always* accompanied Holy Ghost baptism" (Wacker, 2001, 5, emphasis in original). Seymour took this message to the Azusa Street Mission in Los Angeles where he lead a revival that rocked the neighborhood, the city, and eventually the world, as the Pentecostal movement was born. Populated by both African Americans and whites, the lively meetings prompted one *Los Angeles Times* reporter to write,

> Meetings are held in a tumble-down shack on Azusa Street near San Pedro Street, and the devotees of the weird doctrine practice the most fanatical rites, preach the wildest theories and work themselves into a state of mad excitement in their peculiar zeal. Colored people and a sprinkling of whites compose the congregation, and night is made hideous in the neighborhood by the howlings of the worshippers, who spend hours swaying forth and back in a nerve-racking attitude of prayer and supplication. They claim to have the "gift of tongues" and to be able to comprehend the babel. (April 18, 1906, p. 1; quoted in Synan, 95)

During these early years, the movement of the Spirit created a relative egalitarianism during worship. The Spirit visited black and white, women and men, adult and child alike. Yet, what began as an interracial phenomenon eventually succumbed to the rupturing forces of racism. By 1924 all the denominational branches either spawned or transformed by the Azusa Street event became segregated (Synan, 169). The heirs of the original saints were divided also by doctrinal controversies, such as disagreements over the role of tongues in salvation and the never-ending topic of discussion among Christians, the Trinity. While most Pentecostal denominations baptized in the name of the Trinity, the Apostolic branch baptized in the name of Jesus alone, believing that the book of Acts dictates such as the practice of the early church. This stream of Sanctified Churches came to be known as "Jesus only" churches, or Oneness churches, and is the stream in which Healing Waters stands.

Responding to illness with miraculous healing was at the core of the origins of Pentecostal believers. They resembled their fore-bears, the radical evangelicals, in their affirmation of the " 'four-fold gospel' of personal salvation, Holy Ghost baptism, divine healing, and the Lord's soon return" (Wacker, 2001, 1). Services included demonstrations of the Spirit besides healing, such as speaking in tongues as well as "trances, dancing, prostration, screaming, laugh-ing, weeping, and violent jerking" (Wacker, 1986, 521). However, it was the moment of healing that lay at the heart of the worship service.

"The common heartbeat of every service," as David Edwin Harrell has said of a somewhat later period, "was the miracle—the hypnotic moment when the Spirit moved to heal the sick and raise the dead" (Wacker, 1986, 521; quoting Harrell, 1975, 5).

The radical evangelicals also provided the theological under-girding for divine healing. "Christ's atonement on the cross pro-vided healing for the body just as it provided healing for the soul" (Wacker, 2001, 3). Their reading of Isaiah 53:5: "He was wounded for our transgressions . . . and with his stripes we are healed," con-firmed that Christ's atoning work in his body on the cross provided for both spiritual and physical healing.

While their radical evangelical forebears had also prayed fervently to God for healing, Pentecostal worshippers offered a specific form of prayer called "prevailing prayer" that "would *auto-matically* bring healing to the body" (Wacker, 2001, 26, emphasis added). The believer's job is to pray for healing and believe that it has been fulfilled, and God would do the healing, by contract.[10] One was obligated to believe that the healing had happened even if there is evidence to the contrary. One Edith Shaw prayed for healing yet continued to have a severe fever and began to doubt the efficacy of her prayer. Wacker gives us Shaw's words:

> Then the Lord spoke: "These are not symptoms of diphtheria, for I healed you of that last night . . . I healed you when you prayed . . . I want you to act just as you would if you felt perfectly well, *because* you *are* well." Shaw captured the essence of prevailing prayer in a single, revealing sentence: "I saw that God's Word

was true and the symptoms were the devil's lie." (Wacker, 2001, 27; quoting Edith Shaw in *Trust*, June-July [1915], 16–17)

While God might be the source of all healing, God does not cause illness in most cases, according to Pentecostals: the devil does. "Everyone knew that evil spirits caused most illnesses. Therefore in many cases divine healing involved exorcism of the tormenting spirit[11] which required placing one's hand on the 'afflicted part' and in the name of Jesus commanding the demon to depart"[12] (Wacker, 2001, 92). While other traditions might assert that God sends illness to chastise or to teach a lesson, according to the Pentecostal, illness came from demonic sources.

Wacker maintains that Pentecostalism holds together both supernaturalism and pragmatism (1986, 532). Adherents trust God to meet their needs, including miraculous acts of healing that shatter the laws of nature, while maintaining a this-worldly pragmatism, a "determination to master life's perils by harnessing and disciplining one's faith" (530). We see both supreme confidence in God's intervention as well as coordinated, rigorous, and sustained human effort in service of surviving the trials of human finitude, including illness. Wacker holds together the supernatural and the pragmatic in the healing tradition with the label "sacrament." "[F]or Pentecostals, divine healing and other miracle experiences have effectively functioned as sacraments, palpable symbols of those rare but unforgettable moments of Grace in the life of the believer" (1986, 532).

Healing Waters Church can be understood as a place constructed for the wedding of ecstatic immersions in Almighty God and the quotidian tasks of a community that cares for its sick. It constructed this place out of material born during slavery, when people of African origin transformed the master's religion from one that taught obedience to human authorities to one that preached the subversive message that slaves are fully human. Not only did their transformation of religion serve their survival, but so did social and familial networks of care that transcended connection by birth, as well as folk healing methods that served the health needs of slaves. Many of these traditions were preserved in the Sanctified Church that refused to relinquish either its life-giving ecstatic worship form or the leadership of women. Finally, the fire of the Pentecostal movement with its affirmation of the centrality of healing in worship gave Healing Waters some of the characteristic theological claims that undergird its healing ministry. Though this particular congregation was formed only in the latter fourth of the twentieth century, it continues to be shaped by strong, usually unnamed streams from the past.

WORSHIP AT HEALING WATERS

Practices of care for the sick are often understood as activities that take place outside the worship hour, at the bedside in homes and hospitals, in the pastor's office, or in living rooms. At Healing Waters, care also happens during the worship hour. Furthermore, because worship is the heartbeat of this church, nothing in the life of this congregation outside of worship, including caregiving, can be understood without exploring worship. Practical theologian Dale Andrews argues that the inseparability of worship and pastoral care is also true of most African American churches. "[B]lack preaching and the worship experience evolved as major facets in communal care, providing survival and growth resources for black wholeness" (Andrews, 28). Invoking the familiar healing, sustaining, guiding, and reconciling[13] functions of pastoral care in general, Andrews states, "Care for black wholeness which includes healing amid sustaining and guiding, and the reconciliation of humanity to God, to self, and to each other, has been among the fundamental facets of black preaching and the worship experience" (29). In a similar vein, Edward Wimberly notes that preaching and pastoral counseling work together in the process of meaning-making, helping people to "replot," or reinterpret, their stories (Wimberly, 16).

The Shout

What people from mainstream Protestant churches notice most immediately in Pentecostal worship is the holy dance, the "shout." When I first saw it I did not know if it was lament or fervent petition or involuntary movements that were disconnected from the will of the dancer. What I have learned is that shouting is primarily a form of praise. Pastor Hanford opens some doors to the internal workings of the shouting person.

> When you want to tell God thank you for what he's already done, and you're sitting, and if it's a song and you can relate to the song, or if it's preaching the Word of God, and you can relate to what the preacher is saying, you want to give God glory. You want to give him praise, you just want to worship him, you want to thank him in the highest. Whichever way I can just let him know, "God, I appreciate you for being my Lord and my Savior and you did this for me, you did that for me. You opened doors for me. You made a way for me. *You healed my body.* You opened up my understanding to your Word your way. And I want just to thank you." And before you know it, the exercise part of dancing—you are dancing to the glory of God. (emphasis added)
>
> It's just like you get right on up and you give him the praise, whichever way you want to. Give him the glory. I don't have to think about it. I just think about what he's already done. How he woke me up this morning, and I'm still in my right mind. I do have arthritis in this limb, but nobody had to bathe me. Nobody had to dress me. Nobody had to feed me. "God, I want to give you all the glory for what you have done," and I got in the car and was driving. Nobody ran into me. I didn't run into anybody. "God, thank you for that!" I just want to give him thanks for everything. He said, "In everything, give him thanks!" Everything, I don't care what it is. In *everything*, give him thanks! And when you sit down and the Word is going forth and you can relate to the Word: "O God, you did this for me!" And you can't sit down on him any longer; you want to express it. So you just emotionally want to express it to him. Even if it's that I have to dance on my feet. Even if I have to run and say "Hallelujah!" or "Thank you, Jesus." Some way and somehow it's coming out of me. Thank the Lord!

While Pastor Hanford described shouting as praise for what God has already done, one church leader adds that sometimes it is praise *in advance* for what God has not yet done, but surely will.

I've been to the point . . . when I have come into this church, because I was married at one time, and going through [having a hard time] at home, I had been abused mentally and physically. And I would come into this church, and when I would walk in here, and I would just start giving God the praise right then. And then when the praise and worship get to going, and I ain't thanking God for what he already done; I'm thanking God for bringing me out of the situation that *I'm already in*, that I'm in. So I'm going to give God some praise *in advance*. You see what I'm saying? I know it's going to happen. I know. (emphasis added)

While the act of shouting is certainly an act of praise, there are times when pain is not far away. Another church leader refers to praise in the midst of trials.

People walk in here burdened. They done come through a lot. So that's the time Jesus don't want us to be heavy burdened, so as we are going through the storm. He don't want us going through the storm feeling all grievey and moody. *He want us to go through the storm praising him.* And that's the way you have to do. And when you praise him, you know what you going through. (emphasis added)

Her husband adds,

When they do this dance, they be thinking about what they're worried about, and they get joy out of that. That spirit gets in them in the dance, and they be dancing in the spirit. They get joy out of it. That's why they be streaming in the aisles.

When asked about how much of the dance is voluntary and how much is being involuntarily possessed by something outside yourself, most say it is voluntary, but add something to the effect, "I can't help myself, I just get up and start praising God."

You can have a bad cold and be coughing, and I'll say, "Well, I'm going to church, but I'm going to sit quiet." Don't never say that. [laughter] Before you know, you are up on the floor. That's the truth.

Having the rhythms of your shout picked up by the organist is key to the escalation of the sense of the presence of the Spirit. I once asked the organist how he knows when to start playing the organ. Does he visually scan the congregation all the time? Does he listen for the sound of feet on the wooden floor? Does he watch for a cue from Pastor Hanford? He said that God tells him what to play and when. "I just listen for the Spirit," he said. I asked him about a time when a woman was shouting, and he did not play anything at all. He said that God told him not to play. I asked if Pastor Hanford sometimes tells him not to, and he said, sometimes God tells her to tell him not to play. Cheryl Sanders notes, "The organ takes the lead in providing the rhythmic and tonal texture of the worship experience" and she describes "a three-way conversation involving preacher, congregation, and musician" (55). This is clearly the case at Healing Waters. The organist has to be on, listening and responding, for three hours every Sunday.

In all my time at Healing Waters, I have seen less than five men shout. On almost every Sunday, it is exclusively women. Some have said men think it is not manly to shout; some have said that women are simply more sensitive to the movement of the Spirit. Whatever the reason, on one occasion I had a glimpse of how it might be different if men did more holy dance.

Healing Waters does not have a baptismal pool, so, on one designated Sunday, several of us joined the baptismal ceremonies of another church, and I had a chance to see another Sanctified Church at worship and prayer. There were two big men at the baptismal pool who were responsible for the full immersion of new believers into the water. After all the baptisms were finished, one of the men at the pool became filled with the Holy Spirit. He was bent over at the waist when the other man grabbed his hands and stretched them out to the side and started pressing hard. Their arms were shaking with the force they were exerting. It occurred to me that, if shouting and praising were mostly a male activity, the times when the Spirit was high might be quite different. I wondered if there would be more muscle, more male energy, even more aggression.

There are also times when the sacred borders the mundane. I once saw a teenage girl wanting to get past a shouter who did not notice her. She waited, patient but bored, to get back to her seat next to her. Finally, in the middle of the ecstasy of her holy dance, the woman did notice her, and, with squinted eyes, moved a little to let her pass, and then resumed the dance. Another time, during an interview with a woman who was a church leader and Pastor Hanford, the leader was praying for me with great fervor, and Pastor Hanford was offering supporting responses. Right in the middle of a word of fervent support, Pastor Hanford noticed her young grandson was touching something he should not have. Pastor Hanford said something like, "Yes, Lord, we want to thank you Lord . . . Charles, put that down! . . . we praise you Lord. . . ." Without missing a beat, Pastor Hanford moved freely from one realm to another.

Sacred Space

Like many churches, when you walk into a service of worship at Healing Waters you are aware of entering into sacred time and space. Victor Turner has described sacred space as a place of "liminality," a place "betwixt and between," a place on the borders of the mundane and the sacred (Turner, 94). To participate in ritual is to participate in a liminal space, a place on the threshold of a new reality. Liminality in Pentecostal worship begins with a physical and ritual separation from the outside world. This separation makes the ecstatic worship inside the building possible. An older woman describes "the anointing" associated with that space.

> Some mornings I just want to lay back in the bed and don't even feel like putting my clothes on. Then I think about it and I say, "But, wait a minute, devil! I'm going to get out of here and I'm going to church!" And you know, when I do that, *as soon as I walk through that door, I can feel the anointing.* Everything that I felt before I left home, it's gone, and I can just feel the knowledge of the Holy Ghost. (emphasis added)

Many elements create a sense of the sacred: the music, the dancing bodies, the fervent voices raised in prayer and proclamation, stained glass, pulpit furniture, the various "uniforms" of worship: choir robes, clergy robes, hats, mothers' white dresses, ushers' nurse uniforms, or, indecipherable to the visitor, the occasional red blouses and black shirts of some of the women. One author has referred to these signs of the sacred as Pentecostal forms of "icons," both visual and auditory, which he defines as "windows, or doorways into prayer . . . intersections between the human and divine," with the goal of "coming into the presence of the Holy" (Albrecht, 111). The very bodies of the other worshippers are visual icons. "Instead of sacred icons fashioned on wood and in plaster intended to draw the faithful into worship, Pentecostals are encircled by fellow believers, together they represent living, active, human, embodied icons." Human bodies also function as "kinesthetic icons," where it is the *movements* of the human body that draw the worshipper into the presence of God. "According to Pentecostal ritual logic, God is expected to move, but so are God's worshippers. . . . They move even as God moves" (113).

Not only are bodies and their movements iconographic, but they also serve ritual ends, as both *performers* of ritual (ritual subjects) and as *instruments* of ritual (ritual objects). Referring to a leader in another Pentecostal worship service, one author wrote:

> In praise leadership, Verna uses various objects: hymnal, an overhead projector, and screen, and, occasionally a tambourine. . . . However, the primary ritual instrument is Sister Verna's body. . . . In performance, she is both ritual object (instrument) and ritual subject (actor). (Seamone, 18)

At Healing Waters, it is not only hymnody, sacred language, and elements of water, bread, and wine that are intrinsic to the rituals associated with the sacred, but also human bodies themselves. Furthermore, these are not rigid, bowed bodies; rather they are bodies in motion. Therefore, those whose illness has rendered them painfully aware of their embodiment, enter into a world where, far from being despised, bodies are as sacred and blessed as any saint's relic.

As a visitor, I was familiar to an extent with many of the indicators of sacred space found at Healing Waters. But there was one marker of the sacred, one marker of a space set apart, that I had to learn. I am calling it "the suspension of rules of etiquette." I learned about it through smiling.

At first, when someone came to pray with me, or to hug me, or if Pastor Hanford called me forward to speak a word of God to me in worship, I would smile politely in response. Yet nobody else was smiling, neither Pastor Hanford nor the person praying with me. They were very, very serious. It became clear that this time of prayer, or summons from the pastor, was less an interaction between me and another person that required certain kinds of etiquette and more an entrance together into the presence of the Holy. Rules of propriety gave way to the sacredness and intensity of encounter with God. Yet what is going on between the two human beings is very, very intimate. It is as though the shared belief that this is about the Spirit and not about us makes us feel safer being vulnerable in one another's presence. If the human-to-human interaction is not the focus, if people are more aware of being naked before *God* and not in front of one another, then we are more willing to be utterly vulnerable in worship.

There are other suspensions of, if not etiquette, then everyday behaviors, that help to create a sense of the presence of the holy, a clarity that this is a time set apart. One Sunday, Pastor Hanford, who was not presiding at that moment, got up from her chair and called all the ministers to the front, facing the congregation, lining up about six of them. She said something big was going to happen today, she could feel it. At first all the ministers just stood there while Pastor Hanford talked, but one of them began to rock back and forth at the waist, like traditional Jewish worshippers at prayer. I thought, any minute she is going to break loose. After everybody else calmed down, she did. She started with a long shriek. She walked back and forth in front of the church, then she got on her hands and knees and crawled halfway down the aisle. These were God's words, not hers. The whole church was silent except for her voice, and a guest who would give a little response. There was no music. Pastor Hanford just sat there, calm but intense. Nobody looked uncomfortable. It was just intense. We waited a long time until she became quiet again. Finally she sat down, someone handed her a Kleenex, the music started playing again, and worship resumed.

These suspensions of day-to-day codes of behavior contribute to the atmosphere of worship. This is hardly quotidian time or space, this is a "zone" where the divine is encountered. Perhaps the rich metaphor of "a home over Jordan" about which Homer Ashby writes best captures this alternative, liminal space of worship.

> Deep River, my home is over Jordan.
> Deep River, I want to cross over into campground
> Oh, don't you want to go to that Gospel feast.
> That Promised Land where all is Peace.
> Deep river. (10)

Ashby describes this as "a place of refuge, safety, and protection. It is a place of promise and expectation. Home across the Jordan is where *full humanity is realized* in the company of others." Crossing the threshold of the door to Healing Waters is a way to cross over Jordan metaphorically.

Liminality and Healing

Yet these elements that contribute to the creation of holy space are not only for an encounter with God, but also for the purpose of reaching practical goals, such as healing sick bodies.[14] In addition to the more lofty practices of "celebration" and "contemplation" during worship, Albrecht includes "transcendental *efficacy*" as one of the modes of worship (116–20, emphasis added). "When Pentecostals pray in this mode, they expect an answer" (118). This is worship with a particular goal in mind, such as "healing, miracles, or Spirit baptism" (118). Speaking of Pentecostal churches today, one scholar states, "Pentecostalism is all about healing. You might almost call it self-help. It's a really therapeutic tradition. . . ." (Griffith). This efficacious mode may emerge at Healing Waters when the congregation gathers at the altar after the sermon for anointing with oil by one of the ministers. Or there may be a laying on of hands by several leaders whom Pastor Hanford would call forth for that purpose. Or, at any time during the service Pastor Hanford may sense that something is wrong in someone's body, and she will call them forward to discuss it, offering a warning of future illness, a diagnosis, or a suggestion for a healing practice at home. This is worship in a mode that expects results, including the healing of the sick.

Pastor Hanford has participated in many such transformational moments in worship. She tells of a healing during one service.

> There was this lady came to the church that night, and she was spitting up blood . . . and a little bit came out of her nose. And the Bishop had his wife to read her that [text from Ezekiel]. He said, "Keep reading. Read that scripture." And he told the lady, "Look at me. If you can repeat what she's saying to you from the Word of God, we are going to see a miracle." And after a while, she would repeat it, and she would act like she was going to pass out or something of that nature, and he said, "Repeat it. Just keep saying it over and over." *And the Lord stopped that blood flow right in that church.* (emphasis added)

Worship at Healing Waters creates a "borderland," a place on the edge between the sacred and the mundane, a liminality, a "'space' for something different to emerge . . . 'room' for change and innovation" (Albrecht, 121). Albrecht names three possibilities that can emerge out of liminality: community, challenges to the status quo, and transformation. It is in the final category, transformation, that he locates healing. All of the shouting, praising, suspension of etiquette, all serve to create liminality, the place where the out of the ordinary can happen. It is the setting for all sorts of transformations, including the transformation of sick bodies into well bodies.

Worship as Congregational Improvisation

Given all the community building, challenges to the status quo, and transformations that take place, it is not hard to imagine that the atmosphere of worship at Healing Waters is charged with drama. Michael S. Weaver refers to the "theatricality of the Black Church"

(Weaver, 53), with its various roles and performances, interactions of "word and gesture" (55). Worshippers never really know where the Spirit is going to lead; it is like a play unfolding before them. Then, at times, you are in the drama yourself, pulled in by inner tuggings of pain or praise, pulled in physically by a worship leader, or pulled in by the Spirit of God. You might be telling the congregation your story, or your story might be unfolding at that moment as you are healed of your disease. Drama is everywhere.

It is a drama where time and the divisions of time, bodies and the movements of bodies, voices and their testimonies, are scripted by tradition, ritual, worship bulletin, and ministerial direction. But all of these structuring elements defer to the will of the Spirit. If the Spirit is present in a big way, the intensity of shouting and praising may last a long time. I have seen some of the ministers trying to calm things down because the service is going long. But they cannot always contain it. Eruptions keep happening even through periods that are usually mellow, such as the calming down period after the altar call. A worshipper might suddenly be moved to march down the aisle with a prayer cloth sweeping the devil away or to tell the choir to march down the aisle, fast, or the pastor herself might call someone forward to heal them, diagnose them, admonish them, praise them, give them a word of advice from God. The divisions of time are the Spirit's, not humans'.

The structures of worship could be understood as the pillars around which souls, bodies, and voices improvise. One writer has called sanctified worship jazz (Paris, 73–79). He defines four "performers" in the "jazz ensemble" that is Pentecostal worship: the *congregation* who acts as both performer and audience; those who act as "*MC*'s" and play managerial and performance roles; the *preacher*; and those responsible for maintenance functions, such as *ushers* and *musicians*. Both the jazz band and all the players in Pentecostal worship "create[s] [their] performance as a collective enterprise" (73). Like Pentecostal worship, "a band's efforts collectively and sectionally interlock around the composition, integrating the individual solos into a unified whole. At their most vital, these efforts transcend the limits of the score and the shortcomings of individual players, and the performance as a collective creation soars. . . . As in church the band has 'stars' and major solo voices, but they are dependent on the support and cooperation of the ensemble in order to create good music" (73–74).

The jazz metaphor works well for worship at Healing Waters. There is a certain "melody" to worship that is unchanging, but the weekly services improvise on that melody in varieties of ways.

Into this drama the sick enter as actors, as performers in an ensemble that is beholden to a degree to an external score, but not completely. The sick enter as those just as empowered as any to contribute their own "riff" on the old standards of worship. If they are healed in worship, they become a central actor, perhaps providing the climax to the day's performance.

Yet even if they and their illness are not part of the high point of worship, they still are creators of the performance. One particular Sunday a woman, Mrs. Wilson, came to church to say that her husband was very sick. The reality of his illness penetrated the workings of worship in many ways at many points. At the beginning of the service, one of the deacons prayed for the "sick and destitute" and named Mr. Wilson in particular. Immediately afterwards one of the ministers came to Mrs. Wilson and hugged her, acknowledging the difficulty of her husband's illness. Later in the service Mrs. Wilson stood in her place in the choir and gave the congregation an update on her husband's health, saying that she gave thanks to God that he is still alive and in his right mind. She drew applause when she said she did not want to be asked what she needed, she just wanted people to do what God told them to do. Pastor Hanford praised Mrs. Wilson for asking for help, and she encouraged the congregation to pay her a visit. Later in the service, Mrs. Wilson had the opportunity to sing a solo, with the refrain, "He set my feet on higher ground," and everyone knew what she meant. Finally, she went forward for an anointing at the altar at the end of the service. Her husband's illness intersected with worship on five occasions in multiple forms: prayer, testimony, ministerial recognition, anointing, and musical offering. She, and her husband, in his absence, were active creators of the worship service as they brought their troubles and their faith to the service, and as it was received and transformed by fellow worshippers.

HEALING WATERS IN AN UNJUST WORLD

The reality of ill health in Healing Waters Church cannot be fully explored without naming the context of social injustice that victimizes many of the worshippers. Inequalities of access to quality and timely health care, dangerous and inadequate housing, poor nutrition, unaffordable medications, and hazardous working conditions are inscribed on many sick bodies of the poor, working poor, working class. "[P]overty is at the base of most of the health problems of African Americans" (Townes, 61; citing Dixon, 27).

Some have criticized ecstatic, Pentecostal worship as contributing to a quietistic faith that fails to address such injustices. Earlier studies saw the ecstatic displays as forms of "sublimation" (Alexander, 1991, 26). It was seen as "a symbolic rebellion on the part of the socially disenfranchised Pentecostals [which] . . . functions as a catharsis, a safety-valve, accommodating them to their social condition" while leaving that unjust condition intact (Alexander, 1989, 26). Pentecostal worshippers, largely of the lower classes, are expressing their opposition to a society that devalues them through their holy dance and tongues, it was claimed. Yet, the argument went, this form of protest is ineffectual. It is a "catharsis" which "drains" or "deflects" their hostility in ways that do not overtly challenge unjust conditions and thus leaves the social structure unchanged (1991, 26). It effectively vitiates any real social action to challenge social injustice.

Rather than a disenfranchising catharsis, I would argue that worship at Healing Waters is better understood as the subversive creation of an alternative realm where black bodies and souls are beloved and redeemed in a world where they are often the object of indifference at best, violence at worst. Lee Butler describes aspects of the experience of living in a black body in America.

> As African Americans, we face a difficult task to be "at home in our own skin." . . . We have never been fully accepted in the United States, and accepting ourselves has been problematic at best. . . .

> Consequently, if we are not conscientious, our dark bodies can feel like jailhouses of shame and ostracism rather than homes of warmth and compassion." . . . The African American experience has been a struggle to find a place to call home. (Butler, 23, 25)

Yet in the worship hour at Healing Waters, worshippers do find "a place to call home," in Butler's words, some reprieve from "mental and emotional homelessness" (25). Rather than worship as an avoidance or anesthesia to the pain of racism, it is a home from which resistance can emerge.

Dale Andrews confirms the political and liberative implications of home or "refuge" in a hostile, dehumanizing, and often violent world (34; quoting Frazier, 44–46). "The dimensions of this psychosocial image ["refuge"] were not devoid of sociopolitical activity. The refuge function of the Church was not escapism. . . . At its heart, the church-as-refuge was a place for the critical affirmation of human value and human needs, which included liberation" (35–36).

Bobby Alexander uses Victor Turner's understanding of ritual not as sublimating but as "redressive" (1989, 113). "[R]itual is a primary means by which men and women redress the problematic aspects of everyday social life by providing an alternative arrangement for social interaction" (113). In this space, social roles and requirements are relaxed, hierarchies of the outside world lose their sway, and participants experience greater equality and mutuality in their interactions (114). "The relaxation of some of the requirements of social structure in ritual liminality invites participants to reconfigure the components of existing structure, now experienced as arbitrary, to envision and experiment with alternatives" (115). Liminality makes possible the entrance into not only the ecstatic, but also the countercultural—the shouting, dancing, running up and down the aisles, all of which are counter to European American norms of proper behavior, such as "poise, dignity, and composure" (117; referring to Williams, 168–69). In Alexander's study of one African American Pentecostal church he concluded that the worship-driven proselytizing thrust was a form of concern for social injustice. The effort to bring outsiders into the alternative social and normative reality of the church was a way of effecting social change. Far from being a diversion from attention to the world's injustices, Alexander concludes that Pentecostal worship funds efforts for social reform (121). "The relative freedom of ritual liminality allows these Pentecostals to elaborate, and experiment with, alternatives to the existing power structure" (123). The behaviors in worship, both the egalitarian social behaviors, and the shouting, jumping, dancing, crawling, and running, further the work for transformation of the outside world.

In worship at Healing Waters, there are signs of the harsh outside world. Once there was another church that was selling "Angel Food," which could be paid for with cash, check, credit card, or *food stamps*, a form of payment as legitimate as any other. We regularly pray for people in prison, people on drugs, the sick and destitute, women "on the streets" (code words for women who are sex workers). A thin, ill-kempt woman who was clearly an addict came into church one time and was cared for in her prayer, praise, and pain. Sometimes there is donated food for the taking downstairs in the church basement. Sometimes adults' limited reading skills mean stumbling over reading the Scripture from the pulpit. On one occasion Pastor Hanford shared the tragedy of one family whose sorrows were directly connected to social injustices. They had just returned home from burying their son (high death rates for young black males). The father had lost a leg to diabetes (a disease of poverty) and used a wheelchair to get around. Someone came to the door and asked for money (much more frequent in poor neighborhoods). When the father gave him everything he had, he was shot in the face and killed (rates of violence in poor neighborhoods). Now the family had to go back to bury their father. Carol Watkins Ali has written that "two of the most detrimental issues threatening the collective survival of African Americans and our ability to self-determine are *genocidal poverty* and *nihilism*" (Watkins Ali, 137, emphasis added). At Healing Waters Church, poverty is never far away, and it provides some material relief from the effects of poverty. Most significantly, however, it addresses the threat of nihilism in situations of human suffering.

Though one enters a liminal space, a holy space, a space where the Spirit of God is moving, the violence and injustice of the outside world is never far away from the worshipper at Healing Waters. The victims of this violence enter a space where black bodies are rendered sacred icons, sick bodies are transformed into active creators of ritual, bodies ravaged by years of poverty are honored as singers, dancers, shouters to the glory of God. There are clearly redressive, countercultural elements of this worship that nurture visions of the time when the Commonwealth of God covers the earth as the waters cover the seas. On one Sunday, there was a moment in worship that is representative of the subversive and liberating nature of worship at Healing Waters. This moment is described below in Chenita's story.

CHENITA'S STORY AND WORSHIP

It started during a "comma" in the flow of the worship, a brief pause before the next word, a time of gathering ourselves in preparation for the next ph(r)ase of the worship.

Breaking into the silence came the sound of, "pound, pound, pound." I looked over and there was Chenita facing the wall, head down, stomping away. No music. No pastor's words. Nothing in the background. Just pounding. Nor was it in response to any music or words. It just appeared, like an unexpected knock on the door. Or the neighbors starting to hammer a nail into some wood. Pound pound pound.

"Oh no," I thought. "The organist doesn't hear her. Or he hears, but for some reason he isn't going to honor what she is doing. She is going to be embarrassed for doing the wrong thing at the wrong time. She was supposed to wait for the right cue. Now they will ignore her."

Chenita is a woman whom I had interviewed the day before. She had been a drug addict, in and out of jail and prison, had sold her body, lived on the streets. She started with marijuana, moved on to powder cocaine, then crack, and finally heroin. At the beginning of her drug use, her father had tried to spare her selling her body by teaching her how to shoplift, showing her the hidden cameras, the blind spots, how to roll the clothes into a compact bundle. But his intentions failed.

Several years ago, though, on a Christmas day, while in jail, wretchedly sick from heroin withdrawal, she returned to Jesus. A week later, on New Years Day, still in jail, she received the Holy Ghost while talking to a minister from another church on the phone. Her offerings of praise, alleluias, and prayers were so loud that the jail officer threatened to put her in another cell if she did not stop. With the help of Healing Waters and God, she has stayed clean.

On that Sunday in church, as she began her praise, the organist was right there with her after only a brief second. Soon others chimed in with their shouting. There were five or six women joining in. There turned out to be a flight of the Spirit through the place. They had not ignored her. They had honored her, and they had joined her. She had issued the invitation, prompted by the inner workings of her soul before God, and invoking the familiar ritual sequence.

Chenita had received no invitation, no cues, whether musical, verbal, social, ritual, or otherwise. She broke into the silence with her body. Her praise, pain, resistance, defiance, declaration of her allegiance shattered the "comma" in which we were all pausing, interrupting our regrouping for the next item on the worship agenda. Healing Waters was the setting for the declaration of her voice, her body. She claimed the authority to bring everything to a halt and, unbidden, pound out her soul on the floor of the church, into the air, into the bodies and hearts of the whole church, before her God.

The transformation in this woman's life, the role Healing Waters has played, the Godness of it all, was overwhelming.

This transformation has not spared her life pain. Only a week earlier she was driving alongside a lake and a strong voice pulled at her to drive into it. "The devil," she said, was trying to get her to kill herself. She pulled into the house of her aunt, a leader at Healing Waters, for support. She was not home. Then she called her pastor, who prayed with her, and got through the crisis.

The odds against addicts making it are small. There are enormous social, psychological, and financial pulls toward returning to drug use. Drug counselors at the women's prison in Raleigh report that 80 percent of women addicts will be back in prison within three years. Yet somehow Chenita has resisted. God, Healing Waters, her aunt, her pastor, have made the transformation in the jail cell a lasting one. Her formerly addicted body, emaciated body, commodified body, in the context of Healing Waters, hijacked worship in an uninvited, but roundly welcomed, pounding of praise. And the body of Christ rejoiced with her.

<h2 align="center">CONCLUSION</h2>

This is a community with deep roots in African slaves' worship and caring practices, in the Sanctified Church's refusal to be associated with white-dominated denominations and in Pentecostalism's emphasis on healing in the liminal space of worship. It is a site of both "refuge and liberation" (Andrews, 89). It is the site of the "adaptive genius of a people" displayed in both "a response to external pressures and a unique and creative way of fashioning that response" (Ashby, 87). In this context there are particular belief-practices that pertain to illness, which will be discussed in the next chapter. These belief-practices do not function independently or in a vacuum. Their particular force, or impact, or function is connected to the context that I have just outlined. It is a context where the body is radically redefined over and against the dominant culture: The body is nothing less than the site of God's transforming power, and the body is integral to the human response of praise and gratitude.

2

HEALING WATERS'
BELIEF-PRACTICES

*A*fter finding Healing Waters, I was eager to talk about it. One of the people I turned to was a University of North Carolina scholar who has studied African American sanctified spirituality.[15] I thought he would be interested in finding a place new to him that he might explore as well. Three minutes into my description of the church he said, "You aren't talking about Healing Waters, are you?" I was surprised to learn that, not only had he heard of it, but he had worked closely with Pastor Hanford on his major book, had known the Hanford family for years, and considered them close friends. He had Pastor Hanford speak in his classes and had taken students to her church many times. The point is, this is a church that has been the object of white, academic scrutiny before, and now I was adding my own account of their life together.

The risk is, of course, that scholars' descriptions, intentionally or not, can serve pernicious ends. What Edward Said said of the Middle East and Middle Eastern studies (called the Orient and Orientalism in British scholarly circles) describes the risk in white scholarship about African American people and communities:

Knowledge of the Orient, because generated out of strength, in a sense *creates* the Orient, the Oriental, and his world. . . . The Oriental is depicted as something one judges (as in a court of law), something one studies and depicts (as in a curriculum), something one disciplines (as in a school or prison), something one illustrates (as in a zoological manual). The point is that in each of these cases the Oriental is *contained* and *represented* by dominating frameworks. (Said, 1979, 40; summarizing the language of British statesmen Arthur James Balfour and Evelyn Baring Cromer; emphasis in original)

In this depiction, "The Oriental is irrational, depraved (fallen), childlike, 'different'; thus the European is rational, virtuous, mature, 'normal'" (Said, 1979, 40). Elsewhere, Said refers to Claude Levi-Strauss' phrase that anthropology is the "handmaiden of colonialism."

One of the ways scholars have tried to mitigate the risk of making oppressogenic claims about other groups, particularly when there is a power differential between the investigator and the studied group in the investigator's favor, has been to refuse to make objective and universally true claims and to recognize the limitations of their observations. I believe a way to begin to discuss Healing Waters is to recognize that it will inevitably be done from a particular perspective, that there is no value-neutral place to stand in approaching it. My vantage point will always be that of a white, Presbyterian, feminist woman. As such I will always have biases, blinders, and blunders in my interpretations. I share with all interpreters of other contexts doubts about how much "bracketing" of one's own perspective is possible in order to "capture" accurately a modicum of truth about what we are describing. Some claim that not only is "bracketing" one's own perspective *impossible*, it is *undesirable,* and that moral judgments about other contexts are appropriate (Prothero). They might say it is desirable, for example, for the feminist to "unbracket" her beliefs and to critique clearly what appear to her to be problematic sexist strains through a culture. Yet others describe a stance of "empathy" toward the group being studied, understanding empathy as "the painstaking attempt to comprehend the experiences and passions of diverse others, eventuating in one's own moral transformation" (Griffith, 2004, 18). Empathy suggests a modesty about the certainty of the investigator's own morality and truth claims. Such reserve gives room for the voices of the other context to speak on their own terms, and even to change the investigator's own claims.

Taking into account these various perspectives on bracketing and empathy, I will describe my approach as having three moments: a moment of "empathetic description," when I attempt as well as I am able to get inside the belief-practice world of Healing Waters and to describe it on its own terms. The second is a moment of "appreciative interpretation" when I use my own language to describe the strength of a particular belief-practice. Finally I move to a "cautionary warning," when I discuss a belief-practice's susceptibility to corruption by sin, which I am defining as idolatry, a turn to the finite for salvation. While not in a position to make judgments about whether a belief-practice has, in fact, been corrupted at any of the congregations studied here, I am capable of cautionary statements about ways they could *possibly* be. By referring to ways they could "possibly" be corrupted, I do not mean, "ways that *maybe* they are corrupted." Rather I mean, ways they are vulnerable to corruption.

Inhabiting these three moments, I have a certain advantage over other social scientific investigators, such as the scholar from University of North Carolina. From the perspective of a secular cultural anthropologist, I have an advantage as a Christian investigator of Healing Waters—I share a commitment to the same sacred texts, core statements of belief, and institutional expressions of these texts and beliefs. Speaking as a theologian, I have the advantage of sharing an experience of the redeeming power of God in Jesus Christ as given witness in Scripture and church. In spite of these advantages, my stance as both investigator and one who shares a common faith is complicated and fraught with risk. At its most benign, I risk simply being inaccurate. At worst, I risk portrayals that reinforce racist, classist stereotypes. Furthermore, I risk taking the stance of a tourist whose desire is to observe the "quaint" Other as a spectacle, to plunder the goods of the "foreign land," and to colonize their traditions.

There is an additional risk as well. Since I am focusing on a practice, care for the sick, which is neither overtly political nor an obvious challenge to oppressive socioeconomic structures, I risk "[i]dealizing narrow roles such as caregiver or grateful believer as the epitome of one's faith experience [which] can unintentionally reinforce norms of 'place' and one's need to *stay* in one's place" (Frederick, 80). While I will argue that there is a subversive, countercultural element to many of the practices I describe, there is nevertheless a risk that such a description would lapse into a trivializing romanticization.

Nevertheless, I have engaged in this study with the hope that my efforts are in service of a good that can only be accomplished when people of good will begin to meet, talk, and connect on holy ground. The challenge is to express appreciation and even awe for the practices of Healing Waters without romanticizing and thus caricaturing them, and to highlight the countercultural and subversive elements of these practices that create spaces of redemption, healing, and liberation.

BELIEF-PRACTICES OF HEALING WATERS CHURCH

If you are a member of the Healing Waters community, here is a summary of the belief-practice world in which you experience your illness:

> God reigns in the world, but the devil is alive and well. To tempt people to deny their faith, the devil makes people sick. Healers use such things as prayer, various material things, laying on hands, and rebuking to get the devil out and to get the Spirit of God in. Some of these things happen in homes, some in worship. The sick person's role is to believe that God has already healed them, to go to the doctor but believe that it is God who heals, to be faithful in the midst of their illness so that God might get the glory.

God Is Good and the Devil Makes You Sick

While God is all powerful, human beings still live in a world where
the devil is also alive and well. One of the church leaders, Annette,
who is also known as a healer, said,

> I've had so many experiences with demonic spirits. They actu-
> ally talk to you, and they know you. They know whether or not
> you are a child of God. They know whether or not you are afraid
> of them. And if you are afraid of them and if you are not a child
> of God, they don't hear you or obey what you are commanding
> them to do, even if you are using the name of Jesus. Because you
> are afraid of them. So demons talk. They talk back to you. I've
> had them say to me, "Why are you so faithful? I don't want you
> in here. Go on, get out!"

Believers must stay strong in their faith to be protected from
demons. She continued,

> If there is someone who is demonic-possessed, and then those
> spirits come out, they have to go somewhere—you understand
> what I'm saying? And then if you're not a strong believer, you
> know, it could attack you.

If some teach that God makes you sick, that is simply not true.
It is the devil who is the source of illness. Pastor Hanford added,

> There are a lot of people who think God make us sick. God will
> not make you sick and then turn around and heal you. That's not
> God. He don't ever make any of us sick. That's the work of old
> Slewfoot. . . . God don't make us sick. Never has, never will.

The devil does many things to try to draw us away from God,
including making us sick. Again, Pastor Hanford said,

> He will buffet us in so many different ways. Come on. Why?
> Because he's already upset with us, because we chose to follow
> Christ. OK? He thought he had us all sewed up. Uh-huh. But he's
> finding out now, "No, you have no control over me. I'm on the

Lord's side. I'm the King's kid. I'm covered under the blood of
Jesus and now you can't touch me. I have my mind made up to
follow Jesus. To take up my cross and follow him." So in carrying my cross, I'm going to face a lot of things, a lot of obstacles,
maybe a lot of different types of sicknesses that I've never witnessed before: high blood pressure, diabetes, arthritis—first one
thing and then another.

In talking about her experience with breast cancer, an older
highly respected woman claimed that the devil was trying to stop
her good works by giving her cancer.

The devil said to the Lord, "You just turn me loose on [her name]
and I'll make her stop." Because the devil knows I'm a lovely
person and I love to do and love and to be doing for the Lord.
So *he wanted to stop me from doing what I was doing.* But even
through the cancer, he couldn't stop me. So, hallelujah! Thank
you, sir! Because he couldn't do it! He tried (Thank you, Lord),
but he couldn't do it! I thank God for it.

When worship is particularly Spirit filled, the devil is especially prone to attack. A woman known for her healing said,

I was here in the service one day and *the anointing was so high
here.* And Susan, I don't know what happened, but I just passed
out. The pastor was sitting in the pulpit. And I was just out. And
I could hear them all around me. We have two LPN's and an RN
here, and they were taking my pulse, and I could hear them say,
"I can't get it. Her pulse is real faint. I can't get a pulse on her.
Her heartbeat is weak. What are we going to do?" and I'm just
like a wet dishcloth, and I could hear our pastor—and this is in
the midst of the service—saying, "Get her to the hospital." And I
had enough energy to say, "No!" That's all I could say. I did not
want to go to the hospital. And one of our ministers here came
up to me and laid hands on me, and when she laid hands on me,
God start to bringing me back. And the Word of God say that he
has called us to lay hands on the sick, and "when we lay hands
on the sick, they shall recover." And God gave me back my right

mind and he gave me back strength in my body. But *I was being attacked by a demon*, and I had no strength in my body. I was not even able to drive my car home. My prayer partner had to take me home that evening from the service. (emphasis added)

Yet the devil is not given all the blame for illness. When I asked Pastor Hanford why a person may get sick, she replied,

A lot of times we bring things on ourselves. We're not eating properly. We're not getting the proper rest and so on and so on. Sometimes we bring a lot of sicknesses on ourselves for the lack of knowledge of things.

Casting out the devil, or exorcizing the presence of the devil from the sanctuary or from our own bodies, may seem to be a fear-inducing return to a primitive, harsh worldview. It nevertheless has some advantages. First of all, it loosens the grip of self-blame when illness strikes. Many who are ill labor under the burden of guilt in addition to the burden of their poor health. In an atomized society that teaches that one's lot in life is individually determined according to one's willpower, hard work, and personal morality, those who are sick often assume that it is personal failure or sin that has caused this illness. Blaming the devil for one's illness shifts the blame for illness from the individual to an external, malevolent force. This is a recognition that something greater than individual human choices is at work in illness. Furthermore, the devil is particularly prone to attack people who are making positive strides in their relationship with God or serving God especially well. Illness strikes those who are making progress. Therefore, far from being a sign of one's sin or unworthiness before God, illness can be a sign that one is doing particularly well in the life of faith. In a world that wants to blame the sick for their illness, at Healing Waters the message is different. Not only are you not to blame for being sick, but you must be doing something right.

Second, blaming the devil for illness maintains the truth that there is, indeed, a relationship between evil and illness. This is not a claim that illness is God's punishment for your individual sins; in fact Pastor Hanford goes to great lengths to denounce this claim. Rather, it is the beginning of a way to name an evil greater than individuals that make us sick. It opens the door to a discussion of the relation of illness and social evil: pollution that disproportionately affects the poor; the absence of a health care system for the poor that is characterized by ease of access, affordability, and timeliness; dangerous work places (pesticides, dust, and fungus) for many low-wage earners; dangerous low-income homes (tainted with lead and allergens, and vulnerable to fire); a paucity of affordable grocery stores in poor neighborhoods. Again, this connection between social sin, the devil, and illness is not articulated directly at Healing Waters. However, devil language creates a space beyond simply individual responsibility for illness, a space for naming social sin.

Third, blaming the devil for something is a way, first, to name it as bad and, second, to stir resistance to it. It is a way to name something as worthy of rejection as well as bestow the power to reject it. I have seen this language function as a way to name injustice, selfishness, unkindness, and cruelty in others *and in themselves*, and to create a sense of outrage and power to distance themselves courageously from it. If illness is from the devil, then, it is not something to forebear gracefully or, even more extreme, a form of suffering that is useful because it brings you closer to God. Rather it is something to be rejected and fought with all one's physical and spiritual power, and with the power of the believing community around you.

However, if devil language in illness etiology can be empowering, it can also be disempowering. While it opens the door to a discussion of social sin as a source of a community's illness, it can also vitiate efforts to organize against it. If a community insists on an otherworldly, personified devil, and cannot make the imaginative move to connect the devil to social sin, then a community will have little reason to reject social sin with the vehemence with which they reject the devil.

The belief in the devil as the source of illness can also invite avoidance of personal responsibility in the causes, cure, and/or management of illness and reduce motivations to choose alternative behaviors in the future. If *all* responsibility for one's illness is divorced from one's past and present choices, and laid at the feet of the devil, then why should one make different choices in the future? The reality of illness is that it is often "multifactorial," that its origins are rooted in factors over which individuals have little control, such as genetics and social evil, but also in factors over which individuals have some control. All choice is not absent from factors such as diet, exercise, and drug and alcohol use, though they are strongly influenced by location in class and culture. If the sick person is to claim as much power as possible in the context of illness, it is critical that she be truthful about her arena of control, even if it means recognizing some responsibility for the onset of the illness and responsibility for its management or cure. For the caregiver, the line between conferring power and conferring blame is a fine one, but one that must be negotiated.

And God does not leave us without healers in our midst.

Some Have the Gift of Healing

If it is the devil who makes you sick, it is God who will heal you. Healers use material things as "points of contact" between God and the sick person. Most typical is anointing with oil, laying on of hands, prayer cloths, and prayer. Annette told me,

> At one time, Susan, my breast got as hard as a rock. I mean it was hot, as though someone had set fire under it. And I could not stand for my bra to touch my back where my bra rested on my back. I didn't go to the doctor. I kept my breast *saturated with anointing oil*. I just kept my breast anointed, and I just kept believing God would heal my breast. (emphasis added)

When asked about what she does at a typical home visit, she answers,

> Immediately, I start in praying. That's the most important thing to do is always to pray. . . . And so as we start praying, you know we anoint ourselves first, the ministers or preachers, we anoint

ourselves first. . . . We take our oil with us. And we anoint ourselves as the Lord leads us, and then we begin to pray.

Pastor Hanford also hands out prayer cloths to be placed on
the part of the body that is sick. (Acts 19:11-12: "And God did
extraordinary miracles by the hands of Paul so that handkerchiefs
or aprons were carried away from his body to the sick and diseases
left him and the evil spirits came out of him.")

> I would have these things [prayer cloths] already fixed up, pray
> over them, put them aside until the Lord say, "Use your prayer
> cloth." . . . We use a piece of cloth as a point of contact, just like
> we do the oil—as a point of contact.

But some healers are called to use other things. Annette told me
about being lead to bay leaves for healing purposes.

> God give me to use the bay leaves at one particular time. When
> he first started dealing with the bay leaves, I thought I was going
> crazy, because you see, I never read any of this. God gave this to
> me and with the bay leaves. . . . I remember years ago when our
> pastor's wife had this severe cough—she had this terrible cough. It
> just worried me that she coughed all the time. She would sit in the
> pulpit and just cough, cough, cough, through the whole service.
> And it would just bother me so bad, so I went home one night
> and I laid down and I said, "God, if it is your will, please give me
> what I can do to help her concerning this cough." And I went on
> to sleep. And in my sleep, God gave me the bay leaves and told
> me how to make it—to put in the leaves in the water and for her to
> make a tea out of it and to pour a little fresh anointing oil into this
> tea. So I told her what God said and she did it. She made the tea
> with the oil and drank it and God did it, God healed her.

> . . . He give me to work with salt—table salt—that was one of the
> things that he gave me to use when I was sick. . . . So the Spirit
> of the Lord spoke to me and said, "Get up! Make you some warm
> salt water." So this is what I did. And I went and laid back down
> and, Susan, it was like three to five minutes, God had healed me

through these things that God had give me to take. [*SD: So nobody taught you these things. Not your mother or Pastor Hanford?*] No. And that's why I even had one girl to tell me, "Annette, I got this book and it's about herbs" (because they know that God was using me concerning herbs) and she said, "I want you to read this book. This is a good book." I told her, I said, "No, I can't read it. I appreciate your thinking about me, but I can't read that, because God deals with me in that area." And sometimes when we get mean—if I would get into stuff like that—then I would feel like that it was Annette doing it and it's not God.

If the healer is not in good shape, the person will not get well. This woman continues,

I've even said sometimes, "Why did this person get sick? Why didn't he get healed when we prayed for him?" . . . Maybe you didn't pray enough. Maybe you didn't pray long enough. Maybe you didn't fast. Maybe you didn't read and study God's Word long enough. . . . If the gift that God has instilled in you is not up to where it's supposed to be, that's not a problem with God, that's a problem with you.

Not only is being a healer hard spiritual work, but it can also be hazardous to the healer's health if the healer is not fully prepared and in good spiritual shape. Pastor Hanford described the consequences of not being prepared.

[Let's imagine that] I'm picking up this sickness from this individual. Why is it coming to me, to my body? Because I'm weak spiritually. I'm not ready to lay my hand, but because I want to be seen, because I want folk to lift me up on a pedestal, I'm putting my hand on somebody, trying to impress you. Hey, I got what it take. Honey, after while it will tell on you. [*What happens?*] I will get sick. The sickness will be transferred to me. . . . If you're not prayed up, if you're not fasted up, if you're not in the Word as you are supposed to be, you, in your weak time, [you will get sick.]

Becoming a healer means being willing to suffer. Annette tells how her health suffered for having accepted the spiritual gift of healing others.

> I lay in my bed a couple of weeks ago, and I could hear the voice of God saying, "Do you really want this [the spiritual gift of being a healer]?" I said, "Yeah." He said, "Do you really, really want this?" I said, "Yeah." He said, "With this comes suffering." And I told my pastor, "I never had problems with no blood pressure." And I got up one morning, Susan, and . . . I said, "I'm going to have to call [in sick] . . . because I cannot drive." I was sick. I was dizzy in my head. I had to take a shower and sit down. Everything I did I had to do in bits and pieces and sit down, because I was sick.

Also, being a healer means taking illness into your own body for the sake of another's healing.

> That's why when we work with demonic spirits, when you say that you are called to work with demonic spirits, you better know that you are called, because demons are real. They will and they can kill you. [*Do they ever make you sick?*] They make you sick. Yes, ma'am, because when you are calling those demons out, with my experience, when God uses me to call out some of the demonic spirits, when they come out, then what the person has experienced, I start to experience it. [*Like what? Can you give me an example?*] Well, not too long ago, I was working with this lady and God had us to anoint her tongue. When we began to anoint her tongue, she started to bringing up stuff, and God has me sometimes to lay across a person's stomach as a point of contact to help draw or to bring about deliverance in that person. So when they started, then I start, and that's part of their deliverance. Whatever's in them, it comes through them, up out of them and God uses me to bring it up. [*You mean, like words? Or vomiting?*] No, substance. Yes, substance. Yeah. Yeah. [*OK, so it's in her body then it goes to your body, and it comes out—*] It goes to me and it comes out. Right.

Again, healing another may be hazardous to the healer's health, even when she is in good spiritual shape. Pastor Hanford tells of visiting the home of a sick person with Annette.

> We walked into this house that was full of old demon spirits, all kinds of spirits. And I could see them, the shadow of them. And Annette started praying, and I was the one that was able to go in the back. And when I went to the back where they were, they all rushed out to the front and they attacked Annette. [She] was like a dead woman, laying on the floor. She was cold and her whole complexion was changed like she didn't have a drop of blood in her. And we had to do what? Stop and pray with her that God would restore her back to us. And I tell you she lay there for a little while—I don't know how many minutes—but it took some minutes before she come through.

While the individual healer's praying and anointing is very important, the prayers of the congregation also play an important role. I asked what Pastor Hanford does first when she hears that someone is sick.

> I get on the phone, and I call all the people I know that can start praying then and pray through. I start a prayer vigil over the telephone. I'll call Sister Carver on her job; I'll call Sister Maxwell on her job; I'll call Sister McDonald on her job; I'll call Brother Arthur Boyd at his home. I'll call my son, if he's not with me. I'll call my daughter Lavonne, and she'll get around and call some others. And I'll call Minister Donald. Mainly, I get in touch with the ministerial staff first and the missionaries. And we have this vigil of prayer going around for them.

She makes it clear that the role of the healer is important, but it is the faith of the believer that is more critical to healing.

The church has engaged in healing practices for centuries. Yet mainstream Protestant churches have almost completely excluded them from church life, for good and bad reasons. The good reasons include a reluctance to narrow the good works of God for the sick to a specific result: physical healing. The bad reasons include a classist phobia of anything that resembles those known by the derogatory designation "holy rollers," considered ignorant, unedu-cated, and "unscientific." Fortunately, here and there, Protestants are reclaiming and reinterpreting ancient healing practices in wor-ship that recognize the difference between healing and physical cure, for which the sick are invited to be open to the varieties of ways God's redeeming power is available to those who are sick.

At Healing Waters, intrinsic to the experience of being a healer is the recognition that being a healer means becoming vulnerable yourself. There is nothing risk-free about giving yourself to the healing arts. When you challenge the devil you are making yourself vulnerable to all sorts of retribution. In a world that expects cheap, cost-free fixes, at Healing Waters the healers recognize that their art is personally expensive. Furthermore, these healing practices require not only spiritual risk but also bodily risk. Healing another's body implicates the healer's body as well. If some contemporary "mind-body-spirit" healing practitioners use their "power of prayer," a mental or meditational form of intercession for others' healing, at Healing Waters healers offer their own bodies for the sake of anoth-er's healing. This belief-practice reinforces a radical connectional-ity between the body of the sick and the body of the healer, so much so that the healer can directly receive the illness of the sick. It is a connection based on shared vulnerability to illness, shared finitude, where one gives her body for the healing of another. This is a central strain in Christian theology. Not only does it have christological implications but it also embodies a Pauline ecclesiology, where an individual's illness implicates the whole church, where sickness in one part of the body of Christ affects the whole body.

The use of material things for healing is also an important fea-ture of Healing Waters healing practices. It is a form of sacramen-talism that eludes many more austere Protestant denominations. The world becomes a cornucopia of objects that can be transformed into "points of contact" with God, as Pastor Hanford says. Herbs, cloths, table salt, oil, water, all bespeak the breadth of objects from the created world that connect us to God. "Pentecostalism, which claims to be an iconoclastic tradition, is saturated in sacramental objects" (Griffith, on prayer cloths). Many of us who are Protestant are nervous about the world, worried that something might capture our devotion and lure us into attachments that turn something finite and partial into something infinite and absolute. As a Presbyterian I am shaped by a religion that, in comparison to Healing Waters, appears to have an impoverished material culture, a minimal sense of the divine mystery abroad in the created world, and few habits that continually instantiate me in a physical world shimmering with the divine. I am formed by a religion that provokes no infusions of the Holy Spirit to move us into physically strenuous wild ecstasies of tongues or dance and where moving bodies are icons of God's movement in the world. At Healing Waters, sacraments are everywhere, and those who are sick are sustained by them. Perhaps most important to those who are ill is the recognition that their own body is a site of divine action. The body, not just spirit, mind, emotions, attitudes, or outlook, is a place where God's redeeming power moves powerfully. Mainstream Protestants usually leave the body to the doctor.

Yet does not the Protestant vigilance for idolatry maintain some usefulness? Is it not possible that material objects of the healers' craft would become the object of faith and not the mysterious divine who is greater than any piece of the finite world? Could not what Pastor Hanford so carefully calls a "point of contact" with God slide into being a god? Other possibilities for idol-making exist as well. What about the healer herself? Could not a person who is terrified in her illness cling to the healer as the one in whom she places ultimate confidence? And, with a number of "successes," is not the healer vulnerable to lifting herself up to a place where only God belongs? Again, I cannot possibly judge whether these idolatries are present at Healing Waters. Yet as a cautionary note, I would invoke the warnings of the Hebrew prophets and the reformers that the temptation to idolatry is both powerful and dangerous.

God Has Already Healed You

There are several offshoots of the belief that God has already healed you. One, the believer's job is to believe it. Two, the believer is to praise God for healing even in advance of it. Three, if, however, you are *not* already healed, it may be so that God might be manifest in your illness. Four, getting medical care is not a sign of unbelief; you simply have to believe that, no matter how the healing happens, it is God who accomplishes it.

Believe

Like their early Pentecostal forebears, worshippers at Healing Waters believe that there is a contract with God: God's obligation is to heal, and the petitioner's job is to believe. As one woman said, "We believe that if you get to praying, that God is going to move. He's *obligated* to move" (emphasis added).

Also, consistent with their forebears, the belief is that you are healed *even now,* because it says in the Bible, "by his stripes you are healed," and that means you are *already* healed. You, the sick person, must simply believe this. Pastor Hanford said,

> And if you come [to God], you need to believe that he's going to heal you, because the scripture say, "by my stripes ye are healed," that means right now, you are already healed. So the person has to believe that. When they come, they must believe that God has already healed them. Then they need to say, "God, I accept your healing. I believe you have healed me."

When your illness is the devil's retribution for your decision to take up the cross of Jesus, the proper response of the stricken is to believe that God will heal you. After telling me about her affliction as the devil's doing, Pastor Hanford described her faith response:

> But because I know who God is and I think about when he was crucified and the wound when they pierced him in his side and blood and water came out. . . . I am healed because of him. [*Even if your high blood pressure is still there?*] Yes, even if it's still there. I am healed. I still say, I'm healed. Even if diabetes is still there. I'm healed. But you know what? It will soon be gone, in Jesus' name. Yes, it will.

In this case, the belief is that, though the physical evidence of healing has not yet appeared, it will soon arrive.

The devil can tempt the faithful to abandon their faith not only by afflicting them with illness, but also by striking someone they love with illness. And still, the believer must believe to the very end. Pastor Hanford said,

> I often say this: When Slewfoot can't get me or you, he will tug on your heartstrings. What is your heartstring? Your child or your children. All of a sudden you say, "What is he doing with leukemia? Nobody in the family has leukemia." And then we can count it all joy, because you can look at it as if this is just a test. And you can know, children with leukemia are often sick for years, they are often sick for a long time, and then sometimes it's not a long time. Sometimes death overtakes. But still, I'm believing God who is the author and the finisher of my faith. Because I believe God can heal and deliver. I'm believing God is going to heal my child and deliver him out of the hands of that sickness, all iniquity and all trespasses and everything that he is going through. I'm believing God is going to bring him out. That's according to my faith in Christ Jesus. I believe God can do anything but fail. He said so. He said in one portion of the Scripture, "Lo, I am with you always, even unto the end of this world." And that's long enough for me. So I'm going to keep right on believing that he's going to zap that leukemia right away. Even though the child can get to his weakest point, he can get down to his lowest point, like he's on his way out, God will raise him up.

I asked Pastor Hanford about her husband's diabetes that never went away. He was a man of extraordinary faith, and yet his diabetes took his four limbs and eventually his life.

> He knew God would heal him. And he said, "Even if he don't, when I rise on the other side, I will be healed." See? You know, he was a man who believed God could do anything. And he would thank God for his healing all the time. "Even though I'm not feeling good, thank you, Lord, for healing me." [*For heal-*

ing me . . . even though I'm not really feeling it in my body yet?]
Un-huh. Even though I'm still feeling pain, thank you, God, for
healing me.

The reality of God's already accomplished healing is consistent
with the reality of persistent illness. A person can be healed, and
still have the illness. Even if healing does not mean the illness goes
away in this life, it will most certainly be gone "when I rise on the
other side." Regardless of the physical evidence, the believer's job
is to believe in the boundless power of God. Pastor Hanford testi-
fied to the strength of her husband's faith: "He would always say to
the Lord, 'Even if you don't heal me again, I know you can.'"

Believing also seems to be a way of surviving the trials of illness that persists, as Annette poignantly describes the act of simply
"holding on to God" when nothing else is working.

I just learn to deal with whatever is happening in my body and to
hold on to God, and say, if God don't do it now, he'll do it later.

I have seen the adherence to the requirement to believe result in
great calm. In situations where truly, one has little control over out-
comes, when circumstances are uncertain and unpredictable, believing that God will answer one's prayers has brought equanimity and
strength. Such a stance enables living with human powerlessness
because the future is in the hands of a gracious and powerful God.
It engenders a courage to continue to focus on the tasks of today, to
continue to love, work, and serve without having all the answers,
without an explication of how the future will evolve. It engenders a
radical trust in God that does not require satisfying rational objec-
tions. Anxieties over finitude that are raised to the fore in times of
illness are addressed with a grounding in a universe where God
dwells throughout.

Yet the vulnerability of admonitions to believe is that one's
belief becomes one's idol. The focus shifts from trust in God to
trust in one's faculty to believe. The risk in focusing on belief in
God as key to receiving God's blessings is that the person who
is sick becomes not only anxious about illness, but also anxious

about the strength and quality of their piety, because their very life depends on it. Similarly, the focus on one's belief as the key to unlocking God's blessings is a form of works righteousness. We earn God's grace through our high-caliber believing, rather than receive it as a gift freely given.

Furthermore, when does believing that one is healed in the face of contradictory physical evidence, evidence generated not only by medical authorities but also by one's own body, become a form of damaging self-deception? When does this become the sort of self-deception required by idol-worship (Farley, 1975)? Idolatry requires self-deception in order to continue to invest in the idol, to give it unqualified devotion in the face of evidence that it is not God, that it cannot save us. There are risks to this deception. One can fail to do the work of saying goodbye, fail to recognize and receive *unexpected* graces from God because one was so focused on the internal believing faculty, and fail to receive God's healing power in this-worldly resources for healing.

Praise

Not only is *believing* God part of the healing contract, but also *praising* God. Once the pastor had asked us to pray for her sister who has cancer and who had lost a great deal of weight. The prognosis sounded grim. But she continued in her report saying that her sister had gained three pounds recently, adding, "I thank God for those three pounds."

Much has been written about the "logocentrism" of mainline churches whose worship is centered on the preached Word. Our worship is sedate, our praise is measured, our petitions are tempered with reason. We value control in our response to God. Have we so truncated our worship and prayer life that a vital part of human life, the realm of emotion, is unwelcome in mainline churches? The cry of the psalmist in praise, pain, rage, and anguish is rarely part of mainline Protestant discourse with God. Yet at Healing Waters, worship and prayer are ablaze with emotion.

At Healing Waters it is praise that is the primary emotional response to God, praise for what God has already done and praise "in advance" for what God will do. Why is this significant for the sick? Because bitterness and anger can occlude the goodness that is undeniably still present in the life of the sick person. Illness does not always obliterate all that is good. Furthermore, bitterness over the failure to find a *cure* can make the reception of *healing* more difficult, if not impossible. To be overwhelmed with the pain and disability of illness at the expense of recognizing places of goodness is detrimental to both mental and physical health. Healing Waters' discipline of praising God is a way of regularly naming resources that remain to those who are sick, resources that are easily forgotten when in the throes of illness.

The discipline of thanking God in advance is one that could be understood as a discipline of hoping. Don Capps defined hope as not simply wishing something would happen, but "the perception that what is wanted will happen" (1995, 53). Intrinsic to hope is confidence in the fulfillment of the desired end. Otherwise, it is not really hope; it is a wish. This, to me, is at the heart of the belief that "God has already healed me." It is an expression of radical hope. It is a refusal to believe that God has been defeated by one's illness. It is a radical trust in the claim that nothing, not even this illness, can separate us from the love of God in Christ Jesus our Lord.

Like the admonition to believe, the vulnerability of the focus on praise, is, again, that it would become an idol or a form of works righteousness. Praise can invite a sort of fanaticism. When are the grimacing faces immersed in vigorous shout a sign of praise for the God who makes all things new and when are they a sign of a desperate attempt to wring a blessing out of a stone idol? How much of the physical exertion is a spontaneous outburst of joy and gratitude and when is it a heartbreaking, futile attempt to dance before a mute, wooden idol in order to be saved? The sufferers from illness could look to praise themselves as what will save them, rather than God.

That God Might Be Manifest in Your Illness

When I pressed Pastor Hanford more about why God did not make her husband's illness go away, she referred to Scripture and to the phenomenon of God being manifest through ongoing illness.

And you think about Job, in the book of Job, and you think about how in the Scripture where it says, "What did this man do that he is blind?" He didn't do anything, but it was *so that God could manifest himself through him.* He [her husband] felt like he had to wait until God manifested himself through him. And a lot of times, the Lord would manifest himself through him. Jay would . . . go into the hospital, lay there and rest, and the Lord would talk to him, and he would come back and tell us what the Lord said to him while he was on that bed and pop up like a spring chicken, feeling better in his body. And then something else [another illness] would happen, you know. So he said, "I'm just waiting on the manifestation of the Lord in my body."

The power of his faith did, in fact, lend strength to his parishioners. A woman who was a church leader reports,

I think when we saw him go through what he went through and keep the faith and never complain and get up there every Sunday and preach from that pulpit and they had to lift him up and put him on that stool, we gained strength from that. Because we were thinking why were we complaining about a headache and this man preaching the gospel with no arms and no legs to us every Sunday. And not only preaching but living the Word of God.

An older woman also wanted to let God be manifest in her illness so that God might get the glory.

So when we are going through things with our body . . . he doesn't want us to come before the congregation moping. That's not helping the congregation, and that's not helping God either. It makes him grieve. Because he's done be through it. He wants us to be joyful, *so he can get the glory* . . . [The congregation was helped because] they could see the spirit I was in. They saw that I didn't ever walk into the church with my head hanging down because I had cancer. So I would always say something to inspire them. And they would come to me after church and say, "I declare, you inspired me today—because of the way you

carry yourself and you don't even act like you have cancer." See,
I didn't act like I had it, but I did have it. I just didn't dwell on
the fact that I had cancer, but I would just go like I ain't got it,
but I had it. That's what inspired them. . . .You know, everybody don't take things alike. I was determined I was going to go,
whatever. I was determined that me and God was going to work
it out together.

For me, it is here that Healing Waters shines most brightly, in
its offering of the transformation of one's sick body into a beacon
of inspiration. Believers show a determination that their body, even
though sick, should be a source of power for another. At Healing
Waters, they have not relinquished the sick body to the definitions
of a mechanized biomedical model that considers the sick body
a sign of failure, nor to the definitions of the larger culture that
valorizes youth, beauty, and vigor. Rather there is another estate
for the sick body: the opportunity to manifest the power of God.
What could be more sacralizing? The admonition to praise God in
spite of one's illness transforms the sick body from that which is
in decay and pain to an instrument of praise, even, as noted above,
an icon. This is not an icon of a saint without blemish. Rather it is
an icon of the saint whose body bears the marks of pain and suffering, and yet who maintains a confidence in God's presence. Upon
entering Healing Waters, sick bodies can be a mediator of the truth
of the crucified Christ, as they dance before the Lord in and through
their weakness.

Arthur Frank speaks of the "communicative body" (1995), the
body whose suffering is made available for others' healing, the
body that chooses solidarity with others in pain. This is the sick
person who turns to the neighbor in compassion, aware that if we
are not all united in our strength, then we are surely one in our
shared weakness. I believe the communicative body is behind the
belief that we have a responsibility to make God manifest in our
illness. Our illness is not ours alone, nor is the strength that we find
in it ours alone. They are meant to be shared, that God might be
manifest.

That God might be manifest through illness is a way of valorizing courage as a response to ill health. It is a way of naming the reality of finitude, the reality of tragic illness over which we may have no control, *and* the possibility of facing it with grace and strength. At Healing Waters there is a deep awareness that we are created vulnerable by virtue of our embodiment. In spite of mainstream Western culture's fear of human fragility and its attendant denial of sickness and death, at Healing Waters finitude is everywhere. There is frequent recognition of our mortality, finitude, our limitations of health, time, and energy. In this church, we all acknowledge that we are all vulnerable and that we all depend upon God for every breath we take. In the context of this full acknowledgment of finitude, Healing Waters holds out for the manifestation of God in our illness.

Get Medical Care, but Remember That It Is God Who Heals

Pastor Hanford explains the relation of modern medicine to faith in God's healing power. First of all, she defends the legitimacy of doctors by pointing to their presence in the Bible.

> If a person said to me, "No, it shows a sign of weakness as far as our going to the doctor and taking what the doctor prescribes for us," is this: There were medical doctors in the Old Testament and in the New. And they used simple medications like figs to make a poultice to put on a sore or something, and that fig would draw it to a head or take all the impurities out.

She also recognizes the legitimacy of saying,

> "I'm not going to the doctor. I'm just going to rely on Jesus." [If] you really rely on him, that's good. Make sure you have that faith to walk in that stature. What I mean is, you're not taking any doctor's medicines, you're not going to the doctor.

But then she goes on to say that going to the doctor can be a way to get an accurate diagnosis of what is wrong so that you can pray accurately.

But it's a little doofus to me if you're getting sick, and you don't know because you can't diagnose what's wrong with you, you don't know what's going on in your body—you need to know what's happening to your body, because our bodies go through a lot of changes, both spiritually and physically. But physically, now, I want the doctor to tell me what he found so I can name it to God and give God a chance to heal it. And I believe, I totally believe, I know that God is a healer for anything. He can do anything but fail.

One way to express your faith in God while following the doctor's orders is to pray over your medicine.

I'm hypertensive and have high blood pressure. And there is medicine that they want you to take in the morning and at night before you go to bed. Now I say to God when I lift my medicine up—my husband taught us to always lift your medicine up to the Lord—and say, "Lord, purify this, and it has been said to us that this medicine will bring my blood pressure to normal, but God, because of my weakness at this point, I'm looking to you, the Author and Finisher of my faith, and I do want you and I know and believe that you can heal this body, but right now I'm taking this medicine. I want you to purify this medicine. I am going to use this medicine as a point of contact." C'mon. God works through that medicine. He works through that medicine. And whichever way we pray and say, "Lord you let this medicine bring this pressure down to normal," and you take the medicine, and your pressure is down to normal, because God is the healer.

I sensed her ambivalence about taking medicine, that taking medicine is a sign of a weak faith. I pointed out that her faith is strong, that she is the very model of faith, and yet she still takes the medicine; therefore it must not be weakness that leads her to take medicine.

Well, I know. I know. I know. And a lot of times—well, doctors don't know, but I skip and don't take the medicine—I just lay down for about two hours and a half, and when I get up, I'm different. Even the pressure in my eyes, sometimes is puffy, and I ask the Lord to bring down the pressure in my eyes to normal.

There are times when modern medicine and faith work together, when faith can bring great reassurance to one who is making decisions about a difficult medical procedure. One man told me about facing the doctor's recommendation that his leg be removed.

When they were saying they were going to have to amputate my leg—you know, for years, I would say I'm not going to let them do that. . . . When they told me that, I was full of pride and I didn't want that, because how am I going to get around? I was thinking all the negative things. And I came to this church, to a service, and the woman that was preaching called me up to the front and had me to sit in a chair right in front of the church. And she told me that God told her to tell me that "it is well." And so when she told me, I said, "It is well? My leg is well?"

And she said, simply said, God said, "It is well."

. . . [W]hen I came in here [to the church], I was thinking about that surgery. I was worried about it. I was worried real bad, and when she told me that God said, "It is well," I felt, "OK"—it was a sigh of relief. When she told me that, I left it in God's hands then. I said, "Well, I don't need to be worrying about it." What was the use of my worrying about it? God said he was going to take care of it. God said he was going to take care of me. And sure enough, that's what he did. That's right. That's so right.

He explained how the visiting preacher's words were fulfilled, even though his leg was still gone.

So I went in on Tuesday and they did the procedure, did the operation, and a lot of people right then would have said, "Well, if God said 'It is well' what is your leg doing cut off? Why did they cut it off anyway?" They said, come back in a couple of weeks and we'll check it again and take the bandages off and check everything. . . . So I went back to the doctor, and they had sent in a medical student. He was telling me, "You've just got to brace yourself. This is going to be painful." . . . So as I was laying back, I began to pray: "Lord, I'm leaving this in your hands. Fix this for me." . . . I didn't feel a thing. The next thing I know, he dropped everything and ran out in the hallway and got all these doctors. My room was full of doctors. And they were looking, and they said, "This is amazing." I was lying there, and I sat up. I looked, and my leg was completely healed. They said, "This is incredible." And they started squeezing it. Just squeezing it. . . . [I]t was just as if it had healed a year ago. And still they weren't satisfied by that, so they said, "Come back next week." And I came back the next week and it was healed, sure enough. I counted those days, and it was 17 days from the surgery until they pulled those things out. And they had told me, "It will take about eight weeks before you'll be able to do anything." But while they were talking to me, my memory kicked in . . . on what that preacher said: "God said, 'It is well.'" And that's what happened. . . . And that's why I come and give God the praise like I do. If a lot of people were in the situation that I'm in and knowing how God can take you out of stuff and bring you through stuff, they would be jumping around dancing, because it wasn't nobody but God.

The woman who told him, "all is well," did not declare that he was already healed, but invoked a deep and radically open trust that he and his leg were in God's hands. It is reminiscent of Julian of Norwich's benediction, "all shall be well, all shall be well, and all manner of thing shall be well." He received a peace and the courage to do what had to be done.

Not only do individuals seek modern medical care without hesitation, but also the church observes "Health Sunday." On one such Sunday there was an announcement stating, "Free Screening: Blood Pressure, Blood Sugar, and Cholesterol" at a local grocery store. There was a flyer in the worship bulletin calling worshippers to "reduce your risk factors for stroke" and listed warning signs and preventive measures. Clearly church members are comfortable with modern medicine.

Pastor Hanford wrested medication from the realm of mecha-
nistic medicine to the realm of God's mysterious power to heal. She
redefined it as a "point of contact" with God, placing it in the same
category as prayer cloths and anointing oil. For her, God is immanent in all the created world, including the fruits of scientific, biomedical thinking. In the terms of Reformed theology, she affirmed
the sovereignty of God who can work through any means at all, the
God who is not limited to any ecclesial, liturgical, or ritual form to
address the pain of the sick body. In this belief-practice we see an
amalgam of the practical and the mysterious. Pastor Hanford says it
would be "doofus" to ignore modern medicine. Yet this practicality
is merged with a deep awareness of the mystery of God's power to
heal the body, to heal relationships, to grant peace, courage, fortitude in the midst of suffering.

The mystery of God's healing power is mediated through
medicine, but at Healing Waters, healing is always greater than the
repair of the body-as-machine. This congregation teaches an awareness that there is much that is good and powerful that is beyond
rationality and human control; there is much about redemption that
we cannot predict or understand, that is of a different order than
the rational. Experiencing this mystery has to do with letting go,
with loosening our grip, and simply receiving it. Grasping for the
fruits of reasoning, explaining, and planning have their place in the
life of faith at Healing Waters, but not as a substitute for the grace-
filled encounter with mystery. This stance infuses the approach to
ill health at Healing Waters.

The risk, of course, is that the affirmation of God's sovereignty
to work through *any* means would weaken to an idolatry of healing
through only a *few* means: practices called faithful. The risk is that
believers would claim that the healing, sustaining power of God
would only be available through certain channels such as believing,
prayer, praise, and certain material objects. A fundamentalism, an
idolatry, of certain practices called spiritual would replace a radical
openness to the varieties of God's modes of acting.

God Leads You to People Who Need Care, Even to Strangers

There are multiple ways church members offer practical help during times of illness. Preparing meals, visiting the home of the sick person, reading scripture to them, taking communion to them, visiting the hospital, and spending the night there if necessary.

A particular older woman is one of the central purveyors of practical help, and I asked her what in her faith leads her to help others. I was moved by her response.

> Because one time in life—not one time, but a lot of times—you get hurt in life. The people who you trust sometimes will hurt you so bad, and I always tell the Lord, "Lord, I am not going to hurt people like people hurt me, but I just want to help and encourage them." Because when people hurt you to your heart, that's a hurting thing, and I don't want to hurt people like they hurt me. So that is what I would always do is tell the Lord, "I don't want to hurt people, and Lord, you just make a way for me to help others in need." Because God always wants us to help the poor. That's what we always say. We are poor, and we help the poor. But if I can help you, then that is what I would do.

> One time, I used to go house to house and I would do missionary work. Like I would get there and I would clean the house. I would go into the church on Dowd Street, and I was sitting up in there, and they were taking up the offering in the church, and the Spirit spoke to me and said, "Get up! Go next door." The lady next door was so sick she couldn't come to the door and open the door. So she left the door open for you to come in. And the Spirit said to me, "Get up and go across there and clean her house!" And I had on my white dress. And I got right up and I didn't even tell my husband, 'cause he was in there. I got right up and when I got up into the back, one of the other mothers coming in said,

> "You going somewhere?"

> I said, "Yeah." I said, "Girl, I got to get out of here." I said, "The Spirit told me to go over there and clean that house!"

She said, "Well, can I go with you?"

I said, "Come on."

And both of us went over there and rolled up our sleeves. We cleaned refrigerator and the stove, and we called back to the church and told one of the members to go to the store and bring us something to kill bugs with. Because she couldn't clean her house, you see, and a lot of stuff was needed. So we told them to go to the store and bring it over to the house. We got some Pine Oil and we cleaned that house out. And when church let out, we had that little house clean. [*And you did this in the middle of the service?*] In the middle of the service! God told me to go and clean her house! And I obeyed. . . . [I]f God tells you to do something, you just go and do it! And we defrosted the refrigerator. We cleaned the refrigerator out. We sprayed the stove and cleaned it. We cleaned the floor. That kitchen looked like a brand-new kitchen when we got through.

So that's how I come in [to giving practical help], just helping people, because I love people. I love people. People will hurt you, but I love people. You have to forgive those that hurt you, too. You have to forgive them. . . So helping people helps me. It helps me live a long time. I've done outlived my mother and my daddy, 'cause they didn't live as long as I did, because I'm 74 years old. And they never made it there.

When asked about her faith that moves her to help others, she first spoke of deep personal hurt, then, in one sentence, an account of a transformation that was at once a refusal and a claiming: "I don't want to hurt people, and Lord, you just make a way for me to help others in need." Then she spoke of an extraordinary act of service to a stranger. Being hurt, refusal of the option to hurt others, taking up the task of helping others were woven into her faith. If ever there were a testimony to the miraculous power of God, it is in this story. While some in Healing Waters would point to other miracles of bodily healing, I lift up this account as a miracle story of the healing of broken spirit not only for personal peace, but through and for compassion for others.

In another instance Pastor Hanford was taking her husband regularly to dialysis, and she noticed that a woman she did not know was having problems with reliable transportation to and from dialysis.

> So I looked at Sister Armstrong one day and my heart just went out to her. I said, "From this day forward, you will not have to worry about a way home or being picked up on a Saturday. Do not be worried about this anymore." And I did it so quick, because the Lord just instilled in me to get Annette and Missionary Tonya Brown in this church. They divide the time. They take two Saturdays—one takes two Saturdays this time and the other takes two Saturdays the next time—and they pick her up. [*And this is a complete stranger.*] They didn't know anything about her—had not met her, had not seen her. I had only seen her because my husband started dialysis and she was one of the ladies in dialysis with him. I know nothing else about her. And the Lord has been blessing her ever since. And blessing Annette and Sister Brown for being so humble, making that sacrifice of their time to go take her, have her there before time, and then going back to pick her up. If she needs them to shop for her or do some errands, they do it. And I said, "Thank you, Lord." . . . I said, "I have a job for you." And Loretta told me she saw me coming to her in a vision, saying, "I have a job for you to do." This was coming from God. This is not me, assigning them. I was led by the anointed of God.

Again, a complete stranger has received regular transportation to her medical care for years because of the response of faith of three strangers.

The practical care offered for one another during illness is expansive. In more affluent congregations this care would likely be provided only by the nuclear family or hired caregivers. The illness would be confined to the realm of the private and the paid professional. Yet in this setting, the church is family. These practices of care affirm the redemption that unfolds in mutual care, the redemption available only in the open acknowledgment of the shared vulnerability of finite existence that depends on the Creator. Those without the resources of the upper middle class have fewer places to hide from the fragility of finitude, and thus they are in a position to recognize what is true of all humanity, that only God will save us, and that we participate in God in our acts of care for one another.

While some might claim that the work of caregiving belongs to the private and thus is no challenge to social injustices, Marla Frederick challenges the notion that the private is nonpolitical. She describes the activities of African American women in Halifax County, North Carolina, "between Sundays":

> While work in private areas often goes unexamined by scholars, on the assumption that it is nonpolitical, the day-to-day struggles of women's lives in Halifax reveal tremendous agency on their part as they wrestle with defining holy and satisfying personal praxis as well as just and humane political praxis. . . . Gratitude and empathy reveal the levels of *continuous and often unrecognized work that women perform ritually in public life.* In these instances women are not necessarily confronting school boards or petitioning about government policies. They are instead maintaining the best possible quality of life for themselves, their families, and those in need of care. (Frederick, 213; emphasis added)

Like the work of women in Halifax County, the caregiving activities that seem to be confined to the realm of the private can also be understood as both political and a participation in public life.[16]

Otherworldly churches have been accused of being ingrown, indifferent to the needs of those outside their boundaries. Yet here we have examples of moving beyond the congregation and into the lives of strangers. These are not programmatic responses that require budgets and executive directors, but they are the more risky, messy kinds of responses to human need that many refuse. Paul Farmer speaks of the flaws of "white liberals" who desire social justice for the poor, but who are unwilling to make personal sacrifices for it (Kidder). There are those at Healing Waters who live their commitment to welcome the stranger in the form of time-consuming and unglamorous work, loyalty, and freely given support.

The risk in this belief-practice is in the bargain to which Pastor Hanford alluded: If you do good works then God will bless you. This removes the acts of compassion from the realm of selfless generosity to the realm of exchange. The person receiving care, then, loses the status of beloved "Thou" and becomes an ancillary "It" in a transaction between the caregiver and God. The care receiver is then a marginalized thing in service of an exchange between two other players. It is true that engaging in self-giving love has its rewards, most prominently participating in the redeeming love of God revealed in Jesus Christ. Caring for the sick can enable an encounter with God in and through a deep encounter with the other. Furthermore, caring for the sick in the congregation etches in the minds and bodies of the caregiver the affirmation that, when their hour of need comes, they will not be left alone. Yet when it is corrupted, these rewards are replaced by a self-serving illusion of bartering "good works" for "divine blessings." Therefore this is a belief-practice that requires vigilance that it not be corrupted by self-serving bargaining with God.

CONCLUSION

No church is free of its idolatries; all belief-practices are vulnerable to corruption. Healing Waters is no exception. I have tried to give an insider's look at what some of these belief-practices are, interpret them with a "hermeneutic of generosity" (Paul Farmer in Kidder) and speculate on the form their corruption might take.

This discussion serves the caregiver in several ways. One, it leads to more accurate empathy. If there is a workable knowledge of some possible features of a sick person's cultural and theological background, then the pastoral caregiver can more accurately hear the illness meanings and the associated feelings. The caregiver is more able (drawing again on the *Dictionary of Pastoral Care*'s definition of empathy) "to enter *the perceptual and emotional world of the other*" (Hunter, 354; emphasis added). Second, this discussion guides the caregiver in the difficult task of discerning how well a particular illness meaning is functioning. By giving both sympathetic and cautionary readings of these beliefs, I have displayed for the caregiver both potentially helpful and potentially damaging ways they might function. Finally, of course, the caregiver must make that discernment, but it is my hope that this discussion has been useful in that process.

The following anecdote serves as an example of the importance of tending to culturally and theologically specific illness meanings. A white male student chaplain was describing in class a pastoral encounter with a patient, an African American woman, in the hospital. She suffered from an illness that was quite serious, yet he reported that she expressed joy and confidence in God's power. He was moved by the depth of her faith and her capacity to rejoice in God in the face of such a grave illness, and he believed it was his role as a chaplain simply to affirm her faith. As I listened to his story of this woman, I heard evidence of a belief-practice that I had identified from my interviews at the African American church for the writing of this book. It seemed possible to me that she was operating out of a belief-practice that is like a contract with God: The sick person's part of the contract is to believe in God and praise God, and God's part is to do the healing. She interpreted her illness and discerned the appropriate faith response through this lens. This reading of the woman's situation suggests a pastoral response different from the one the student chaplain offered. Instead of a pastoral reading that leads simply to affirming her faith, the knowledge of belief-practices in *some* African American churches leads the pastoral caregiver to consider certain questions: Is the face of confidence and joy this patient presented a form of works righteousness which is based on a desperate attempt to wrest healing from God? Is it based on fear and desperation more than deep trust? Of course the student chaplain's reading may have been accurate and the line of thinking I am suggesting off target. But if the alternative reading I propose is more accurate, then his decision simply to affirm her faith would have reinforced a desperate attempt to earn God's favor. Knowledge of a range of belief-practices could have refined his ear to her words and expanded the range of possible pastoral responses.

Illness meanings are particular to individuals, and are hybrids from personal, familial, ecclesial, cultural, and ethnic sources. I have not attempted to spell out specific illness meanings that each of the belief-practices in this chapter might produce in an individual because that would be impossible without knowing the person. It is my intention to establish that the caregiver who is familiar with the formative belief-practices of a person who is sick will be better able to offer quality care.

3

First Downtown Church

*U*pon first moving to Durham, our family was immediately drawn to First Downtown Church. There were telling markers that this was the local "liberal" outpost for the denomination: It was the church whose banner was "downtown by history and by choice," it housed an urban ministry, one heard regular social justice sermons, the pastor's wife had organized peacemaking trips to the then Soviet Union, and the congregation actively included lesbian and gay people, though quietly. It was the obvious choice for our family. Our daughter was baptized at First Downtown, and we worshipped there for five years until I took a job in another church. We have since returned and are regular worshippers there.

Our weekly drive to church holds so much of Durham's past and present. We pass the lumberyard with building supplies for the exploding construction business. We pass Duke Hospital with its multiple attendant research and clinical structures. We pass the historic Erwin Mills, part of Durham's past textile industry. We see tobacco warehouses, some abandoned, some part of trendy urban renewal efforts. On the left of our route is the large building for North Carolina Mutual Insurance Company, the multi-million-dollar historic and black-owned business. On the right is the Catholic church with its burgeoning Hispanic membership. Upon leaving the freeway and approaching the church, centers of county activity come into view: the county courthouse, county social services, the county library, and the county health department. Most worshippers drive toward the front of the church but then glide past it to the back parking lot. There are few pedestrians on the street on any day of the week. The church faces an abandoned Health Department building that developers have considered for various purposes.

If one should enter the front door of the heavy stone Gothic Revival building, its doors elevated seven steps above the sidewalk, one would enter a shadowed foyer that holds remnants of the past: old books and carved furniture with a Gothic flair. This would have been the entry of choice for past decades.

Today most churchgoers approach the church from the back parking lot, walking through a grassy area on a short sidewalk lined by large crepe myrtle trees, brash pink in the summer. To the left is a small brick-walled courtyard that holds a garden and a columbarium. To the right is the education building, whose architecture confirms it was built in the mid-sixties. It houses a day-care program during the week.

Inside this large, bright foyer are signs of the church's current vitality: pictures of new members, a table for the youth fundraiser, posters for the CROP walk, reminders of the installation of the presbytery's new Hispanic minister, a display of stoles donated by closeted gay clergy, and newspaper clippings about members involved in current city events. Parents are rushing kids to Sunday school, older people are moving to the new elevator, and most are aiming for the door to the sanctuary.

The most commonly used door to the sanctuary is an inconspicuous one that opens into the very front, side corner of the worship space. Worshippers walk past the baptismal font and into a worship space that would hold 450 if the balcony were filled. The high ceiling draws the eye upward and the stained glass windows glitter in the sunlight. The chancel of the church is raised by three steps, warmed by golden wood furniture and light rose-colored marble floor. The choir sits in the very front, facing the congregation.

The markers of the sacred are the windows, the organ pipes, the communion table, the pulpit and lectern, and the large cross hung high over the chancel. The most prominent indicator of the transcendent is the enormous, cavernous space above the worshippers. A classic Gothic cathedral also has high ceilings, but its interior space is limited by sidewalls creating a long, narrow nave. In this church, the sanctuary is almost square, without the space-limiting proximity of the sidewalls. The looming, virtually square area emphasizes the sheer volume of space above the worshipper. Worshippers look short. Even in the raised side pulpit, many preachers look short.

In the midst of multiple signs of current vitality, most obviously the presence of engaged and involved people, the past is always visibly present as well. In the hallways and parlors there are oil paintings of past leaders, heavy carved furniture, a framed copy of the original minutes of the founding meeting of the church, and plaques dedicating rooms to former members. An oil painting of a tobacco baron, philanthropist, and generous benefactor of the church building—hangs in a room named after him. The present vigor of the congregation takes place against the backdrop of a long and remembered history. A telling indicator of the present vitality of the congregation is the response of the congregation to the illness of a woman named Sandi.

The Story of Sandi

Pastor Jennings, a clergywoman, and Sandi had forged a strong relationship over eight years. One of the paths that they often traveled together was Sandi's memory of her mother's death to breast cancer when Sandi was 18 and her fear that she would meet the same fate. At age 39, she did receive a diagnosis of cancer of the breast. Afraid and disoriented, she went from the doctor's office directly to her pastor and asked with urgency, "What am I going to do?" For her, the question represented grasping, desperate flailing for control. She explains what the question meant to her: "How am I going to change this? What can I do? I meant to fix it, change it, not let it be. There was no answer for me. I was helpless. I was out of control with the biggest thing that I had ever feared all along." Her pastor answered without hesitating, and with firmness and gentleness, "We are going to do what we always said we would do: call in the troops. You won't have to do this alone." It was not a promise of control over the illness, but it was a firm promise of presence.

Soon Sandi had to make a major decision about how to treat the breast cancer. With the help of her pastor, she gathered her friends to help her make the decision. At a gathering moderated by Pastor Jennings, she laid out her choices before women mostly from the church, but also a few from other groups. This gathering at her house opened with prayer by Pastor Jennings, and then Sandi asked the group directly, "What should I do?" While she knew the decision was finally hers alone, she also wanted the collective wisdom of the women around her. There were some health care professionals there, some breast cancer survivors, and dear, dear friends. All those present were hand picked by her. When Sandi did make her decision, it was not solely based on a rational consideration of the medical facts, nor solely on moments of solitary prayer. But it was a decision made in the context of the wisdom, experience, and support of a company of women of God.

The time came for her first surgery, a lumpectomy. Just as she was leaving for the operating room, she kissed her husband, walked toward the door, and gestured to Pastor Jennings to come with her. Pastor Jennings remembers sheepishly that she soon fainted as the procedure started.

By this time, a care team was capably organized by a good friend from church, Linda. Many, many people had volunteered to help, but Sandi had trouble remembering exactly who had volunteered, what they offered to do, and when they were available. Linda did as Presbyterians often do in times of need: she reached for a book: *Share the Care* (Capossela and Warnock), a highly detailed plan for organizing a caregiving team. She soon was handing out packets to team members with forms to fill out that listed interests, schedules, skills, etc. There were eventually about thirty-five people on the team.

Over the months that followed, this care team worked like clockwork. Each week had co-captains and a set of volunteers. There was a regular schedule of help, and if something unexpected arose, if Sandi needed extra child care, for example, she only had to make one phone call to one of that week's captains. The team also organized special events. For her fortieth birthday, they threw a party and made matching t-shirts that celebrated the team. She continued to meet in smaller groups to discuss major treatment decisions, such as breast reconstruction. Team members signed a blanket to comfort her for the duration. "So I was always surrounded with those names and those prayers, and truly comforted. [The blanket] was baby pink and I love pink, it was soft." On the occasion of her last chemotherapy treatment, she received a bouquet with flowers from team members' gardens.

When her hair fell out, she wore a wig or a hat. One Sunday, however, she was teaching her third and fourth grade Sunday school class and her hat became hot and uncomfortable. In an act that was part rebellion and part radical trust, she decided to speak to the kids about her hot head. She told them, "You know what? I am really hot. And the reason I'm so hot is because I've got this hat on. If I were at home where I knew I wasn't going to scare anybody, I would just take it off so I could be comfortable." And then one of the children said, "Well, we don't mind, go ahead and take it off." So she did. They looked at their teacher for a moment, commented on her resemblance to a popular basketball player, and then went on with the class. To them, it was a nonevent. Undoubtedly Sandi's words to them were issued without fear or shame, and they responded with innocence and acceptance. It was a moment of redemption, the transformation of her body from representing the shame and demise that usually belongs to a bald woman with cancer, to a woman who still belongs and, though different, is neither feared nor despised.

Sandi speaks of "coming out of the closet" with her baldness. At one point, as she was driving through town with her bare head showing, she said to herself, "O my God, I really *don't* care what they think." She remembers it as a lasting liberation in many aspects.

> Since my hair didn't have a damn thing to do with what I was, inward or outward beauty, it has nothing to do with who I am. And my 50 pounds of fat don't have a thing to do with who I am. I felt like my body was kind of freed.

She began to go the grocery store, meet with friends, appear at church events with her head bare. She felt freed from definition by stares, undeterred by the problematic meanings cancer has accrued or gendered notions of beauty. Sandi was acutely aware that she wore her wig not to protect herself, but to protect others from the discomfort of seeing her. "It [others' discomfort] is awful, it's bigger than the fear." A woman from the church shot a photo of a profile of her head and shoulders. We see her smooth head, with only tiny, soft baby hairs barely present on her scalp. Her neck is bare and her head is slightly lifted, and the viewer is reminded of Nefertiti, the queen of Egypt, in all her beauty, dignity, and royalty.

In the midst of an experience of feeling out of control over her body, her illness, and the effects of the treatment, Sandi felt empowered by the care team. "I knew I had a captain if something came up." She remained in control over the care she received. They had not taken over her schedule, meals, and children and left her with the task of being grateful. She was not infantilized or rendered an invalid. She did not have to defer to their construals of what was best for her in order to continue to receive their care. She did not have to enter into the painful bargain, "You be the good patient, cheerful and compliant, and I will continue to care for you" (Frank). Rather she felt the very essence of support: caregivers offering concrete help without taking over, carrying out the agenda of the care receiver, not their own. At first Sandi relied heavily on the group for emotional and practical support. As she adjusted her life and expectations to the reality of the diagnosis and treatment, she grew more independent from the group. "They wrapped me in security when I needed it. I was like an infant: if you respond immediately to their needs, then they are stronger later, and don't need as much attention. The group was a little like parenting, a little like God."

Sandi's illness and the team's response to it have had lasting redemptive effects. If she had lived for years under the shadow of her mother's breast cancer, she was now freed from its paralyzing effects. "I didn't feel scared of death anymore because I had witnessed first hand that God would not leave me or forsake me." In these words, we see how she had fully appropriated the language of Scripture to describe her newfound discovery of God who will not leave, will not forsake. In the form of a care team, Sandi was drawn near to the very heart of God's mode of presence to the suffering, in the form of steadfastness, a refusal to abandon, and a love that is stronger than death.

Sandi also experienced what might be called a "fall from control."

> It was little by little I realized that ultimately I was not in control. None of us is. And that we are really in God's hands like everybody says. I don't think God says, "breast cancer, earthquake." I don't think of God as throwing bad things our way. What was going to happen was going to happen, and it was that I was going to go through it and that I was going to continue to go through some bad things. I stopped trying to control things. And was more comfortable in my skin, allowing life to happen like it happens. Allowing the true beauty around us . . . it just unfolds around us. I'm going to do whatever I can with as much grace as I can do it with. Some of us try to force it and make it and set a stage instead of allowing ourselves to act freely with whatever is really there. That is a burden.

One wonders if Sandi would have felt safe enough to let go of her lunging, grasping for control if she had not had the safety and security the care team had offered. It is likely that she was able to let go of her grasping for illusory human power long enough to experience God's power because she was surrounded by the safety of the group.

The yearlong lifespan of the care team had lasting effects not only on Sandi, but also on the team. Some reported a new feeling that God is steadfastly present in their lives, too, as well as a new confidence that God would be there in redeeming power should they become vulnerable. For them, it was an invitation to move beyond illusions of life as unending cheer and success. Pastor Jennings noted that "Sandi's willingness to be vulnerable was key" to the impact of the care team experience on both Sandi and the team. As a pastor, she knew that "a major obstacle to caregiving is others' unwillingness to be vulnerable." Sandi had opened her pain and fragility to others, narrating it along the way with honesty, humor, and in gritty detail, and in so doing created a space for all to experience God. Here is what Linda, the lead organizer wrote:

> I will be forever grateful to have so intimate a friendship that I can be allowed to carry her on my back to good health—for that is what I am prepared to do.

> And what a gift to us all, that she has brought us together to do the carrying as a woman-family and not alone, for the burden is always lighter when two or more are gathered—in his name and for his splendid child.

It also must be said that Pastor Jennings had already created a safe communal space for women to speak of their struggles without fear of rejection or ridicule. She was particularly skilled at "plugging people in with each other," as Sandi said. Many of the women in the group had already experienced her as one who does not withdraw in the presence of intense suffering, is willing to endure the powerlessness to make any of the suffering go away, while searching for and exercising what power there is within the limits of the situation.

Sandi's is a story of being made and remade in community. It is a reminder that we are created and recreated, redeemed, in and through our communities, and our bodies are, too. Surrounded by damaging cultural messages about beauty as the sole form of legitimate female power and the valorization of infinite youth, Sandi was a *breastless, bald woman* with *cancer*. Her stigmata were threefold. Yet her community, including the community of the children in her Sunday school class, persisted in defining her as beloved and desired, and they all experienced a power vastly different from that offered to women in the larger culture. While her care team was a subset of her church community, it also included dear friends outside her church. This is a reminder that we are created in multiple communities, that we have multiple subjectivities, and that being restored to health may mean invoking the recreative powers of more than one community. The church is not the only locus of activity of our sovereign God. Yet her church was the source of this locus of redemption of her body and soul, and she used the language of church and Scripture to describe her experience. This is a story of a church providing the language and social support for a woman to come face to face with her finitude. "It was a beautiful time after that initial month."

Asking the same question of First Downtown that was asked of Healing Waters, where did this church come from? How did it come to be? If I started the story of Healing Waters with the trials of slavery, I will start the story of First Downtown Church with the grueling life of the lowland Scots in the sixteenth century. Though Presbyterians in America also came from England, Scotland, France, and Germany, the predominant numbers were the Scots-Irish. So I will start my story of the origins of First Downtown Church with the story of the Scottish who migrated the twenty or so miles across the English Channel to the northern part of Ireland.

SCOTS-IRISH PRESBYTERIANS

Life was grim in Scotland in the seventeenth century: small mud houses, primitive agriculture, frequent diseases, lawlessness, and general insecurity. After 1603, an opening was made for settlers in the northern parts of Ireland, where the soil was rich and where the British were attempting to solve the problem of the "wild Irish" with settlers from England and Scotland (Leyburn, 83). The Scots were England's hope, and many were ready to leave their home country. "[T]he poverty of Scotland, the adventurous nature of the

Scots, and the appeal of a good bargain" lent themselves to success
for Britain's recruitment project (Leyburn, 93). But it was not only
economic conditions that lead to their quitting Scotland; it was also
religious conflict with England's king.

> The curious fact . . . is that the trials and sufferings of the Scottish
> Kirk . . . were not caused by differences on important points of
> creed. *The crucial issue was church government.* Presbyterians
> might have been as Calvinistic in their beliefs as they pleased
> if they had yielded to the monarchs and the supporters of the
> episcopacy by admitting bishops over dioceses. . . . *Most of the
> difficulties of Presbyterians . . . would have been avoided if the
> Presbyterian form of government had been given up.* (Leyburn,
> 106, emphasis added)

The centrality of form of government to Presbyterian identity is one
that persisted over centuries, and will show up in the story of First
Downtown.

Over the decades, the character of the typical Scottish resident
of the north of Ireland changed. This person developed habits of
pride, strong church discipline, and "penuriousness" (Leyburn,
153). Adjusting to the new circumstances in Ireland inculcated
"both self-reliance and adaptability" (153).

A little over a hundred years after the first Scots migrated to Ireland, they were ready to move again, this time to America. A combination of drought, economic setbacks from the British crown, and
religious restrictions led to the first large-scale migration to America in 1717 when five thousand Scots set sail (Leyburn, 168).

Over the next sixty years, there would be five pulses of migra-
tion, each one following economic downturns in northern Ireland
(Leyburn, 169). By the end of the fifth migration, it is estimated
that 200,000 Presbyterians had arrived from the north of Ireland.
They entered first through Boston and then through the mid-
Atlantic ports. The third wave of immigrants pushed south into the
Shenandoah Valley of Virginia and eventually into the Carolinas.
Later waves arrived in America through the port at Charleston and
moved northwest into the piedmont of North Carolina. With each

wave of immigration their Presbyterian clergy went with them, providing a link to the values and social structure from their past.

> The Presbyterian Church was, then, for many Scotch-Irish pioneers the one effective social institution in the community, a real focus and center of community life. . . . The minister, and to a less extent, the elder, was the voice of the community conscience. (Leyburn, 293–94)

Not only did the church provide links to the past and stability in the present, but also the character of its people lent itself to building lasting institutions for the future.

> The Presbyterian Church had gradually and imperceptibly become what it was to remain for more than a century—a denomination of the staid, sober, settled people of steady character, of that element generally known as middle class. The church continued to found schools and colleges, to eschew emotionalism and revivals, to esteem both self-discipline and social discipline. (Leyburn, 295)

Immigrants to North Carolina in the eighteenth century would have found Presbyterian churches already founded by Frances Makamie, a Scots-Irish minister educated in Scotland, considered the founder of the American Presbyterian Church. In 1758 the Presbyterians formed their first General Assembly, which included the Synod of the Carolinas, which itself included the Orange Presbytery, the home of the future First Downtown Church of Durham, North Carolina.

SOUTHERN PRESBYTERIANISM

Eventually, the careful, scholarly, and disciplined traits of the Presbyterian clergy were put to use in the defense of slavery. In fact, "Southern Presbyterian ministers led in the defense of slavery" (Alvis, 4). In January of 1861, a sermon at First Presbyterian Church in Augusta, Georgia, raised many of the theological themes commonly used in defense of slavery (Wilson, 1861). Using historical-critical methods, the preacher laid out a careful argument

from Scripture, quoting from the Ten Commandments, the Leviti-
cal Code Ephesians, Timothy, Philemon, and even Jesus, and argu-
ing from the silence of Scripture as well. He used arguments based
on the biblical affirmation of the universality of hierarchy, including between men and women, and "that no household is perfect
under the gospel which does not contain all the grades of authority and obedience, from that of *husband and wife*, down through
that of father and son, to that of master and servant" (8, emphasis
added). He drew on the vision of the "divinely sanctioned" strati-
fied southern household with the master-husband on top and each
level responsible for the care, feeding, and salvation of the levels
below (Fox-Genovese and Genovese). Slavery, then, was a means
of bringing the gospel to the fallen people of Africa. He concluded
the sermon with a vision of the last days when it will become clear
that the institution of slavery has saved both slave and master, both
lower and superior race:

> And, oh, when that welcome day shall dawn, whose light will
> reveal a world covered with righteousness, *not the least pleasing
> sight will be the institution of domestic slavery*, . . . appearing
> to all mankind as containing that scheme of politics and morals,
> which, by saving a lower race from the destruction of heathen-
> ism, has, under divine management, contributed to refine, exalt,
> and enrich its superior race! (Fox-Genovese and Genovese, 21,
> emphasis added)

Four months after this sermon was delivered, the denomination
was torn apart. The General Assembly of the Presbyterian Church
of the Confederate States of America was constituted, largely on the
grounds of the strict separation of church and state. In an address written by Presbyterian theologian James Henley Thornwell, "unques-
tionably the greatest theologian in the South" (Fox-Genovese and
Genovese, 217), the spirituality of the church was invoked. ("The
state aims at social order; the church, at spiritual holiness. The state
looks to the visible and outward; the church is concerned for the
invisible and inward" [Minutes, C.S.A., 1861, 7].) On the issue of

slavery, the address stated that "we would have it distinctly understood that, in our ecclesiastical capacity, we are neither the friends
nor the foes of slavery—that is, we have no commission either to
propagate or abolish it. The policy of its existence or nonexistence
is a question that belongs exclusively to the state. We have no right,
as a church, to enjoin it as a duty or condemn it as a sin. Our business is with the duties that spring from the relations—the duties of
the master on the one hand, and of the slave on the other. . . ."

Even after the Civil War, a defense of slavery was mounted
by the Presbyterians. In a book composed of columns printed in a
publication of the Presbyterian Synod of Mississippi, *Plantation
Life Before Emancipation*, we see an additional argument put up by
defenders of slavery: that their slaves were much better off than the
poor in the North.

> Compare . . . the suitable and substantial clothing and bed cov-
> ering supplied the slave with the scanty and sometimes ragged
> raiment of the poor in our great cities, and even laborers in our
> factories; . . . compare hours of labor in the open air, not pushed
> to exhaustion and comparatively short, with the long and drastic
> work of many artisans, against which there is a constant demand
> for restrictive legislation; . . . and it will be perceived *that no
> laboring population in the world were ever better off than the
> Southern slaves; and that there never was a falser accusation
> made against the Southern planter than this, harped upon by
> abolitionists of old, and repeated sometimes by Northern preach-
> ers now, that "he kept back the hire of the laborer."* (Mallard
> 36–37, emphasis in original)

As a further jab at their Presbyterian brethren in the North, this
author added that, though there were abuses of slaves, "[t]hese
were clearly exceptional cases, and rare, and no more indicative
of general treatment of slaves than the conduct of the father who
sat his child upon a red-hot stove to help him to recite the Shorter
Catechism, is of the Northern Presbyterians' treatment of their children!" (Mallard, 44).

After the Civil War, most former slaves left white denominations. The few who remained Presbyterian were not permitted "to
hold significant leadership positions" (Alvis, 7).[17]

HISTORY OF FIRST DOWNTOWN CHURCH

First Downtown Church was founded only six years after the end
of the Civil War, when Confederate and Union troops first shared
Durham's tobacco while their generals negotiated the surrender. Its
first pastor was educated at Hampton-Sydney College in Virginia,
before the war, and undoubtedly trained in the slavery-endorsing
theology of Thornwell. During the war he served in the Confederate Army.

Some of the most significant early business leaders and builders
of the town of Durham were also the early leaders of First Downtown Church, George Watts and Dr. Richard Blacknall. Watts
was a partner of the Dukes as they built their tobacco empire, and
Blacknall was a prominent community leader. Their presence as
creators of large corporate entities during the earliest years of First
Downtown undoubtedly made conditions ripe for this congregation
to be shaped in the next few decades by powerful social forces of
"incorporation" (Weeks, 101). These "incorporating" forces were
transforming businesses from groups oriented around the local
extended family and other loose filial connections to tightly organized hierarchies run by a board of directors, with a CEO at the top
and managers who directed the workers at the bottom. Nationally,
many of the owners and managers of these corporations were Presbyterians, and they exerted a powerful influence on the development of the structure of the denomination.

The earliest, foundational years of First Downtown Church
were also subject to these forces, and George Watts was one of
those who were both at the center of the creation of an enormous
and extremely powerful corporation, the American Tobacco Company, the corporate empire of the Dukes, and also at the center of
creating First Downtown Church. He entirely financed the current
Gothic Revival building with the brick and stone sanctuary that
seats over 400 worshippers.

However, for many churches in America, the "incorporation of the church proved costly" (Weeks, 111). "What had been
extremely informal and family-oriented congregations . . . became
tightly structured, hierarchically oriented congregations managed
by pastors with staffs, regulated thoroughly by a denomination
that resembled a major corporation. The congregation came to be
viewed . . . as a small (or medium-sized) corporation. . . . The session . . . served as a board of directors; the pastor as chief executive
officer. The various staff, and sometimes the committee members,
comprised the work force" (112). Though today First Downtown is
significantly more relaxed in its hierarchies and organization than
in the past, some organizational remnants of the historical development of "incorporation" remain.

In distinction from a profit-oriented business, however, First
Downtown has from its beginning been characterized by an impulse
to move beyond its own boundaries. First Downtown became the
seed church for three other churches in Durham, "missions" to
the workers in the factories and mills owned by the Dukes, Carrs,
and Watts. During World War II, First Downtown provided hospitality and meals to soldiers and sailors in training at Camp Butner
just north of Durham. In the mid-fifties the congregation overtured
the Presbytery to allow the ordination of women. In 1955 the church
adopted an open seating policy for all who sought to worship there,
while even ten years later some southern Presbyterians were still
blocking the entrance of African American worshippers.

A defining moment was in 1960 when the congregation made
the decision not to move to the suburbs. As more and more members moved away from the center of Durham, there was pressure to
move out of downtown. When the church made the commitment to
stay downtown, it marked a new era to an old orientation to serve.
The congregation turned its gaze to its increasingly poor neighbors through such efforts as Presbyterian Urban Ministry and the
First Presbyterian Day School. The decision to stay on its current
urban site is the origin of their motto, "downtown by history and
by choice."

Today, First Downtown Church sees itself as having a distinct identity in Durham. Defining identity as "a set of shared perceptions of members about themselves, their congregation, and its mission," Carroll and Roozen would probably describe this church's identity as closest to "Old First Presbyterian" in their typology of possible "identities" of Presbyterian churches (357). First Downtown Church shares with "Old First" churches a "strong sense of Presbyterian identity" and a "sense of being prestigious churches in their communities" (357). For example, it self-defines as the "flagship of Presbyterianism" in Durham on its website. They share an "emphasis on acts of charity and service [and] education, nurture, and a gradual approach to salvation" as opposed to an emphasis on a one-time conversion experience (357). Both Old First churches and First Downtown "emphasize meeting needs in their local communities (e.g., senior citizen programs, substance abuse programs, and tutoring and recreation for community youth)" more than an emphasis on a program to meet the spiritual needs of church members (364).

Unlike Carroll and Roozen's "Old First" churches, however, First Downtown Church is eager to engage in "contemporary issue-oriented Christian education" and "encourag[es] member action on the relationship of faith to contemporary issues" (364). Its orientation toward current issues is part of its perception that it occupies a place of central importance on the ecclesiastical landscape of the whole city. The pastor reports that forty-one different groups hold meetings at the church. First Downtown's website quotes a local rabbi who designates the church as "the central religious address in Durham." The church lived up to this self-perception when it hosted a citywide service where James Forbes preached. The service was sponsored by Protestants, Catholics, Jews, and Muslims. Several city and county officials sat in the pews of First Downtown for this highly visible event in the life of Durham's faith communities. When John Hope Franklin, internationally recognized historian of black history, read from his book for the local community, the reading took place at First Downtown. Senior Pastor Spaulding's name often appears in the local newspaper as a commentator on issues of religious or moral concern in the community. The church enjoys a prominence not only within Presbyterian circles in the town, but also on the interfaith scene, as well.

CARING ACTION OVER RIGHT BELIEF

In many ways, First Downtown's care for the sick can be understood in terms of what Nancy Ammerman calls, "Golden Rule Christianity": "This category of religious persons is best defined not by ideology, but by practices. Their own measure of Christianity is right living more than right believing . . . these Christians are characterized by a basic 'Golden Rule' morality and a sense of compassion for those in need" (197; citing Hoge, Johnson, and Luidens). Like Golden Rule Christians, First Downtown does not press evangelism or a personal relationship with Jesus Christ as the core of Christianity, nor, as it is at Healing Waters, a transforming, ecstatic experience of God. Rather this group believes that "people should seek to do good, to make the world a better place" (197). While more evangelical churches stress "prayer, Bible study, and witnessing" at one end of the theological spectrum, and more activist churches stress working for social change at the other end of the spectrum, this group of Christians stresses "service to people in need," both within the congregation and in the larger community (198).

Caring practices constitute faithfulness, not assent to a set of doctrinal tenets. "'Meaning' for Golden Rule Christians consists not in *cognitive or ideological structure*, not in answers to life's great questions, but in *practices* that cohere into something the person can call a 'good life'" (Ammerman, 202, emphasis added). At First Downtown, when asked the very difficult "great life question" of why people get sick and suffer, it was most often answered in one of two ways: either by making it clear what they *do not believe* or by stating what they *do not know*. Statements of what they do not believe were mostly refutations of the belief that illness is God's punishment for sin, a belief that is still heard in popular religiosity.

I don't see it as God punishing people. I also don't like it when people say, 'God must have had a reason for somebody dying.' . . . I don't think God says, I'm going to strike you with this so that you'll learn lessons X, Y, and Z.

Well, it's not because they sinned.

Who knows? I don't think that it's God's will; I don't think that it's punishment. It's none of those things for me.

I certainly don't buy "the sins of the father are visited upon the later generations."

I don't think illness has much to do with your goodness or your badness.

The second way to answer the question of why people get sick and suffer was to state what they did not *know*. This is consistent with Reformed theology's modesty about claiming to understand the ways of the sovereign God, reinforced in the early twentieth century by neo-orthodoxy's emphasis on the mystery of God.

I don't know. It's a mystery to me. I don't have any idea.

I don't know that I can answer that.

Who knows?

I don't have any answer to that question. I don't know. I don't have any idea."

I wish I knew, I have no idea. No idea.

While theological matters are the subject of study groups and Sunday morning adult education, a rationally cohesive and cognitively available doctrinal system is not the primary manifestation of their faith. Pastor Wilson gave the clearest statement of the faith orientation of this sort of Christian: the response to suffering should be alleviating it, not composing a propositional statement of belief about it. She stated,

There is not an answer to why people suffer. If we think we have an answer, it is probably trite or trivial, or, at worst, wrong. A better question would be, "How do we deal with suffering?" or "what do we do about it?"

Ammerman reminds us that Golden Rule Christians have been (unjustly) criticized as a sign of the secularization of the church, a sign that lax, incoherent beliefs, a vague and pliable moral code, and an ill-defined and uncertain Christian identity have won the day (196; citing Hoge, Johnson, and Luidens). It has been said that decades of accommodation to the dominant culture have resulted in a watered down form of religiosity that ultimately is indistinguishable from the larger culture. However, when groups such as Golden Rule Christians are found wanting, the standards of religiosity and faithfulness by which they have been evaluated have been set according to evangelical indices of orthodoxy, such as engaging in certain forms of personal devotional, Bible study, and evangelism (Ammerman, 197). In Golden Rule Christians, Ammerman sees "not a rejection of orthodoxy, but a different orthodoxy" based more on right practice than right belief (201). "Everything we have seen thus far tells us that developing a coherent theological system is not what Golden Rule Christians are concerned about" (202). The primary means of knowing God and communicating God's love is not through facility with propositional statements, but through caring actions.

As Ammerman noted, though Golden Rule Christians emphasize practice, they are not disinterested in matters of belief and systematic reflection. In fact, at First Downtown the members are very interested in cogitating over the ultimate meaning of things and groping for explanations for suffering and life's big questions. My interviews surfaced two pieces of evidence for their interest in systematic reflection. One, the number of books cited and sages quoted. In almost every interview, while grappling with the reality of suffering from illness, a book or a well-known thinker was quoted. I heard quotes from Bonhoeffer, Sartre, Browning, John Dominic Crossan, Elizabeth Kubler-Ross, and, most frequently,

Harold Kushner's *When Bad Things Happen to Good People,* as well as others.

A second piece of evidence is the frequency with which a statement of "I don't know the answer" was nevertheless followed by an attempt at an answer. It was clear that people spent time grappling with possible cognitive responses to the problem of human suffering, even if none of them was completely satisfying. They tentatively proffered explanations such as: suffering is God trying to teach me something; suffering is a way to make us more compassionate; suffering gives us "permission to lean on others"; God teaches others how to suffer through our suffering; suffering is "a wake-up call" to make life changes; suffering is "God's way of enlarging the kindness that's within us." The people of First Downtown are interested in the cognitive realm, the realm of belief, but not in an orthodoxy exclusively defined as conformity to Scripture or doctrine, and not at the expense of commitment to particular practices as a central expression of faith.

First Downtown Church is interested in practices, and in particular, *caring* practice. This care extends to one another within the congregation and to the town community. Most prominent in their community ministries is their decades-long involvement in urban ministry. Several members are also involved in AIDS care teams and Habitat for Humanity, all local efforts to "provide care and comfort for people in need" (Ammerman, 203). The church has sent multiple teams to the area devastated by Hurricane Katrina. Many individual members also show traits of more activist forms of exercising Christian faith in their involvement in local progressive political organizations and in community organizing. Within certain subgroups it is a common understanding that local and global suffering have their roots in social injustice. The church recently took the first steps to become more involved in an IAF (Industrial Areas Foundation) community organization that works for lasting social change. This is a departure from Golden Rule Christianity, which usually confines its practices to service and does not emphasize efforts to bring about structural, social change.

ILLNESS AND THE LINKS AMONG PEOPLE

If what was most striking about Healing Waters are *healing* practices in homes and in worship, at First Downtown it is the *sustaining* practices of community, as the story of Sandi illustrates. Though cure and care are not mutually exclusive, the former church emphasizes cure, the latter focuses on care. Stating this more formally, if what happens in *ritual* at Healing Waters' is the locus of that church's response to illness, then at First Downtown Church the feature most significant for care is the giving and receiving of supportive care—formally in *programs* and informally in *networks of affection*. In other words, care has to do with the arrangement of people within either programmatic or affectional structures rather than with ritual activity. At First Downtown, the power, the efficacy, the force, of the church's response to the sick is found in what happens in the spaces between people, whether that is a space defined by formal program or informal affection.

Program

Within the programmatic structures, one occupies the space of a caregiver or a care receiver. Throughout one's tenure as a member of the church, one can occupy the position of either, depending on whether one is ill or one is a member of a service-providing group, such as the Pastoral Care Committee, the Deacons, or the Session. But within programmatic arrangement of people, there is a segregation of roles: one would not be a care receiver and caregiver at the same time.

When asked about their caregiving activities, interviewees often responded by referring to the job description of an organized subgroup within the church and to whether or not they were currently an active member. One caregiver said, "I've rotated off the Deacons, so I don't have institutional reasons to [engage in caregiving]" and later added, "It does seem that everything has to be institutionalized at [First Downtown]."

Out of curiosity for how she would respond, I asked a woman whom I already knew to be a very active caregiver in the church whether she did much caregiving in the church. Her response was,

"I am really not on a caring committee or anything like that." When asked further if she uses any of her medical expertise, she said, "I don't have any connection" with the sick in the congregation that draws upon her expertise. This comment suggests that, since she is not on a committee, she believes her ample caring activities should not be counted as part of the church's ministry to the sick. One wonders if the strains of the "incorporating" forces of the past are echoed in her assumption that holding a designated position in the organization is what makes a person's efforts an official part of the church's work.

During another interview, a woman spoke eloquently of the relation between her faith and her care for the very sick and dying that she practices in her profession. Yet, when I asked *why* she had participated in a church group that discussed her congregation's care for the sick, rather than responding out of her broad repertoire of spiritual and theological language, she spoke in bureaucratic terms:

> I was pulled into that discussion because of chairing the pastoral care committee and because of this session-charged obligation, which the pastoral care committee was simply supposed to carry out, of connecting officers within the church individually to persons within the congregation who were shut in, disabled, sick, in order to provide them with pastoral care.[18]

In this congregation, when the enterprise of caregiving is mentioned, often an image of a program within a church bureaucratic structure is evoked, instead of a shared, mutual, common activity that naturally arises out of faith, gratitude, or call. Surely this emphasis on program and bureaucracy was reinforced by the churches' inception in the midst of the rapid growth of corporations in Durham, where major players in both business and First Downtown were the same.

Affectional Networks

However, there is a great deal of shared, mutual, common activity that does arise out of faith, gratitude, and call. In addition to formal programs, there are strong affectional networks where there is no formal designation of who gives and who receives care. These networks tend to be subgroups within age- or gender-defined groups, such as the young families' group or the women's circles. Here there is a sense of mutuality based on the bonds of feeling and commitment between peers, and the segregation between caregivers and care receivers is not as pronounced. One could be a recipient of care and a giver of care at the same time.

Though care receivers spoke with deep gratitude for the caring activities of committees and staff, what evoked the most profound expressions of gratitude are the outpourings of affection, support, and practical help by these informal networks of affection. One can speculate that it is assumed that the clergy would offer support, and that it is done well. But the caring actions of the laity were experienced as sheer grace. The very presence of God was attributed to the activities of this network of the faithful. This was the most common response to where God was in their particular experience of illness: "in the community."

However, some expressed disappointment and hurt over being left out of the caring activities by networks of affection. One woman said that "the pastors do a good job but it doesn't get beyond them, unless you are connected in some way to a social network." A man who was very grateful for the care he had received noted, "I find that people who have been lost out the side door, some of our friends, they weren't always able to get into the group."

Therefore, it could be said that the weakness of any church that looks primarily to affectional networks as the locus of God's care for the sick is that not everyone is included in one or another of these networks. When the experience of the presence of God is limited to mediation by limited, sinful human beings, then one will inevitably be disappointed. The question then becomes, does this congregation, which emphasizes right practice over right belief as a measure of faithfulness, and who largely construes faithful practice as a form of caring, adequately point beyond itself to the God who is both immanent and transcendent, who is indeed in this community, but is not exhausted by its actions?

CONCLUSION

The extraordinary strength of First Downtown is a sustaining inter-subjectivity that transcends formal program and is available through interpersonal networks of affection. It is a form of interconnected-ness that, members report, mediates nothing less than God. It is countercultural, as seen in the response to a bald, breastless woman with cancer. It allows people to relinquish a grasping for control, to recognize that personal well-being is not up to the individual alone but is also the concern of this congregation and God. This relinquishment is often the result of a deep assurance that, at some level, one is safe: from abandonment; from the threat of a discon-nection; from being regarded with disdain for being self-absorbed; from shame, ridicule, manipulation, accusations of weakness or self-pity or self-indulgence.

4

FIRST DOWNTOWN CHURCH'S
BELIEF-PRACTICES

*T*he ethnographer writing about her own community faces significant challenges. It is very difficult to develop the naiveté, the unbiased eyes, the freedom from an internal map of a community that was formed through direct experiences in that community. This is a congregation that I love, where my daughter was baptized, where I have witnessed many moments of mercy and redemption, courage, and kingdom-building. Therefore, it is clear that it is impossible to attain freedom from bias. What the ethnographer can do when encountering her home community, however, is view it from the perspective of someone who has visited other lands, the perspective of the traveler who has returned from a journey through other ways of being Christian, worshipping God, and caring for the sick. The ethnographer of one's own community, whose eyes have been forever altered by visits to other places, can return home and see one's community with a freshness that would be impossible without having left. It is my hope that that is the perspective I bring.

Like my discussion of Healing Waters Church, my approach has three moments: first, a moment of "empathetic description," when I get inside the belief-practice world of First Downtown in order to describe it on its own terms. The second is a moment of "appreciative interpretation," when I describe in my own

language the strength of a particular belief-practice. Finally, I move
to a "cautionary warning," when I discuss a belief-practice's vulnerability to corruption by idolatrous impulses. Again, I do not put
myself in the judgment seat regarding these belief-practices. I do not
at all wish to suggest that these belief-practices have in fact been corrupted by idolatry in this congregation. I only discuss the possibility
of their serving idolatrous ends, how they *might* be corrupted.

BELIEF-PRACTICES

Like my treatment of Healing Waters Church, I offer here a summary of the belief world of First Downtown Church gleaned from
interviews with members and staff.

> The most important way God is present to the sick is through the
> church community, through both networks of affection as well as
> structured programs. God also works by giving the sick internal
> strength and through modern medicine. There is much that we do
> not understand about *why* people suffer. We do know, however,
> that people get sick for "natural" reasons, such as exposure to
> bacteria or genetic vulnerability, as well as problematic inter-
> nal dispositions, such as stress or pessimism. They should seek
> medical care, though not everyone in the world has access to it.
> Church members take care of the sick because of what Jesus said
> and did. This care should extend to the sick outside the congre-
> gation. It includes practical help as well as sending cards and
> remembering the sick in private prayers.

The Community Mediates God

God is mediated through people. After describing a moving encounter with a woman dying in the hospital, I asked Pastor Spaulding
where God was in that moment. He replied, "My own belief is
that God was in the interaction." When I asked a man with cancer
how his faith helped him deal with the uncertainty of his future, he
replied that it was "not through faith itself" that he was helped, but
it was "being part of a faith community" that was significant. He
also spoke of valuing the sense of belonging he had in his Sunday
school class.

> When I hadn't been around this fall for different reasons, some-
> one from the group came over to me and said, "We miss having
> you there." There is a sense of being valued as a person and valu-
> ing other persons. I'm not alone. I'm not a lonely person.

He concluded, "So faith for me has been within those communities
[that are within the congregation]."

The summary statement for what the community actually did
that mediated God was "support." Immediately after identifying
the faith community, not faith, that was significant to him in his illness, the man cited above identified "*support* in a number of ways"
as what the community did to mediate God. Again, when I asked
a caregiver about how a person might experience God during their
illness, she replied simply, "Through community." Then she added,
"I think God reveals God in community, in those *support networks*"
(emphasis added). When I asked Pastor Spaulding about specific
practices of caring for the sick, he replied, "I think the whole business of trying to be a *supportive* community to those who are sick
is a real challenge." One woman described tearfully the importance
of this pastor's actions after her husband died. "Pastor Spaulding
was quite a *support* for me afterwards. He could just give you that
look, of 'I'm here, if you need me.'"

Community mediates God, and this happens through support.
The specific practices of support include sending cards, visitation,
and practical help, and praying for others.

Sending Cards

Sending cards to those who are sick is the most widely observed
practice of response to illness. One older woman in the church
made it a practice to send cards monthly to each person who was
sick or unable to attend worship. She was mentioned with admira-
tion by many people as an example of the way that congregation
cares for sick people. I asked her to describe the cards.

> Well, I go to a shop and get the same thing for everybody, mostly.
> Then I'll just write on there mostly "wishing you a happy day"
> and then sign it "Presbyterian Women" and then sign my name.

Other cards were more personalized. When Ned's illness kept him from attending worship on Christmas, he received a specially created card.

> Lo and behold, here came in the mail a card that [a church member] had made with two photographs of the Christmas service. That was just terribly meaningful for me . . . that came at a very good time.

Another man received cards from the children's Sunday school class that he had taught for years. Another younger woman received both cards and e-mails and that was a "pleasant surprise" for her.

One researcher considered the related practice of sending sympathy cards to the bereaved. He concludes that these cards are a way to express care for the grieving person while keeping distance from death (Lippy, 177). The prevalent practice of sending cards to the sick could be viewed in the same way: it is a way of performing the social requirement to express concern for the sick without getting too close to the finitude that illness exudes.

However, there is another possible explanation for the prevalence of the practice of sending cards that may be more accurate. Sending cards may be a way to express care while maintaining a distance, yet it is a distance not maintained out of a fear of the silent death rattle that all illness sounds, but out of a caring respect for the sick person's privacy. Illness is kept a private affair in many churches because, in a culture where frailty and dependence are signs of moral failure, the exposure of one's illness is to be avoided. In this line of thought, it is respectful to maintain one's distance from the sick during their time of dependency because some consider dependence to be humiliating and embarrassing. In the dominant American culture, dependence implies failure: both a failure of competence and a moral failure. To fail at being able to care for oneself implies one has the moral failings of carelessness, laziness, and even selfishness. Therefore it is an act of kindness and respect to maintain some distance and allow the sick their privacy.[19]

The expression of care while maintaining distance in the act of sending a card also respects the sick person's control over who they see, when they see them, and under what circumstances. Such control is relinquished in a hospital setting.

Certainly the practice of sending cards is not an act of idolatry, and it was often cited as very moving to receive cards and letters and a source of great comfort and connection to the nurture of the church. However, one can discern the potential for idolatrous underpinnings to the practice of maintaining distance from the sick in order to avoid viewing respectfully the other in the indignity of their illness. The underlying idol is the lone, self-sufficient individual who can and should survive alone. The threat of idolatry here is not the material greeting card, but is the belief that independence and self-sufficiency are the moral norm, and that fragility and dependence are a departure from the status of "a good person." The two theological fallacies at the heart of this belief are, first, the assumption that finitude is a mark of sin. The measure of our finitude becomes the measure of our sin. The second fallacy is that needing others to survive the hardships of finitude is a moral weakness. On the contrary, human beings are created for interdependent life in covenant community and thrive as interdependent members of the body of Christ.

The second fallacy described above, that needing others is moral weakness, is no doubt rooted in American individualism—the belief that I am who I am through my virtuous hard work, I create and maintain myself through the sweat of my brow. This claim is not only empirically false, but it is also rooted in racist, sexist assumptions that render invisible the sacrifices of African Americans and women of all races whose unpaid or underpaid labor created the material foundations of the American economy and provided for the material needs of the people of this country. Without centuries of unpaid slave labor the American economy would not have flourished in the way that it did. Similarly, there is no lone individual who is exempt from the feeding, cleaning, bathing, washing, cooking, and nursing labor of women of all races. The belief that we are capable of creating ourselves is both false and a racist, sexist, graceless elision of the contributions of millions of our forebears.

Again, the act of sending cards to the sick can only be seen as an act of kindness and hardly an act of idolatry. The argument here is that a faithful congregation will be vigilant to the possibility that maintaining distance from the sick may have problematic underpinnings. Many mainline, middle- and upper-middle-class congregations face the challenge of creating the countercultural ethos of a communion of the fragile, on the basis of the deep belief that we thrive when we are mutually upholding in the midst of the trials of finitude. Privilege renders us vulnerable to the idolatry of the lone, self-sufficient individual because many of us have not been forced by chronic economic hardship to acknowledge fully our core interdependence with others. Our traditions of care evolve in the context of relative economic ease, and we are distanced from the truth that we thrive only in mutual care. Our relative financial independence allows us to live with the illusion that we can make it alone, or that we can purchase all the care we need in times of illness.

Visitation and Practical Help

If sending cards is a way of expressing support while allowing the ill to maintain their privacy, visitation and practical help is based on a contradictory impulse: the desire to enter into the world of the sick and to bear their burdens with them. Members of First Downtown Church engage in both kinds of supportive practices, one that allows greater distance and one where visitors enter the homes of the sick and provide many forms of practical caring.

Visiting the sick is both programmed and informal. The Pastoral Care Committee delivers flowers every Sunday after church. One man said, "Easter Sunday morning, someone came after the service with an Easter lily . . . that was very meaningful." While describing important pastoral actions during his illness, the same man described a pastor's visit coincidentally timed to receive bad news. He was able to quote the pastor's exact words, though he heard them several years earlier.

When Pastor Spaulding came in on the day that I had received [bad] news and we were able to tell him that. And he said, "And this isn't the result you were looking for," and so we did have a prayer together, and that was meaningful.

Pastors visit people in the hospital regularly, and a layperson might accompany a pastor. Those in nursing homes also receive regular visits. Pastor Jennings often prayed laying her hands on the sick person. On occasion she went with another pastor and a layperson to sing to those in bed with illness. "When [my husband] was in the hospital [Pastor Smith, Pastor Jennings, and layman] would go over and sing to him. *This was one of the best things that we had*, the singing."

There are also countless, unreported visits paid in nursing homes to individual church friends who cannot drive, who would otherwise be isolated from the world and human warmth. Often those who were so generous mentioned their acts of kindness, remembrance, and inclusion only in passing. Yet they are received with enormous gratitude and given great significance by the receivers of these caring acts.

Members offer countless forms of practical help to people who are sick. "When I expressed something about difficulty with driving because of the eye, one of the men said, 'Well, look, anytime you want, give me a call,'" one person reported. One mother whose child had been sick described a member of the church who became her daughter's "special friend." She would babysit, come to soccer games, have the whole family over for dinner. Whenever a new baby is born, meals are provided for the family for weeks.

I asked one vigorous older woman, who is well known as a generous caregiver to other older women, what she did to care for those who are sick. Her reply refused to create hierarchy between her and the recipients of her care. "Well, I have some friends," she began.

I might drive her to a doctor's appointment, go to the grocery store for her, go over and write notes for her and maybe write her checks so she sign them and pick up personal items if they're in assisted living or get some of these services provided for them.

Then, I pick up on the things that they need extra personal items and things of that kind.

She described mutual acts of help among several older women.

A recent theme [in our prayers] was the ice storm and how we feel blessed that friends checked with us to see if we might need something. And then when we can do something for someone, we check with our friends. "I'll be going out" or "I'm going out now, can I get something for you?" And, just share with each other how grateful we are to have a circle of friends and also to have people that do check on us and that we can check on.

One widow described her congregation this way, "I think that the people in our church were good medicine for [my husband]." She went on to describe the elaborate acts of one man who was a college classmate of her husband's.

We'll just never forget him. He was from a strong Presbyterian family. He was a deacon in our church for a long time. When he heard about [my husband], when he was at [the convalescent home], this man would come, and he spent hours getting ready to come. He'd bring a trophy, put a piece of cardboard over it, and put on it, "[Husband's Name], Greatest Patient." Then he would send an article about somebody they knew in college, send articles about the football team, send little jokes that only men of that age would pay any attention to. And he'd send pictures of their classmate. He must have sent *two dozen* of those kinds of things. (emphasis added)

Another caregiver describes seeing a friend moving into the ravages of Alzheimer's. She resolved to help her.

I remember talking with her and saying [to myself], "Frances, God loves you and I do, too." I realized to myself that I had darn well better mean that. I had to live that out, and so I felt a very strong call to be involved in her life. I really felt like I was called to do it. It felt like a call. I couldn't walk away from her.

She provided extraordinary care over two years' time. As a part of Frances' care team she prepared meals, took her to the doctor and the grocery store, helped her move to two different apartments, fretted over financial and legal issues, and, what was most impressive, drove with Frances from North Carolina to Massachusetts, a two days' drive, for Frances' daughter's wedding.

Prayer for the Sick

I did not find any in the congregation who were known as caregivers who prayed with the sick. When I asked one person whether she would suggest a prayer with those for whom she was caring, she said,

> Probably not. I should probably carry one along with me so I would remember to do that. That would be a good reminder. I'm not probably as religious as some people might think. I do mine in actions, rather than in words.

When asked the same question another woman answered,

> As far as, quote, praying with each other—if there's a real need, it's like, "put me on your prayer list" or "I'd like to be on your prayer list." In our own way we share our faith, but we don't get together and pray. If there's an illness or a special need that we have, we feel free to say to the other person, "Remember me in your prayers" or this kind of thing. We share our faith in that way.

Another person replied, when asked about praying with the sick,

> I'm just a little uncomfortable with it, with initiating that [prayer]. I don't think that you have to. I think being interested in the person and staying there to talk is, you are demonstrating that you care about them. Even though I guess I am representing the church, I don't feel the need to pray or sing hymns. If they wanted to, I would certainly do it. If they initiated it.

However, it was very important for those who were sick to hear that they were included in others' private prayers. In response to a question, "where was God?" during her daughter's illness, one woman responded,

> Everywhere. The *support* from individuals, and from the church
> as a whole. I knew that she was *in folks' prayers*, I would get
> e-mails and phone calls from people that I didn't know very well,
> that were pleasant surprises to us. Cards and notes. I really felt
> like folks were praying for her. (emphasis added)

The very presence of God was mediated through "support" that was expressed through e-mails, phone calls, cards, notes, and prayer. There was no mention of the content of the cards, e-mails, or prayers. The mere fact of them was support enough, and in this support she found God. One person said, in response to a question about the presence of God in his illness referred to forms of caring he appreciated,

> *having a prayer with me*: it isn't even the words—they could
> have said the wrong words—it was the time together, it was their
> caring for me.

Another form of ministry with the sick has been the formation of a group devoted to knitting prayer shawls. These shawls not only go to the sick, but also their family members, former members, and people who are not able to get to church. They are a tangible reminder that a person is not forgotten, that they still matter. Before a shawl is presented, it is blessed. The leader takes a shawl and prays for the person who will receive it. Then it is passed around and individual members pray silently for that person.

The pastors did pray with those who were sick, and these prayers were important to them. For some, the content of the prayers were important. One woman asked me with misty eyes, "You know how Pastor Jennings prays? She always gets it right." Another referred to Pastor Spaulding's prayers as particularly sustaining for her.

It seems that "knowing one is prayed for" is what is significant about others' prayers. The intimacy of praying together may be too much, and the knowledge that one's plight has entered into the praying heart of another is enough. Participation in the event of prayer is not what is important; rather, it is knowing that another has thought to bring you before the throne of grace, that you are not alone in bringing your burden before God.

One can probe further into the laity's reluctance to pray with the sick. Many were simply unaccustomed to praying with another person and therefore felt uncomfortable and unsure of themselves. Why do some ecclesial traditions include extended, emotional, and repeated prayer with the sick, while others do not? There may be at least two reasons.

One, the Presbyterian fear of domesticating God, the fear of overconfidence in one's knowledge of the transcendent God, and the reticence to claim the skill of speaking directly to that God in the presence of another, is no doubt behind the reluctance to pray in pairs or small gatherings. It is a reticence based on a fear of relating to God as a being like any other rather than the fundamental ground of existence itself. Two, it is also possible that underlying the almost exclusively private prayer for the sick is the assumption that it is somehow embarrassing to be vulnerable before God in the presence of another. Certainly to come before the Almighty is a humbling experience, and to be humbled in the presence of another person is to be avoided. Three, it may be that the disinclination to praying with the sick is a reluctance intensified by living in the evangelical South. When one feels vaguely embattled by a surrounding form of religiosity that is considered premodern and anti-intellectual, there is resistance to engaging in practices that might appear to be acquiescing to it. Furthermore, it could be argued that there is a subtle classism here with the belief that uneducated "holy rollers" pray openly, freely, and with emotion, while educated, rational, Presbyterians do not.

The God who is present through these multiple forms of support is not a magical force from the heavens that intervenes in human affairs. This is the incarnate God, the God who works in partnership with other human beings. This is not the monarchical God who is present as control and domination, but the God who is present as compassion, as mercy—the God whose power is passionate *chesedh* and self-giving love. These Presbyterians evidence a belief in a transcendent God who can never be fully known, and whose mystery must be respected, in their reticence to pray with others. Yet they also evidence belief in an immanent God, intimately present in and through human actions in their faithful care for one another. Their confidence in an immanent God is expressed in their belief that God is present in the community.

"Support" is more than the practical help it imparts. The significance of support is that it is experienced as a gracious challenge to the burdensome belief in the West that we live and die by our own wits and grit. To be in this church where support is freely given and received is to hear the message that it is not shameful to be finite and in need. It is to receive the good news that you are beloved in your weakness, you still belong to us, you are not measured by your success at self-sufficiency. Your primary identity is not in your strength, but in your status as beloved by this community. Support is a way of establishing that you are beloved not because of your strength and what you can give in return, but because you are simply part of this community.

The vulnerability to idolatry in the belief "the community mediates God through support" is that "community" and the "support" it offers can become that to which a person suffering from illness turns for salvation. The affection, care, and nurture of a congregation can slide from being a witness to God to becoming a god itself. "Community and its support" can itself be the object of yearning, desire, and worship rather than the God embodied in that community. The God discerned in support remains God only if the support is a finite and partial glimpse of God who is present in many other ways as well.

This idolatry can blind the believer to the multiple modes of activity of the sovereign, mysterious, infinite God. The vulnerability to idolatry in this belief is that such a strong emphasis on support can limit the perception of the countless other ways churches mediate God. God-perceived-in-support is exposed as idol when the believer is closed to the infinite ways God is present through churches in times of illness: God in the still small voice in personal prayer, God in ritual of all sorts including the sacraments and laying on of hands, God in worship, God in praying dyads, and God in passionate communal lament. Even if "support" has not become an idol, even if it is clearly recognized as an imperfect mediator of God's presence, a congregation still needs other ways to mediate the infinite ways God acts through church life, because *its support will always be imperfect*. Congregations who unwittingly limit God to the experience of interpersonal support can be enriched by finding ways to affirm God's presence when the community fails miserably, as every one inevitably will.

When God's presence to the sick through the church is viewed primarily as "support," it is possible that the receptivity to the God who heals is diminished. Throughout history many Christians have believed that God not only sustains the sick, but also makes them well: God as healer. Many traditions hold to the belief that God can cure disease. Other traditions make a distinction between healing and cure. Even if the disease remains, God's healing power can transform illness into the occasion of call, repentance, reconciliation, or the inbreaking of a vision of God's powerful and redeeming love. Whether or not healing includes cure, Christians affirm God's healing power, and limiting God to support is problematic. God-present-through-support is vulnerable to domestication, a God whose transforming power is tamed in order to remain predictable.

God Is Also Present outside the Church

Though most people described "the community" as the primary mode of God's presence, in the course of our conversations, other modes would emerge. One woman described in sacred terms the work of a secular hairdresser who cut Sandi's hair right before receiving chemotherapy.

> She took Sandi into the back room and almost had this counseling session with her, while she was cutting her hair. She talked about what Sandi could expect, "Eventually it will all fall out, and you will want it shaved. . . ." She kept talking; she was very reassuring. "I've done this for other people in the past." She

asked how she felt about her hair being cut, and her hair growing back and being perhaps different from what she had now. It
was really incredible. It was an incredible experience. *It was this
act of grace.* It was a service, she didn't charge Sandi for it. It
was interesting to me because I never thought of a hairdresser in
those terms. But why not? Why not this kind of *ministry* of working with patients? (emphasis added)

The same woman spoke of another friend with chronic pain who
experienced God through "other revelations."

She is in a meditation group, she experiences God in profound
ways, speaking to her via the lessons that happen, through dreams
for her, and in times of prayer. Sometimes there are messages she
doesn't want to hear, but she knows it's God speaking.

Others experienced God as internal impulse or feeling. For one person, God was "a sense of calm." One woman spoke emphatically
about where God was in her illness: "Oh honey, it was God who
gave me whatever backbone I had to say, no, I don't want that surgery." And then she continued,

God was at least there. Not to mention the doctor who happened
to be [there] who looked at me and said, "This lady needs to go
to the hospital." And the doctors who took care of me there, certainly they were, and the nurses who took care of me there. And
the psychiatrist. And my dear husband who put up with all this
garbage that I would come home from the psychiatrist with, and
say, "Now listen here!" And he accepted it . . . O yeah he [God]
was right there, he or she, was right there all the time.

God is present in nature.

Besides the medical healing, nature is a powerful healing force:
to watch the birds and nature—God's creation—or to take a
walk. One time I was under a lot of stress that could have led to
depression. I just went and sat on a boulder and listened and I felt
God's presence there. I thought about the 23rd Psalm. I thought
about the beauty of God's creation and the peace of it all. That

was a healing experience for me. For the first time I felt a oneness about God's creation. I felt a sense of belonging. It was like
God's Spirit was infusing. If I were sick again or under stress—
just to go and sit and be quiet.

God is present through various sorts of leadings. A woman who
had not attended church for some years said, "I just had this feeling
like there's a reason I need to go back." I asked her to explain what
she meant when she said she felt she had moved to Durham "for a
reason." She said, "Well, technically, my husband was transferred
here. But I think God was moving in mysterious ways because
we needed to be close to a major medical center." She explained
that Duke had the particular specialist a family member needed at
the beginning, and University of North Carolina, fifteen minutes
away, had the world's expert for later treatments. "That's pretty
extraordinary."

Some emphasized God's ubiquity. God is present "all around
the sick person, as well as the ones caring for the sick person."
And,

> I think God is right beside you. I think God is weeping when
> people are sick and dying. I think he is listening and consoling.
> Through people who visit the sick and through ministers and
> nurses, he is helping them get better. He is very sad when they
> don't. I don't think he is "up there" ruling exactly everything that
> happens. I'm not that kind of theology.

The pastor expressed the most encompassing view of God's
presence: "If you believe that God is in the depth of life, in all of our
lives, then there's nothing that we do outside of God's presence."

Finally, God was described as mystery. "For me, God is more
mystery, more sense of wonder, the recipient of gratitude, the most
pointed metaphor for the community."

In these affirmations of the varieties of ways God speaks we
see the Reformed emphasis on the sovereignty of God who can be
present in any way God chooses and who refuses to be limited to
the institution of the church, its leaders, its texts, and its rituals. The
places named were: hairdresser, meditation group, dreams, prayer,

sense of calm, a doctor in the crowd, a psychiatrist, a husband, nature, leadings, ministers, nurses, and in the depth of life. These various sites of God's presence are a testimony to the openness to God's Word beyond the institutional.

The risk for idolatry here is when discernments are loosed from the church, its leaders, its texts, and its rituals, then it is possible that one is worshipping simply an extension of the self. If the heart and mind, eye and ear have not been shaped by representations of a community with a deep history of sapiential knowledge, or, saving wisdom, there is greater possibility that one is merely communing with a Feuerbachian projection of one's own deepest needs and desires. One way to view inherited scriptural, theological, ecclesial traditions is that they are a repository of wisdom that has been honed, produced, and tested by centuries of human suffering, and therefore they bear the authority of the voice of the suffering.[20] These traditions provide a check on the human tendency to make an idol of the self.

Illness Has Natural Explanations

The causes of illness are "natural."

There are dangerous bacteria and viruses in the world.

There are biological causes.

We are made naturally and natural things happen.

Some referred to genetic vulnerability as a source of illness. "There are weaknesses you are born with." Another woman answered quickly and simply when I asked why someone was born with a birth anomaly. "Genetics."

Another way illness is explained is by pointing to unhealthy behaviors that some people choose.

People do things that are destructive to themselves. . . . [such as] eating habits, smoking, just excessive behaviors which lead to illness.

None of us are perfect. We do things to our bodies that we shouldn't do, and we shouldn't blame ourselves for all of the things that happen. Some of the things happen because of the way we care for ourselves or don't care for ourselves. Smoking and alcohol and drugs and eating too much, and just a lot of the things we do to ourselves.

One woman explained her illness as "a strictly medical thing." If she fails to take care of herself, "that's my responsibility and I can't ask God to help me out of it."

Illness can also be explained by emotional causes. I received several answers that included emotional causes in response to the question, "Why do people get sick?"

Too much stress!

Serious and deep disappointment in life does make us vulnerable. Cancer is connected to serious loss.

Oh, a lot of it has to do with your emotional health. One of the reasons I think I'm healthy is because I am an optimist.

If you handle stress well I think you are healthier. And I think that's been shown with clinical studies.

Related to emotional causes was "attitude." "Some people have different mental attitudes about sickness and wellness. I don't think it's all attitude, but people around you can be either good or bad for you in getting well." Another person, when asked why people get well, responded,

I suspect it has to do with their attitude. You hear of people who fight to get over their cancer or whatever, and there must be something to that. Wanting to get well more than you want anything else. And self-interest, probably. I think self-interest is why some people don't get well; it's better to be sick and get the attention. We all like attention.

God's good gift of medical care and the means to afford it is why we get well. I see it as a gift from God and that there are physicians that help us get well. Maybe that's why I don't pray as much when I get sick because I'm thinking, "I'm going to the doctor and God's already answered my prayer that I can afford to, that I have health insurance." I'm not in a country where there isn't adequate medical care, [therefore] God has already answered my prayer.

Only Pastor Spaulding referred to life's unpredictability and randomness coupled with human and divine compassion.

> A part of it, I think, is that there is a kind of randomness to life that is a part of the world we live in. In other words, you can get a germ and your system may be such that it will respond in a different way, and I may get the same germ and it may not bother me, or I may get sick and you may not. Because I believe in God doesn't mean I am immune to those kinds of things. I don't have this sort of "God-shield" around me. I'd better wash my hands, too, when I go around places where there are a lot of germs or I'll get sick like everybody else. That's part of the process. But if I do get sick, people step in, people intervene. So even in the midst of that [the randomness], I don't think it's *just* a natural process. Somehow God is at work in that.

Though illness incidence has a random quality, it is not beyond the pale of God's activity.

Presbyterians are known for their appreciation for the fruits of scholarly pursuits, including science. The sovereignty of God is such that God can be revealed in secular investigations, though only through the lens of the Word of God in Jesus Christ as witnessed to in Scripture can God's Word in science be discerned. Even in the early twentieth century, the fundamentalist B. B. Warfield held that "God gives us the means of medical science to deal with illness, disease, and pestilence" (Smylie, 222–23). Presbyterians evince a freedom to explore the world through the means of science because of their confidence in God's sovereignty over all human endeavors. This congregation is no exception.

This willingness to accept a "scientific" account of illness is, in a way, an appreciation of the materiality of the body. The body is recognized in all its physicality, and it relinquishes parts of its truth only through the measurements, probes, and quantifications of the biomedical sciences. There is a body-denying flavor to some more "spiritual" approaches to health that verge on Gnosticism, which these Presbyterians avoid in their respect for scientific materialism. This acknowledgment of the irreducible contribution of science to health successfully avoids a spiritualization of the body, which makes its fleshly healing secondary to spiritual intervention.

In addition to strictly biomedical explanations, some added "emotional causes" and "attitude." Though no one interviewed cited specific clinical studies, my hunch is that the confirmation by science of the impact of psychological states on health is important to them.

Yet, of course, this confidence in biomedicine and its truths is vulnerable to idolatry. The belief that the body is finally explicable is kin to the belief that the fate of the material world is, finally, controllable. Openness to the partial truths of biomedical knowledge of the sick body and its healing is different from total confidence in them and a slavish adherence to the dictates of a treatment regimen. In this view, the body and its fate, then, is divorced from God's healing, redeeming, transforming power.

Illness Can Be a Time for God's Teaching

A caregiver speculated that "perhaps there is purpose behind the [illness]." She listed, "to know the suffering of Christ, to identify with other people who experience pain, to experience the grace of God. I don't know if I'm supposed to figure out why, if it makes me more compassionate toward other suffering." She continued discussing the changes brought by illness. "It's hard to just go on [as if nothing has changed]. Something's happened that is very sacred, or special or precious and you can't just go on. You are kind of transformed."

Pastor Murray stated that

illness certainly can be a means of grace. Illness can be an opportunity—a call to make significant changes in my life. So, it can have a very real benefit.

For Pastor Spaulding, "[God is at work] in the process of the illness even. You experience God's presence. You'll discover something. Somebody demonstrates some level of caring that is really amazing to you. And it kind of transcends anything you ever imagined."

Another woman bemoaned with some amusement, "I think God is trying to teach me something, and I'm a lousy student. I'm not a very perceptive student."

Pastor Spaulding spoke eloquently of the fact of human finitude, and the equally real fact of God.

> I think ultimately one of the pastoral responsibilities that we have in terms of caring for the sick, the ill and the dying, is to tell people that death is not the scariest thing in the world. The scariest thing in the world is to live and die in a world where there is no God. All of us are going to die someday. To say it's a part of who we are as mortal people, and our mortality is a part of our God-givenness. That's a reality that we need to come to terms with, and that helps us a great deal in dealing with our own ability to take care of other people who are suffering, because we realize that we share their mortality.

One woman spoke of death.

> This is part of God's creation. Jesus' death was one of God's plans. We are mortals and it's part of God's plan that we're going to die. So, to accept it that way and to be able to have the courage of your faith is something I hope I will be able to do.

Though strong natural explanations for illness were cited, there was also the awareness of God's power within illness. The confidence in scientific explanations of illness does not preclude the possibility that God is at work in and through illness to redeem and make whole. God can sacralize illnesses, transform them from an occasion of decay and pain to growth and joy. Pastor Spaulding said in one of his sermons that "God can pick up the broken pieces and make something sacred out of them." Here we see an awareness of God's transcendent power in the midst of the trials of human finitude. It is a statement of confidence that, indeed, nothing can separate us from the love of God in Christ Jesus our Lord, not even this illness.

This belief is vulnerable to idolatrous impulses to make all suffering meaningful. The idol here is "meaningfulness." The final answer to the question, "Why is there human suffering?" will never give itself up to human knowing, and the futile quest to know fully can make an idol out of the full disclosure of the mystery of suffering. This belief could function as an attempt to reduce suffering to human size, to tame its ravages. For some who are ill, there is a desperate search for a reason, a meaning, a purpose to their illness. Many who embark on that search do find that God can transform even this, even these dire circumstances. Yet, when the explanation, the purpose, the reason becomes the object of desire and the goal of the search, the quest lapses into a destructive idolatry. Finally, of course, the search must be for the God who defies explanation, who is present to the one who gratefully receives the often surprising ways that God is at work.

Care for One Another Is at the Heart of the Christian Faith

When interviewing caregivers, the reasons given for their choice to care for the sick in the congregation were almost all christocentric.[21] The response offered most often in response to "why do you care for the sick" was to cite Matthew 25, and often in the King James Version: "Inasmuch as ye have done it unto one of the least of these my brethren, ye have done it unto me." Several offered the image of the church as the body of Christ, "I think your job as a member of the body of Christ is to embody as much of Christ as you can with your actions." "The body of Christ is a very real image to me. There are times when my role is to be arms and legs or whatever is needed to assist." One woman spoke of Jesus' reading the Isaiah scroll in the synagogue. Another spoke of Jesus' healing the sick. Another referred to the "Golden Rule": "I think it's that 'doing for others as you would have others do to you' piece of it, but I don't know that at the time I was aware of that." Another said,

> For me there's this fundamental element in the persona of Jesus
> and in the Christian faith that is nurturing, compassionate and

healing. There is such a fundamental part of the life of Jesus and the message of Christianity that reaches out to the suffering of people and reaches out to people who are in hard places. So it's all in the Bible, the reasons. That's what Jesus did: Jesus took care of people, and I think that's the greatest witness. I don't think of it as a witness, but really I think that's all Jesus did was take care of people.

Some spoke of a very specific call to a particular person: "I really felt like I was *called* to do it. It felt like a call. I couldn't walk away from her" (emphasis added). Others referred to a general Christian call.

It is just absolutely what we are *called* to do as Christians is to care for the sick, the poor, and to love each other, particularly in our community, in our church. (emphasis added)

Others said, simply, it's what we do as Christians, period.

It was just natural. It just felt like if you are a Christian, why don't you do that? I mean, that's who we are.

I had a strong feeling that it was what we as a community of faith should do: be a part of taking care of each other.

Reaching beyond the bounds of self is clearly a core affirmation of those who offered care to the sick. More significantly, one sees the countercultural impulse to reach out beyond the bounds of the nuclear family to carry some of the burden of illness. The respondents' overwhelmingly christological responses challenge the criticism of mainline churches' lack of theological clarity about the basis for their ministries. Rather than a generic, amorphous morality disconnected from a community of accountability and a historically rooted sacred text, these respondents root their actions in Jesus Christ, the Scriptures that witness to him, and the church that proclaims him. Considering the headlong drive toward increasing isolation among Euroamerican middle- and upper-middle-class Americans, one described years ago as the "pursuit of loneliness," it is clear that these caring actions are motivated by a countervailing force, one they identify in reference to the figure of Jesus (Slater, 1970).

The vulnerability to idolatry here is that right Christian living, correctly following Jesus' example, would become a means to earn membership in the beloved community or even God's favor. One's righteousness is the idol. When faithful Christian works are identified at the core of one's faith then one must become vigilant for a lurking works righteousness. Other traditions can idolize other practices, such as the correct orientation of one's heart, genuine belief, or true sorrow for one's sins, as the hallmark of faithfulness. Still others can idolize ritual observance, such as proper participation in confession, Eucharist, and penance. In contrast, the vulnerability here is the belief that correct performance of the central Christian mandate to care for others will lead to salvation.

Care for Others Is a Response of Gratitude

One woman who had received care from the church when her husband was dying began to visit people regularly in a local nursing home.

> I had experienced other people coming to see us, and what it meant to us. I know how sweet it was when somebody, like Sheila, she'd just pop her head in the door for two minutes, and that's all it takes [speaker's eyes fill with tears].

Another woman recalled "growing up in the Depression and my father was out of work most of the time, and we struggled, we didn't have that much." Then she asked,

> The traveling that we have done, the three wonderful children that I have that are well educated, well married, and have healthy children, I mean, how can you not be just totally grateful for all of this when there is so much suffering and trouble in the world? I have to be grateful for that, I have to share that [plenty] because it's so much more than I deserve.

Yet another woman noted that *"so much has been done for me*. It's a way of passing along some of the kind deeds that have been done for me over the years." Her care for others who are ill is rooted in the memory of how the church cared for members of her family when they were ill. She remembered

a family member that was so very ill and to see how my fellow church people responded by ways that they helped her. And then in later years, I had another family member who was very ill and it's the way that church members interact with each other and *the kindness that was shown to my family at that time. I can't go back and do special things for the people who responded, but if there are other church members or friends that I can do*—I might not be able to do the same thing that they did for my family members, but I can help in some way. I feel *that's a way of sharing your faith.*

This belief-practice lives out Jesus' call in John 15:12 "to love one another as I have loved you." Our love for one another arises out of the grateful recognition that we have first been loved by God in Jesus Christ. It is out of gratitude and plenitude that we give.

The vulnerability to idolatry in this belief-practice is that service should become payback, a reimbursement for mercies received. In order to stay in God's favor, to secure a lock on God's mercy, we must adequately compensate God through service to God's children. In a capitalist world where one's success in the marketplace defines one's worth, the commandment "love one another as I have loved you" risks becoming "love one another so that I will love you." In this world, nothing is really free, everything, finally, must be paid for. Again, the idol here is the self's righteous acts. That which will save, in the final analysis, is the self.

Care for Others Because It Is Personally Rewarding

Many who were caregivers spoke of how rewarding it is to care for those who are sick. One woman said simply, "you get far more than you give." When I pushed her for an explanation, she said,

> Well one thing you get is *the good feeling* of knowing you were
> able to help someone and they were grateful that what you think
> was a very small thing you did for them, when they express their
> appreciation, it meant more to them than you thought. And it also
> does something for me. I loved working with them [special needs
> people], and they all knew it.

One man spoke of the joy he brought to old people when he
visited them, "People were always very happy to see you." He also
appreciated their knowledge of history. "They had full interesting
lives that were, they had many years to talk about: the history of
Durham, World War II, things like that." He concluded about his
years serving as a caregiver, "And I got a lot out of that, too."

Two people spoke very movingly about their caregiving as part
of a mutually give and take relationship. The implicit relationship
between caregiver and care receiver was one where each benefited
from the other. The hierarchy between caregiver and care receiver
was flattened. One woman spoke about her care for people with
special needs.

> And you know, I've learned too much from these special people
> to not believe or to realize that they are here for a reason, and *they
> have something to teach us.* They also are God's instruments,
> and that we are mistaken if we think there isn't some purpose
> and meaning in their lives. Sure, it would be nice to do things so
> that people don't have to suffer, yes, I think that's fine, but I also
> think that *there's something wonderful about what they can offer
> us.* And we can offer them, and what we have to share. I think
> I just learned *that everybody's got something to share,* And it's
> just wonderful for someone to have a good time and to just come
> up and give you a great big hug. It's wonderful.

The mutuality is not necessarily experienced simultaneously. There
can be a temporal disconnect between times of giving and times of
receiving. I asked a woman why she continued to visit her friends
with Alzheimer's, even though they recognize her only rarely.

Well part of it is what their friendship has meant to me over the years and you don't stop caring for your friends when they can no longer carry on their end of the friendship. *When they can no longer carry on their part, it doesn't mean you can no longer carry on your part.* So part of it is *remembering the kind of friendship you did have* when they were able to be your friend and some of the nice things they did and good times you shared.

Not only was this woman aware of her past connections to a woman now unable to hold up her end of the friendship, but she was also aware that she was part of a web of connections that would care for her in her old age.

I am grateful that I can still help my [older] friends because the time may come when I have to call out to some of my younger friends. "I need you to do something for me."

In a world of increasing isolation, where the number of close confidants has been diminishing, many middle- and upper-middle-class Americans have a deep hunger to be engaged at a deep level in others' lives. It is a participation in nothing less than the disclosure of glimpses of the divine. I-Thou connection, where the other is encountered without expectation of usefulness, is becoming scarcer. What the respondents said "feels good" may be interpreted as the experience of fulfilling who we are meant to be as connected, mutually interdependent people. I wonder if "it feels good" could be interpreted as "it fulfills a God-given deep impulse to connect." The frailties of illness require that we overcome pretenses of being useful, pleasing to the senses, or entertaining. We come before one another stripped of masks, illusions of self-sufficiency, and any thought of being useful. *Both the caregiver and the care receiver participate in this nakedness.* Certainly the one who is ill is aware of personal powerlessness, but the care receiver also feels powerless in his or her inability to "fix" the problem of pain and suffering. This is the arena for authentic I-Thou encounter.

Another possible interpretation of "good feelings" is that, every time caregivers visit another in need, they are reinforcing the confidence that they themselves will receive care when they need it. Caregiving is a reminder that we live in the kind of community that cares for one another, it is a way of reassuring oneself that, indeed, participation in the body of Christ is truly to participate in mutual interdependence.

The belief-practice that caregiving is personally rewarding can be corrupted by the human propensity to idolatry when caregiving is a means to the end of "feeling good." The "good feelings" here are not the encounter with God in the context of human mutual inter-dependence, but rather other false gods. Such gods can be feeling superior in health/righteousness, the feeling of having paid one's debt for past blessing, the feeling of having personally stemmed the suffering, the feeling of "effectiveness" in the face of human pain. If it is true that we live in an era plagued with narcissism (Capps, 1993), then this quest for "good feelings" makes sense. The nar-cissist's difficulty with feeling anything at all may explain why entertainment displays bloodier violence, more explicit sex, more opportunities for voyeuristic pleasures in talk shows, and greater cruelty and betrayal in "reality" shows. The narcissist would not only be vulnerable to the impulse to visit the sick toward the end of "good feelings" but would also be drawn to situations of extrem-ity, such as illness, in order to feel anything at all. Here the idol is simply feeling anything.

THE STORY OF NED

There is one example of a person who drank deeply of the well of God through the caring acts of the church, and yet who was also aware that God is more than an aggregate of human acts. Ned was a man who lived with cancer for years. He lived with his wife and enjoyed children and grandchildren living in other states. He was an ordained Presbyterian minister but spent most of his career editing a magazine. He had come to a place in his faith where he had rela-tivized traditional sources of authority. "And I don't have to worry about the boundaries of the Presbyterian Church and the Presbytery . . . I don't have to follow the book." "I don't believe the Apostle's Creed. What for me is important when I say [the Apostles' Creed] is that I think, 'Imagine all these centuries, there have been people all around the world who have repeated these words and I stand with them.'"

He gave the congregation the gift of inviting us to accompany him on his illness journey. At one point we received an email asking us to "give him a hand," meaning he was asking for us to send him cutouts of our hands so that he could sense our presence with him. So children, adults, people in and out of the church, sent him their hands. One woman made a quilt with a hand motif.

We also received updates regarding good and bad news.

> Hi everyone,
> [My wife] and I were encouraged by our doctor today that . . . the chemotherapy is working. . . . We are grateful for this extended reprieve! Thank you for your concern and encouragement which mean a lot to us during the bad days of recovery after treatments. Two good weeks out of three is good! I can't wait for blossoms to begin at the Duke Gardens. A pair of Canada geese are back on our pond—maybe goslings this year?

Finally, we were heartbroken to receive the following message.

> Dear friends,
> Living with cancer took another turn yesterday afternoon when our oncologist referred us to Duke Hospice. There are no more treatments for my . . . cancer and my body is breaking down in several irreversible ways. . . . [My wife] and I saved the tears for when we got home. We thought you would want to be included in our news, hard as it is. I will get back to several unfinished poems and a collection of the others. A biblical Hebrew article of mine will be published soon. . . .

Members of his Adult Sunday School class quickly began organizing a care team for him and his wife, but he died three weeks later.

Many members of the congregation were affected by Ned and his wife and their honesty, courage, and capacity to stay deeply connected to each other, to their friends and family, and to their church. I was particularly moved when I interviewed him for this project. I came away from the conversation feeling that I had experienced God. Looking back, I try to understand, precisely, what it was about the interview that left me feeling I had experienced the divine. *Ned* wasn't God. Though he was a fine human being, it was not through any of his *particular excellent qualities* that I met God. Nor did he verbally express a *concept* of God that I found particularly compelling. He didn't proclaim any *good news* to me that I was forgiven or beloved before God. Nor did he perform a particular act of *kindness* and compassion toward me. It had to do with his ability to both perceive and articulate what some have called *"more"* in our earthly existence. He described some fairly average events, being addressed by name during communion, various acts of kindness showed him, and he talked about how he sensed in them something of God. He had some sensitivity, some perceptive faculty, some interpretive lens that opened up to him a deeper or higher level of what was going on, what I am calling a "more." At one point, he had just described several moving experiences of people and art without using any traditional theological language. I asked him how he connected these experiences to God.

> I think they are related [to God] in the sense of the unexplained-
> ness of life, the mystery of life, the beyond the touch. And while
> I can't test it and experiment with it, there's a sense of something
> there that I don't want to let go. But I don't want to give it over
> to creeds or supernatural language. . . . For me, God is more mys-
> tery, more sense of wonder, the recipient of gratitude, the most
> pointed metaphor for the community.

He was neither sentimentalizing, nor romanticizing, nor in any other way glossing over all in human life that is limited or imperfect either morally or materially. Yet he sensed in our worldly existence something beyond the boundaries of sense. One way to describe how I experienced God in this interview was that I was quickened, alerted, reminded of the "more" that is present in the midst of everyday people, places, and things. The way he talked about his life, loves, and illness demonstrated his faculty to discern that "more," and it awakened mine. He was clearly able to speak of griefs, disappointments, angers, and ways life had failed him. But there was something about his level of feeling for people, beauty, knowledge, and goodness, his courage to reject his earlier construals of religion and faith, his realism about his illness and its course, his hope for the future, his gratitude for his wife and his church, that I can only describe as a perceptive faculty for the "more" of human life. He showed what Edward Farley calls courage: a desperate love for this world without trying to use the world to save yourself (Farley, 1990).

There was also a second way in which I experienced God. In the first way I sensed God, it was something that I would have been able to experience had I been watching him talk to someone else, or watching a video of him talking. "Here is a man who knows God," I could have said. In the second way, there was a "more" that happened in the course of our conversation that involved me as a participant and not just an observer. It was a mutual recognition that we both had the same sense of God. It was an unspoken understanding between us that we both have known that "more," and, furthermore, it is the most precious thing in all the world, we have given our lives to it, and, finally, we worship it. For me, it was a moment of communion based not on mutual self-disclosure (I did very little talking), not based on help given and received (there was no caregiving going on), nor on empathetic listening by one to the other (there was none). In fact, the interview was a rather formal occasion of a researcher asking questions of a research subject. What did happen, though, was a togetherness based not on mutual gaze in which we saw the face of God in each other, nor in the quality of our connection, nor in an acute I-Thou intimacy, but rather a togetherness based on gazing in wonder and adoration at the same God.

There is something important here for those of us who emphasize the communal mediation of God to the sick and suffering. It is not exclusively an I-Thou encounter between two people where God is mediated. Nor is it only in a moment of authentic, empathic encounter, where the quality of one person's presence to the other is the arena for experiencing God. God is also mediated, or perhaps quickened or awakened in each other, as we stand together, not facing one another, but side by side in awe before God.

The task of the community is to be intensely aware of its responsibility to mediate God to the sick, but it will always defer to the God that is never confined to the fallen, finite church. It is in this way that churches avoid making an idol out of the goodness of community. Insofar as the quality of the community is one that points beyond itself to the God who is its source, it is a faithful one. A particular form of community is indispensable to the knowledge of God. But it is not only because of the exquisite relations of love, compassion, and communion among its members. It will also be a community that names its shortcomings, its sins, and does not hold out for excellence in human acts of kindness in order to mediate God. It will also defer, refer to God as its members link arms in gratitude and wonder before God.

In the course of this interview with a man who was facing death, the truth of the funeral prayer drew near.

> Give us faith to see, beyond touch and sight,
> some sure sign of your kingdom,
> and, where vision fails,
> to trust your love which never fails.

Cared for by First Downtown Church, Ned looked beyond sight and touch and saw sure signs of God's kingdom.

5

Our Lady of Durham

The Fiesta of Our Lady of Guadalupe

*A*s I stood in the cold December air at 5 a.m., multiple layers of history and culture were displayed before me. It was the third hour of the annual fiesta in honor of Our Lady of Guadalupe, which is held in the early morning to mark the time that she appeared to the simple peasant, Juan Diego, in 1531. At that moment, we were in front of the church after the service, and two lines of ten or so men were dancing to the sound of drums, surrounded by hundreds of worshippers. There was a striking contrast between the two groups' costumes. One group wore dark pants and white, long-sleeved buttoned shirts, with red fringe epaulets. Sashes of red, white, and green, the colors of the Mexican flag, crossed their chests. Some carried long, steel machetes. Clearly they represented an official class, perhaps the Spanish colonizers of Mexico.

The other line of men clearly represented native peoples, wearing feathers, brown tunics and white pants. The dancer in the front was light on his feet, exquisitely precise in his timing. He bounced rather than stomped, defying gravity. This group also carried machetes. In each dance, the two lines would circle past each other, passing close by in parallel but opposite directions. By the end of the dance, the directions switched and the two lines met and danced in the same direction, still in parallel. The man next to me said it represented Mexicans as a *mezcla*, "a mixture," of Spanish and native peoples. The machetes were a reminder of the violence in the first encounters between the two cultures.

The urban setting for this celebration brought other layers of history and culture, centers of identity and meaning, in this small city. There is the church's brand new Emily Krzyzewski Family Life Center, named for the mother of Duke University's fabled basketball coach. Across the street is the steepled Southern Baptist Church building, abandoned by a congregation who relocated in the suburbs. Further down the street is the storefront Tabernacle of Joy congregation, as well as the storefront Ar-Razzaq Islamic Center. Further down the street is the Durham Food Co-op, a reminder of the sizeable countercultural community in town. The longest edge of the church property is wrapped by the curving Durham Freeway, built to link Duke University Medical Center to the Research Triangle Park, signifying Durham's leap from a tobacco to a biotechnical economy.

I also saw signs of popular culture within the crowd: a child holding a "Dora the Explorer" book, English-speaking Latino youth with baggy jeans hanging precariously low, jackets with U.S. sports teams logos, and video recorders.

The mass earlier was lead by a Polish priest fluent in the Spanish he had learned in Mexico and Peru.

Summarizing the cultures and historical eras in that moment, I saw representations of the indigenous Nahual people, the Spanish colonizers, and modern Mexico. I also saw represented important pieces of the history and cultures of Durham: the Duke family and their association with the Methodist Church, the Southern Baptists, the African American Sanctified Church, African American Islam, U.S. Catholicism, countercultural America, pop culture America, Duke University basketball, biomedical Durham, and, finally, a Spanish speaking, Polish priest. Present in that moment were multiple borders, hybridities, and juxtapositions among widely varying discourses.

Prior to this outdoor dance, the indoor activities were entirely devoted to the Our Lady of Guadalupe. When I arrived at 3 a.m., the sanctuary that seats 1000 was three-quarters full, with a large group of people concentrated at the side statue of *la Virgen de Guadalupe* with their backs to the central altar. Immediately in front of the statue was a mariachi band, including singers and trumpet, violin, and guitar. The area around her was so packed that the steady stream of people with an offering often had to pass their roses forward from person to person to reach *la Virgen*. Roses came in plastic wrap, in vases, and in elegantly arranged baskets, and some with at least two dozen roses. A young man with a Mohawk haircut took his bouquet forward. Others held up cell phones taking photos. The mariachi band led several songs, but none were sung with as much enthusiasm as *"Las Apariciones Guadalupanas,"* which told the story of the Virgin's appearances. The song mentioned the site of her appearance by its native name, Tepeyac, and included references to her clearly Mexican character: the song celebrates her hands and face that were Mexican, she brought peace and harmony to the Anáhuac, and she is the mother of the Mexicans. The merging of national identity with religious persona was jarring to my American liberal Protestant ears, so trained to reject the merging of religion and nation.

Soon the sanctuary was packed, with people standing in the back, and the service began. Here and there little boys were dressed in peasant clothes with tiny mustaches, beards, and sideburns penciled in—tiny Juan Diegos. At one point in the service, our attention turned to the back of the sanctuary. Forty or so dancers began processing into the sanctuary, two by two, on their knees. When they reached the end of the aisle at the altar, they stood and backed down a side aisle so that their backs would not face the center altar.

The service also included a sermon, Scripture readings, and finally, communion. I expected the celebration of the Eucharist to be the culmination of the celebration in honor of the beloved *Virgen*, with hoards of people streaming forward to the sound of Latino music. Yet very, very few people took communion. The usher passed pew after pew and nobody went forward to receive the host. Occasionally a single person from a row would go forward. I would later hear several explanations for this small numbers of person taking the Eucharist. One explanation was that most people had not been to confession and did not feel worthy. Another explanation is that the historical scarcity of priests in the rural areas and small towns of Mexico has meant that non-Eucharistic, popular religion became more important in people's spiritual practices.

Every once in a while a worship leader shouted: "*Viva la Virgen de Guadalupe!*" And every one answered: "*Viva!*" The voices were loud, but I saw no smiles and sensed little jubilation. Not the rollicking street party that I pictured when I pictured "fiesta." I would later learn that religious fiestas have the character of a commemoration rather than a party.

Throughout the service I saw a collection of objects on the wall around the communion table that faced Our Lady of Guadalupe, objects there to absorb, soak up the holiness of her presence.[22] There were statues of "*la virgencita,*" candles with her image, pictures, some of whom were large, framed poster-sized images, 2 x 3 feet, that men would carry to place before her altar. At the end of the service the priest sprinkled holy water on them, with one man hurrying forward pulling a tiny picture out of his wallet to be blessed.

Perusing the special songbook for the day, I saw a wide variety of appellations for Mary:

Santa María, Saint Mary
Paloma blanca, White Dove
Madre del creador, Mother of the Creator
Niña santa, Holy Girl
Madre mía de Guadalupe, My Mother of Guadalupe
Virgen celestial Señora, Heavenly Virgin
Virgen sagrada María, Sacred Virgin Mary
Mi Guadalupana, My Guadalupan Woman
Madrecita de los Mexicanos, Little Mother of the Mexicans
Madre amorosa, Loving Mother
Virgen santa, Holy Virgin
Virgencita, Little Virgin

Mi virgen morena, My Brown Virgin
La Virgen de Tepeyac, The Virgin of Tepeyac

Two features were particularly remarkable. The first was, again, the merging of national identity with religious belief, the blurring of the boundaries between honoring *la Virgen* and honoring Mexico. Second, there was an overt naming and celebration of her brownness, the indigenous nature, of Mary, the Mother of God. This was not a secondary feature, incidental to her identity. Rather it was central, and our attention was called to her brownness over and over.

After the service we streamed out of the sanctuary to the parking lot/driveway in front of the church for the dancing. The first group consisted of thirty or so youth, the youngest appeared to be six, in two rows. They wore feathers splayed out like rays from their caps that also bore a picture of *la Virgen*, long capes that fell behind them to below their knees with full-sized picture of the virgin icon, and in front, an apron also emblazoned with her picture. Sequins flashed from their costumes, and they carried shakers with long silvery tinsel attached.

It was dark and cold. I wondered if another gathering of a thousand people at three o'clock in the morning with drums, feathers, sequins, roses, costumes, candles, music, trumpets, guitars, hot drinks, and bread could happen with so little notice.

I assume most of the people gathered there had worked the whole day before, then got up at 2 a.m., went to church, and then would go to work all day again. I looked at one young man's face during the music and wondered if he thought of his family somewhere in Mexico, if he felt displaced from everything that was important to him.

The Evening Procession. When I arrived that evening, it was dark and the procession had already begun, and in the distance a large column of people crossed the road, traffic stopped by two flashing police motorcycles. First came the indigenous dancers, then an SUV pulling a low, flat trailer where Christmas lights illuminated Our Lady of Guadalupe, and then the people. Not thirty or forty people, or even one or two hundred. There was a stream of at least a thousand people crossing the street before me. Almost all of them were short in stature, brown-skinned, and black-haired; some carried children; some pushed strollers. A hand-held loudspeaker led the procession in songs and prayers in Spanish. Our Lady of Guadalupe was represented by a live young woman in blue, and kneeling before her was a live Juan Diego. The procession walked between wooden bungalows as the African American neighbors here and there came out on their porches to watch.

An older woman carried a child of three or four years old, shifting him from one position to another. When I offered to help her carry the child, she smiled, shook her head no, and told me she was fulfilling a *promesa*, "a promise," by carrying the child through the procession. This would be another question I would ask: What is a *promesa*?

The procession was quiet yet powerful. Most were walking silently. Only a few near the loudspeaker were singing and praying. There were no slogans or political chants. There was no laughing and joking. It was a great company of brown people silently exerting their presence in Durham. There were no TV cameras or press that I could see. There were very few onlookers. This was not an effort at communicating a message to anyone, to the city of Durham or its politicians. This was not a parade. This was a large, powerful, public religious event that wound through the neighborhoods of Durham in the dark, occasionally stopping traffic when crossing busy streets, but otherwise revealing its power only through its great, quiet numbers.

CHANGES IN NORTH CAROLINA

This fiesta in honor of Our Lady of Guadalupe is indicative of recent migration patterns from Latin America into the American South. Into the land of tobacco, Southern Baptists, and the "pig pickin'" has been a sudden influx of Latino workers, with the Virgin of Guadalupe, *taquerías*, and signs reading "*se habla espanol*." The Latino population in Durham has increased seven-fold in ten years. The typical immigrant is a young, unmarried, Mexican male with little education and speaking little, if any, English. He is also undocumented. He works long hours in construction, yard work, or service work for restaurants or janitorial services. He sends money back home to support his family. He has come directly from Mexico rather than an established Latino community in other parts of the U.S. There are, of course, many Latinos from Central America as well as older married men with their wives and children, as well as single women, though they are not representative of the majority. Currently some are recognizing a "second wave" of Latinos that includes many more women and children. In addition, many Latino babies are born here. In Duke University Hospital, fully half of the babies born are of Latino origin.

Latinos migrate to the U.S., leaving their homes, land, culture, ways of life, and most painfully, their families, mostly to improve their lives and the lives of their families, especially the children. Urban unemployment, rural farm failures, and grinding poverty have lead them to the U.S. Most send money back home to their families or save money to build a house or start a small business in their home country.

Eighty percent of the Latino parishioners at Our Lady of Durham are undocumented, which means that many of them endured some sort of difficult border crossing. Some paid thousands of dollars to *coyotes* who hid them in trunks of cars or backs of trucks, or who lead them across deserts and rivers to the U.S. Some made the journey without help, enduring heat, thirst, hunger, wild animals, and bandits. Women risked sexual assault. The *Washington Post* reports,

> Rape has become so prevalent that many women take birth control pills or shots before setting out to ensure they won't get pregnant. Some consider rape "the price you pay for crossing the border," said Teresa Rodriguez, regional director of the U.N. Development Fund for Women. (Watson)

Below is an account by "Nelio," a resident of a town a few miles from Durham. This story is a part of a larger study of the migration patterns between a particular region in Mexico and Carrboro, North Carolina.

We got here by crossing the United States-Mexican border in California, but it took us two times to get here. We only got by the *migra* (border police) on the second attempt. The first time, the *migra* found us in the desert near the Mexican-Californian border and sent dogs after us. They arrested us and deported us back to Mexico. The second time we attempted to cross, there was another group with a *pollero*[23] and the *migra* couldn't get both of us at the same time. *La migra* arrested the other group. After walking for a day, we reached a railroad track that transports cargo to Southern California cities. At a place where the train slows down, we all jumped on one of the cars and climbed up the top, where we laid flat so we would not fall off after the train sped up. Yet we knew that *la migra* would be patrolling overhead with helicopters. One of the cars was open at the top, so we climbed into the container to hide. It was made for ceramic tiles, not humans, and it was extremely uncomfortable, jarring us violently during the trip. *La migra* did appear at a point when the train stopped. The police hit the sides of the car with their batons in attempt to flush out migrants; the sound is so deafening that people often can't take it and try to escape from the car, only to be discovered. We held tight and got through it but still had to jump off the train before it arrived at its destination, where more of *la migra* were waiting. We jumped off at one point near Palm Springs when the train slowed down. (Gill, 56)

Nelio's story could be that of any Latino at Our Lady of Durham. The difficulties and the costs of crossing the border are immense.

These recent immigrants, of whom 70 percent are Roman Catholic, have brought their religion to the historically religiously homogeneous South where Baptists and Methodists comprise the majority of the "southern evangelical Protestant establishment" (Tweed, 72). Small southern towns see symbols strongly identified with southern history and identity juxtaposed with symbols equally rooted in Hispanic identity. One writer describes a procession honoring the *Virgen de Guadalupe* passing by a statue with the inscription,

In Honor of
The Confederate Soldiers of Sampson County
"Who bore the flag of a sacred trust
And fell in a cause, though lost, still just
And died for me and you."
                              1861–1865[24] (Tweed, 86)

Commenting on this moment, Thomas Tweed writes, "Even this traditional southern Protestant town—with more than its share of tobacco farmers, gun racks, and Baptists—had begun to feel the effects of the post-1965 immigration" (90).

OUR LADY OF DURHAM

When the bishop recognized just how many Latino Catholics were arriving in the Durham area, he directed them toward the town's small African American congregation. For eight years this church conducted bilingual services in order to meet the needs of all its parishioners. In time, though, the parish council feared losing the distinctive African American character of the congregation and voted to end bilingual services. Soon afterward, on a Sunday morning, a Latina laywoman gathered up the large icon of Our Lady of Guadalupe that adorned the sanctuary and lead a procession of Latino worshippers out of the building. Within days they had found a home in the large Catholic parish in the middle of Durham, which I am calling Our Lady of Durham. Until that point, this congregation had been largely Anglo, with small but significant representation of African, Asian, and Latino populations. Their style of Catholicism was shaped by the social justice concerns of the Franciscans who lead it. The theology and liturgy represented the best of U.S. Catholicism: committed to the world, embracing diversity, and actively involved in peace and justice ministries.

On any Sunday, approximately 1600 Latinos participate in an activity at Our Lady of Durham. There are two Spanish masses lead by a bilingual priest, prayer groups, and various other groups that meet on Sundays. The staff also includes a Latino ministries coordinator, and a Latino Faith Formation secretary and a Latino Ministry Council also provide leadership. Such annual observances as the Day of the Dead and the Fiesta of the Virgin of Guadalupe are a part of the church's calendar, as well as *quinceañeras*, the observance of a girl's fifteenth birthday. Not only does the congregation address the spiritual and liturgical needs of the Latino population, but it also participates in advocacy efforts for its people, sponsoring buses to a large gathering of people dedicated to social justice for immigrants, for example.

The large red brick collection of buildings houses the church, a school, and a community center. Their 7,000 square foot sanctuary has been replaced by one measuring 16,000 square feet. The visitor enters the main church building through any one of a wide bank of glass doors. Directly across the foyer from the front doors is another wide bank of wooden doors. They glide open and lead into a wide but shallow and shadowed entry chamber. A third bank of doors opens silently onto the bright, skylight-lit sanctuary. The one entering passes by the flowing waters of a large, heavy, stone baptismal font. Still the ceiling directly above is relatively low, but the spacious, bright central space lies ahead where the huge, tall ceiling reaches high, lined with light reddish wood. Rather than the elongated center aisle of the traditional Gothic cathedral, the sanctuary is wider than it is long. At the raised center, matching the baptismal font, is a heavy stone communion table. Above it a large cross is suspended by wires from the ceiling, each wire dotted with small spheres that represent celestial bodies. Also on the raised dais, matching the baptismal font and communion table, are a heavy stone pulpit and a single, centered stone chair. On three sides, rows of pews face the table. At the far left, a small platform holds the small group of music leaders. At the far right is an alcove dedicated to the Virgin of Guadalupe.

To this Protestant who has visited Romanesque, Gothic, Baroque, and Rococo churches in Western Europe, as well as ornate Mexican churches, what is most noticeable is the lack of adornment. There is only one small bank of candles the worshipper can light. The walls have large, plain expanses of gray stone-looking cement bricks, without color or adornment. A single, dwarfed banner signifying the liturgical season hangs on one wall. The heavy, squared stone sanctuary furniture has no carving or polish. Though the space feels spare, it does not feel cold. One's eyes are lead to fall on the people in the pews or on the lone priest.

A typical Spanish-language Mass begins with a welcome from the choir leader, the people greeting one another, and an opening hymn. The short procession consists of an altar-server (usually a girl) carrying the processional cross, two other altar-servers called *monagillos*, one of the lectors carrying the Gospel book, and finally a priest. All of this happens without much fanfare, while much of the nearly full sanctuary is still murmuring quietly. On the spacious dais where the priest presides, the only other person in the front is a lone adolescent altar girl dressed in a white alb. Laypeople sit in the pews and come to the pulpit to read Scripture, make announcements, or lead prayers. In addition, eight or so laypeople serve as Eucharistic ministers and a dozen or so teens collect money and bring the gifts to the altar. The heavy lay involvement diminishes the distance between the clergy and the people.

All of the heavily amplified music, accompanied by a piano and a small singing group, has a Hispanic feel. From a distant corner it seems to come from nowhere, and is certainly not the center of attention as in many Protestant churches. The focus is on the spacious, bright, spare center and the people gathered on three sides.

The vast majority of these people have arrived in the United States within the last five years. They are very recent arrivals to a new culture, a new language, and a new way of life. Most of them have left large family networks and thus are isolated from a central locus of support, meaning, and identity. One is reminded of that reality by a row of ten or twelve young men sitting together in a pew. Scanning the faces of the worshippers sitting in the bright, spacious, peaceful sanctuary, one can imagine the invisible presence of recent memories of crossing the U.S.-Mexican border alone or with the help of a *coyote*. What did they endure in the crossing? Did some only arrive recently? Last week? Are some still paying off a *coyote*? One can also imagine a life lived in chronic dread of discovery that one has no documents authorizing his existence in this place. Is it a life of hiding, chronic vigilance? One also imagines the prayers offered for safety, family at home, work, health, and strength to endure.

For the very last liturgical act in the Sunday morning service, the priest moves down toward the people, and ten or so tiny bundles of pink and blue, only a tiny hand or a tuft of black hair showing, are carried forward to be blessed. These are infants born in America, blessed in a church in America. It is as though we are witnessing a border crossing at the very moment: the infants' entry into a religious and cultural life different from the parents who are holding them. One can only pray for a safe crossing and for a warm welcome on the other side.

HISTORY OF LATINO CATHOLICISM

Scholars have traditionally argued that American religion has functioned to acclimate new immigrants to America. By joining in American forms of religion the immigrant has been able to better adjust to America and its ways. Yet some are pointing out that there is also a reverse process in play, that immigrants are bringing their home religion to America and changing American religious life (Rieff, 40ff). In other words, the church does not only help recent immigrants become "more American," but it can also become a place for preserving ethnic identity rather than changing it. In the process, the American church itself is being changed by forms of religiosity that arrive from other lands. The question arises in the context of Our Lady of Durham; what sort of religion have Latino immigrants brought to a congregation that was largely Anglo?

In order to understand the religion that so recently arrived to Our Lady of Durham, it is important to understand the origins of Latino Catholicism itself. The conquistadors and missionaries who brought Catholicism to the New World in the sixteenth century were rather ill-educated and rough hewn "people from the villages" (Espín, 318). They brought with them the religion of the people rather than the university or the church hierarchy. Furthermore, it was religion that had not been challenged by the Reformation or the Enlightenment with which the church later wrestled during the Council at Trent. "This Christianity, therefore, was medieval and pre-Tridentine, and it was planted in the Americas approximately two generations before Trent's opening session" (317). Closely connected to the "cycles and components of village life," the gospel was not presented "through the spoken, magisterial word, but through the symbolic, performative word" (317). In this form of religiosity, "all of reality could sacramentally speak the message of religion."

The indigenous religion that the missionaries found in the New World shared features in common with Spanish Christianity. "[The] sense of meeting the sacred in special times and places, through consecrated words, songs and gestures, was one of the factors that the native cultures shared with Iberian popular Catholicism" (Vidal, 73). Elaborate rituals, processions, and festivals characterized both forms of religion. But the meeting was no peaceful blending over time. "Evangelization was made possible by conquest, that is, by first vanquishing the potential hearers of the gospel" (Espín, 319). The conquest was brutal and bloody. If the Europeans who first arrived on the North American shore uprooted and drove out the native peoples, the Iberian conquistadors slaughtered and conquered the native peoples of Latin America (Goizueta, 2004, 258). "In addition to deaths caused by warfare, forced labor, brutality, military force, and subjugation, many died from endemic disease" (Rodriguez, 3). Their gods were destroyed, loved ones murdered, and social structure broken (Elizondo, 1994, 122). One author states bluntly, "Physical contact between the two cultures (usually in the form of rape) began immediately, producing the Spanish-Indian *mestizaje*, the Mexicans" (2).

Religion in Mexico is also *mestizaje,* "a mixture," a melding of two religions. The first Christian missionary efforts that began in the mid-1520s met with little success. However, in 1531, a simple man named Juan Diego had three visions of a brown woman telling him to go to his bishop with a message: build a temple for her at the site of their meeting (Goizueta, 2003, 141), After the bishop refused to believe the simple peasant, on Juan Diego's third try he opened his simple robe, and emblazoned upon it was the image of the Virgin of Guadalupe. News of the *morenita*, the "little brown one," spread far, and within six years nine million people had converted to Christianity (Rodriguez, 45; quoting Elizondo, 1980; Madsen). She formed a bridge between Iberian Catholicism and the brown-skinned peoples of the Americas. "By revealing a Christian God with a special predilection for Juan Diego and his people, Guadalupe thus makes possible the evangelization of America. . . . Without the hope engendered by *la Morenita* and her message, Mexico would not have emerged, like the phoenix, from the ashes of the conquest" (Goizueta, 2003, 145).

As the colonial period developed and relations with Spain remained strong, the church in Mexico eventually was influenced by post-Tridentine European Catholicism. Yet it was primarily the fair-skinned, urban, colonial elite who felt the impact of doctrinal and liturgical developments in the European university and the church hierarchy. Among the poorer, isolated rural people, the impact of the medieval Spanish Catholicism remained strong. "Dogma and doctrines seem to be so Western, while ritual and mystery seem to be so *mestizo* Mexican" (Elizondo, 1994, 116). In the "official liturgy . . . the conquered people participated in the religious, cultic, and civil life of the Spanish kingdom" (Pérez, 364).

Today, Catholicism in Mexico has both official and popular forms. The majority of people in Mexico, particularly in rural areas where there are fewer priests, are not trained theologically and liturgically in the official texts of Catholicism and thus improvise by creating "alternative paths . . . to circumvent the exclusive definitive power" of the official church (Espín, 309). Popular religion does not require the presence of a priest, and therefore those who create and maintain it are outside the church's purview. Some official church leaders consider popular religion to be "superstitious, magic, primitive, uninformed, and evil" (Perez, 364).

This antipopular religion sentiment on the part of some church leaders, however, is in opposition to statements by John Paul II. For example, in *Ecclesia in America* he stated,

> If properly guided, popular piety also leads the faithful to a deeper sense of their membership of the Church, increasing the fervor of their attachment and thus offering an effective response to the challenges of today's secularization. . . . Given that in America, popular piety is a mode of enculturation of the Catholic faith and that it has often assumed indigenous religious forms, we must not underestimate the fact that, prudently considered, it too can provide valid cues for a more complete enculturation of the Gospel.

John Paul II explicitly affirms one of the most powerful representations of Latino popular religion:

> In America, the *mestiza* face of the Virgin of Guadalupe was from the start a symbol of the inculturation of the Gospel, of which she has been the lodestar and the guide. Through her powerful intercession, the Gospel will penetrate the hearts of the men and women of America and permeate their cultures, transforming them from within.

Latino popular religion continues to play a strong role in millions of lives, and it continues to grow and evolve as people adapt it to new circumstances.

LATINO POPULAR RELIGIOSITY AND THE U.S. CATHOLIC CHURCH

When popular Latino Catholicism comes to the U.S. through immigration, it meets the U.S. Catholic church, which was shaped by earlier immigrants from northern Europe where the Catholic church had already confronted the forces of the Protestant Reformation and the intellectual challenges of the Enlightenment. In response to these challenges, "Northern European Catholicism would become increasingly rationalist, demanding a clarity, precision, and uniformity in doctrinal formulations" (Goizueta, 2004, 256). Through Latino immigration to the U.S., a piety rooted in premodern Spain meets a modernist piety rooted in the more rationalist Catholicism of northern Europe. In some congregations, there is dissonance between Latino immigrants and non-Hispanic clergy who are largely trained in worship experiences "based on monastic,

contemplative patterns in which profound silence, great organization, and rehearsed ritual movement are the norm" (366). This has
resulted in varying degrees of appreciation for the religiosity of
their Latino congregants. One author has noted,

> There is no end to the chagrin voiced by pastors about the piv-
> otal role of *la Virgen*, the saints, processions, statues, holy water
> and ashes, while, they continue to lament, Latino Catholics pay
> so little attention to regular attendance at Eucharist. . . . Pasto-
> ral ministers decry the non-Eucharistic character of Latino reli-
> giosity and develop catechetical programs to "bring the people
> around." (Riebe-Estrella, 513)

Latino Catholics are inheritors of a medieval Christianity's
"unified, profoundly sacramental view of the cosmos. Creation
everywhere revealed the abiding presence of its creator, a living
presence that infused all creation with meaning" (Goizueta, 2004,
262; taken from Dupré, 94). For the Latino, the whole created order
is the site of a possible meeting with the transcendent God. God is
not relegated to the heavenly sphere far away, but was encountered
in the material world here and now (Goizueta, 262–63). Latinos are
inheritors of Baroque Catholicism of medieval Spain.

> There was a universality in which Catholicism experienced God
> in a vastness, freedom, and goodness flowing through a world
> of diversity, movement, and order. . . . The Baroque world was
> also a theater . . . Liturgies, operas, frescos, or palatial recep-
> tions were theatrical, and Baroque Christianity was filled with
> visions and ecstasies, with martyrs, missionaries, and stigmatics.
> . . . The Theater of the Christian life and the kingdom of God
> moved from the medieval cosmos and the arena of society to the
> interior of the Baroque church and the life of the soul. (O'Meara,
> 115–16; quoted in Goizueta, 2004)

In this way of viewing the world, Goizueta tells us that "the God
of Latino/a Catholics is one whose reality is inseparable from our
everyday life and struggles . . . a God with whom we can weep
or laugh, a God who infuriates us and whom we infuriate, a God

whose anguished countenance we can caress and whose pierced feet we can kiss" (Goizueta, 2004, 266).

One particular point of contrast between Latino popular religion and American Catholicism is the place of sacraments and "sacramentals." For historical reasons, many Latinos have had limited access to the sacrament of Eucharist. Because the New World was so large and the number of priests so few, as well as "the racist attitudes of the conquering Spanish who opposed the ordination of the indigenous and . . . even of *mestizos*," people in rural areas and small towns would only have access to the sacraments on occasion (Riebe-Estrella, 513). This history of limited access to the sacraments has led to a greater emphasis on the sacramentals in Latino piety.

Sacraments and Sacramentals

In Roman Catholic teaching, the sacraments are material objects that mediate the saving grace of God. The efficacy of the sacraments does not depend on the state of the heart or mind of either the priest or the receiver of the elements. Rather it depends on the correct application of form to the material elements. So, for example, in the Eucharist when the proper *form* of Jesus' words at the Last Supper is applied to the proper *matter*, bread and wine, then the grace of God is present. This contrasts with, for example, the claim that the efficacy of the sacraments depends on the officiant as the moral example or the humble and contrite hearts of the worshippers. This understanding of the Eucharist is relevant to the church's understanding of God's presence with the sick in this way: "if Christ could be brought down upon an altar in the shape of bread by the mumbled Latin of an insignificant and no doubt sinful priest," then God can be brought to the body of those suffering from illness (O'Connell, 116).

Particularly fascinating to this Protestant, however, is the use of sacramentals among the Catholic faithful. In contrast to sacraments, whose efficacy depends on the proper application of form to matter, or *ex opere operato*, sacramentals do depend on the strength of piety of the one who is using them; they are *ex opere operantis*. The sign of the cross, blessings, salt, ashes, oil, fire, candles, rosaries, scapulars, medals, icons, statues, altars, church buildings, bells, and blessed palms are part of the rich collection of sacramentals that aid the prayer of the Catholic believer.

Our Lady of Guadalupe

One particular sacramental that is central to Mexican and Mexican American people is the image of Our Lady of Guadalupe (Goizueta, 2003, 141). Robert Orsi has noted in this now familiar passage,

> She appears today on bolo ties, playing cards, tattooed on the skins of cholos in East L.A. and South Phoenix, on belts, pillows, towels, cigar boxes, lampshades, "among horns honking, ambulances running, children crying, all the people groaning and dancing and making love," in the struggles of farm workers, in the places of the sick and dying, carved in soup bones, and in ravines on the border between Mexico and the United States, helping her people make the crossing north in the middle of the night by distracting the border patrols. (Orsi, 1997, 25; with quote from Castillo)

She is by far the most prominent form of Mary that appears in the whole sanctuary of Our Lady of Durham, her star-spangled blue robe draped over her shoulders, her face looking down at the people standing before her. In her prominence, in her presence as the dominant representation of Mary, we see a rejection of the requirement that Latinos relinquish their beloved *morenita* upon their arrival in the U.S.

Orsi reminds us, "To become 'American Catholic' once meant, among other things, to turn away from the dark-skinned, full-bodied Madonnas, who seemed to bear the weight of histories too heavy for this culture, toward the thin, pale blue virgins of suburban parishes" (Orsi, 25). This is not required of Our Lady of Durham's Latinos.

It is impossible to overemphasize the importance of Our Lady of Guadalupe to Mexican piety. Historically she has provided critical validation of the humanity of the mestizo Mexican people. As a brown (not white) woman, she appeared to a brown (not white) man, at the site of a native goddess (not the Catholic cathedral) with a message to build a temple to her there (not in the Spanish colonial capitol).

Contemporary theological interpretations of her are varied. Some are critical of her and see her image as supportive of a passive, compliant Mexican persona, particularly Mexican women. Others offer a positive interpretation of her as a "liberator of the poor" (Goizueta, 2003, 140). What may be most interesting about the presence of *la morenita* is not what individuals believe about her in the private space of heart and mind, but how she transforms public space of street and square. Claiming public space, sacralizing it, Latinizing it, as in the procession through Durham on her fiesta day, may be one of her most powerful roles.

Not all of the Latinos at Our Lady of Durham are so devoted to this particular manifestation of Mary. Central and South Americans have other representations of her that are more central to their piety. One man from Central America almost sheepishly explained his presence at the celebration of *la Guadalupana* by saying he had been spending a lot of time with people from Mexico, and he had grown to appreciate her. She maintains a central place at this particular congregation. Before entering the sanctuary, the worshipper passes a large statue of a fair Mary dressed in light blue that was at the center of the former, smaller sanctuary. In the new sanctuary, it is *la Morenita* who is the central representation of Mary.

The Fiesta

The central annual act of the Latino subcongregation within Our Lady of Durham is the fiesta of the Virgin of Guadalupe described above. A religious fiesta is different from a party; it is more of an expression of gratitude to God and often is a celebration of a particular saint. The fiesta often "blurs the distinction between religious and civil celebrations," confirming my observations of such blurring at the fiesta of the Virgin of Guadalupe that something of both private and public import was going on (Goizueta, 1999, 91).

Goizueta's work offers an interpretation of the great power in the procession I observed. What he says of the Way of the Cross could also be said of the procession in honor of the Virgin of Guadalupe. "[B]y 'taking over' public thoroughfares and neighborhoods . . . the Latino community asserts its identity, visibility, and vitality in the face of a dominant culture that demands assimilation" (93). What I saw as power was the assertion, the quiet yet relentless and unswerving insistence that Latinos are in Durham, they will remain Latinos, and they will honor *la Guadalupana*. As such it was a liturgical act that functioned also as a quiet act of resistance to being defined by others.

LATINO CATHOLICISM COMES TO OUR LADY OF DURHAM

In the Southwest there are very old Catholic churches that were founded when the land upon which they sat was still part of Mexico. These churches have had centuries of encounter with northern European forms of Catholicism and had time to form a U.S. Latino Catholicism. Our Lady of Durham is only beginning that process of encounter and maturation. Only ten years ago did Latinos come in large numbers to this congregation.

An often used metaphor to describe Latino communities in the Southwest is that of "borderlands." On the border of two nations, cultures, and social structures, Latinos construct identities, ways of life, and spiritualities. That construction is only beginning to happen in this Southern tobacco town, Durham. If borders are the places of the production of religious forms, then at this moment such a process is underway at Our Lady of Durham. Virgilio Elizondo speaks of the religion of Latino Americans in the U.S. as a "second *mestizaje*," a second mixing after the first mixing between native peoples and Spaniards in sixteenth century Mexico (Riebe-Estrella, 512). In the meeting of multiple discourses, histories, and identities, a sort of second *mestizaje* is happening at Our Lady of Durham.

Gloria Anzaldúa argues that hybrid identities emerge at the borders, a hybridity born of creativity. "Borderland" has become a way of speaking not only of the geographic border between Latino Mexico and Anglo U.S., but also of "a rhetorical device for describing perennially emergent and multiplex individual, social, and cultural formations" (544). "Borders of all kinds are central and formative places in the production of religion" (544). This is where Our Lady of Durham lies, on the creative border.

León describes several borders where different cultures meet and creative responses are formed. Certainly Our Lady of Guadalupe occupies the borderlands between the Spanish and the Aztec cultures. But she also challenges the border between official Catholicism localized in ecclesiastical buildings and popular religion localized in home altars. This is not only a spatial challenge but also a gender challenge: laywomen challenging the authority of the male priesthood. "[F]or many, home altars are sites of concentrated authority where women invoke the symbol and narrative of Guadalupe in their sometimes unorthodox religious practices and thereby trouble the notion of a singular center of official Catholicism. . . . Appeals to Guadalupe—mediated by the home altar—enable Mexican American women to confer authority upon themselves and each other, authorizing themselves as religious specialists" (León, 1999, 546–47).

León points out that "the other side of the border has been so close, and yet so distant." It is true in Durham. The border crisscrosses Durham. The other side of the border is down the street, across town, next door. "In the U.S.–Mexico borderlands, desire, will, and dissent result in creative and strategic religious forms." That creativity, and strategizing, is only beginning at Our Lady of Durham. Yet we see its green shoots just starting to emerge.

OUR LADY OF DURHAM AND CARE FOR THE SICK

I spent most of my time with the Latino group dedicated to visiting the sick. It is heavily influenced by charismatic strains in Catholicism, and its style of prayer and theological bent reflects this influence. The group meets every Sunday morning and visits every Latino patient at Duke Hospital. Sometimes they receive a visitation list from the hospital or the priest; sometimes they divide up the hospital wings and inspect patients' door signs for

Spanish-sounding names. After a brief organizing discussion, before leaving for the hospital, they gather in a circle holding hands. The leader prays in a charismatic style with great feeling, and the group simultaneously offers supportive prayers as well. At some point in the prayer, the leader moves into the traditional Catholic prayers such as the Our Father and the Hail Mary. The prayer is a hybrid of traditional Catholic ritual and strains of Pentecostalism. After the prayer there are hugs and greetings in the name of Christ, and one of them greeted me, a stranger, as *"hermana"* and offered me the peace of Christ.

The group not only visits the sick in the hospital but also visits them in their homes. All the visits include a brief message of faith, Bible reading, and prayer. Sometimes they leave a rosary, a Bible, or a devotional pamphlet with the patient. Financial help is also offered, as one man said:

> Sometimes there is a large necessity to help a brother who has an economic need. Because he lives alone and he has nobody here in this country. And he has wishes to communicate with his family. And sometimes it is just as simple as buying him a telephone card with which he can communicate.

Every week someone from the group goes to a state psychiatric hospital to visit a Latino man who has significant brain damage and who has no family. One week I accompanied a young man from Central America on the visit. After stopping at Burger King to buy a breakfast for the man we would be visiting, I asked him what motivated him to be a part of this ministry. He replied with a story. He spoke of a time when he was far from home working in a European country, and he became very sick. During this time when he was not only very ill, but also profoundly lonely, a woman visited him in the hospital everyday, offering her presence and her prayers. Though they did not speak the same language, he believed the woman was sent by God. This was a very important experience for him, and he wanted to do the same for others who are alone and in the hospital. I remembered the biblical texts that refer to our care for others because we already received care ourselves. "You shall also love the stranger, for you were strangers in the land of Egypt" (Deut 10:19). "Love one another as I have loved you" (John 15:12). Many others in the group also spoke of visiting people in the hospital out of gratitude for what God had already done for them.

A Visit from Our Lady of Guadalupe

One of the women in the group, Rosa, asked whether I would like her to bring a picture of Mary to my house and leave it there for a week. I said, of course, thinking she had one around the house that, from time to time, she would take to some family as a way to bless their home. She said her nephew would bring her to my house on Friday. I later found out that there is one picture that travels from house to house, Friday to Friday, all over town.

At about 8 p.m., Rosa arrived, but not only with her nephew. Two SUVs pulled up in our cul-de-sac. Rosa, six other women, three men, and three children stepped out of the cars with a big picture of *la Virgen de Guadalupe* adorned with an arch of silk flowers over the top. They also pulled out four vases of flowers, one of them with live red roses, the rest silk. They started to sing out there at the curb, handed me the picture, and I realized I was supposed to lead the singing procession.

We got in the house; I lead them to the dining room where I had planned to place the picture. Rosa and the others, still singing, arranged the picture, the flowers, and some candles on our sideboard. We kept singing for a couple more minutes. Then I welcomed them, thanked them as best I could in my halting Spanish. We were all smiling and nodding at one another a bit awkwardly, and I eventually asked, awkwardly, "Well, is it finished?" Rosa pulled out several booklets and said no.

The praying began again, some with prayer books, some without, and I realized we had started saying the rosary. At one point we knelt and stayed on our knees for a very long time. Long after a sharp pain forced me to move from sitting in a chair, several of the older women continued to kneel without shifting. There were about five "mysteries," and each one had the Lord's Prayer, ten Hail Marys, plus other prayers. After the rosary, there was more singing.

Then it was over. I invited them for tea or coffee, but they said no, and left rather quickly. They had been at our house for an hour and a half.

Like in Healing Waters services, I wanted to observe correct etiquette. I offered refreshments, smiles, and words of welcome. However, this was not a social visit. It was about bringing Mary, the Queen of Heaven, the Empress of the Americas herself, to my house. At first I thought the picture was a holy object that was intended to bring favor to our house, a general sort of blessing. But, after talking further with Rosa, it became clear that she did not intend to bring any sort of general blessing. Rather, she was bringing a person that she knew and loved, the Virgin Mary herself, to my house. She was bringing a beloved person to live with us for a week. She was inviting us to get to know the *santissima Virgen*; she was introducing us to a living person.

She said later that our family was like Juan Diego, that first indigenous person to see *la Virgen de Guadalupe*. She told us that we had met her just like he did. Her desire that we know her was touching. When asked whether I now believed in her, I said that I was only beginning to get to know her, but I was very, very glad that she introduced her to me.

6

OUR LADY OF DURHAM'S
BELIEF-PRACTICES

*T*here were two factors that made the investigation into the ministry at Our Lady of Durham's Latino population different from the research into the other two congregations. Most significant was the language barrier: I speak little Spanish and most of the people I interviewed spoke little English. I worked with an interpreter when necessary. All of the events I attended were exclusively in Spanish. The other barrier was my unwillingness to inquire about the immigration status of the people I interviewed. While this may seem like a relatively inconsequential fact to consider when researching a local church's care for the sick, it is relevant to several factors affecting health. The chronic insecurity of living without *papeles*, "papers," documents that establish the legality of one's presence in the U.S., affects health. Also, if one is undocumented, it is possible to return to one's home country, but one faces the ordeal of crossing the border in order to return to Durham. This means one is cut off from the comfort and care of family during illness. As emphasized earlier, the level of immersion in the three churches is uneven.

There is more diversity in this subcongregation than the other two churches I studied. The single uniting factor is the Spanish language. There is great class diversity, and people from many Latin countries. Furthermore, within Latino Catholicism there is diversity: charismatics, for example. The vast majority is from Mexico, the second largest group is from Central America, and also I spoke with people from Colombia, Peru, and Ecuador. Therefore, these beliefs should not be understood as representative of all of the Latinos in this congregation. These belief-practices represent a sampling, rather than a unified fabric of a belief system. They should not be understood as forming together a coherent worldview to which all adhere. They are simply beliefs that I heard repeated in my interviews and focus groups. The belief-practices below resemble a collection of beliefs in a basket more than puzzle pieces that together form a coherent picture.

THE SACRED/HOLY IS PRESENT IN THE MATERIAL WORLD

For the Latino member of Our Lady of Durham, material objects can be repositories of the sacred. The entire physical world can mediate the sacred. The multiple statues and pictures of the Virgin of Guadalupe placed before her altar for the duration of the service were there to bask in the holiness of her "statue" in order to bring some of it home. The man rushed up to the main altar pulling a card out of his pocket at the last minute in order to receive some of the holy water the priest was dispersing.

The Spanish-speaking, Polish priest devoted to serving the Latino community at Our Lady of Durham, Father Jorge, referred to the rich "sacramental imagination" of his parishioners.

> There is a sense that the things of this world, it could be a rosary, a picture, can communicate God's presence. For example, before or after the Mass people will come and ask me to bless things. It could be a blessing of the rosary, or a figure or a picture of Our Lady of Guadalupe, or Jesus, or a saint. Or when a child turns two years old or is just born, the family would also come and ask for a blessing. *When they are sick and at the hospital* oftentimes I would see a picture of Jesus or Our Lady of Guadalupe next to that person; it is important for them. (emphasis added)

He referred to their sense of "God's presence communicating through the little things" and spoke poetically of "touches of the sacred bubbling up through the ordinary." With respect and affection he said,

> I look at a person coming for a blessing, or at the hospital bed [where there is] a person surrounded by different kinds of images, and say, well, that's just another way of expressing a deep truth of Christianity.

He described making a decision regarding whether or not to bless a truck. He hesitated to do so because "its not just a regular truck, its a big, gas guzzling truck. I have a problem with that and what it does to God's creation." But when he saw that it was a truck with ladders and painting equipment, using holy water, he "blessed it, and blessed the work, that the owner of the truck and his family might become more united and strengthened through it."

When I visited the home of an older woman in the congregation, at the center of the main living area was a large altar, approximately five feet wide and four feet tall, devoted to Our Lady of Guadalupe and to "*mis santos*," my saints. There were little white Christmas tree lights dispersed through images, figures, candles, and plastic flowers. Others with whom I spoke affirmed the presence of altars in their homes.

> I have a little altar, yes, and the *Virgencita*.

> I have some *veladoras* [devotional candles] with saints.

> I have my saints and my candles and the angel that guards us. And saints given to me by my mother and my grandmother, the Virgin of Guadalupe.

One family I visited had several dolls dressed as various saints on the mantle, and one of them was Jesus dressed in white as a doctor. On his chest was embroidered, *niño Dr. Jesus* (literally, "boy Dr. Jesus"). In this family the father lived with a chronic disability. His wife pointed to the doll and said, "Here is the doctor of the house."

Surely this is an instance of a radical incarnationalism, a radical affirmation of God's immanence in God's good creation, mediated through multiple sacramentals. As one writer said, the world is "shimmering with the divine."

I had another taste of this sacramental sensibility on a visit to the Basilica of the Virgin of Guadalupe in Mexico City. I had just bought a small medal with the image of *la Virgen* on it. A kind woman offered to take it to the crowded window where the priest was rather mechanically sprinkling holy water on various objects. For her, the materiality of the water was what mediated the sacred to my little medal, not the quality of the interpersonal connection between me and the priest, not my intellectual understanding of the meaning of the medal, not the intrinsic monetary value of the medal, not my personal skill at praying with the medal. Rather, it was the physical contact of the medal and water deemed holy that sanctified the medal.

The risk of idolatry is obvious: these material objects could, literally, be idols. The distance between them and God could be collapsed. Rather than an aid to worship and prayer, they could be the object of worship and supplication. Perhaps more subtle is the risk that the dispenser of their status of "holy" would be deified. The one with the authority to render a material object sacred is at risk of being idolized: the priest. One of the strengths of Latino popular religiosity is that it is an improvised form of piety, relatively independent of the official church's presence, that emerged in remote villages where the priest could visit only annually, if at all. A priest's blessing was not required for the presence of the sacred to be indwelling in an object considered holy. Still, a priest's power to confer holiness on the material is substantial. Such power is often coincident with the power of white race, male gender, university education, ecclesiastical authority, and higher class. Rather than dependence on the God who is beyond all materiality and all human beings, it is possible that material objects and the ordained men who render them holy could become the objects of dependence, the guarantors of salvation.

THE PAIN OF ILLNESS CLEANSES US FROM SIN

Illness has a cleansing effect. Though illness is not connected to sin as God's punishment for it, it is still connected to our sin as a means of purifying us of it. "Through our pain he [God] cleans us from our sins" one person said.

> If we could die, just fall asleep, we would not have to go through so much pain in our body. But we have sins to clean, and that's why we have to suffer pain.

The way illness cleanses us is by engendering regret for our sins.

> If we don't suffer in our body then we don't have any regrets. Because the regret comes through the profound suffering and pain that we experience through our bodies.

However, in order for illness to cleanse us, we must accept its suffering gracefully, and not rebel or despair. Caregivers help the sick with this task. "Our mission is to [encourage the sick] to not despair, to not rebel against their sickness, because God is love," one woman said. Another caregiver said,

> He accepts our pain as a payment for our sin. When we suffer, asking God for his favor, we can't get angry or rebel, we can't do that. We suffer with patience . . . It's a deep cleansing of our soul.

Patience is a key part of maintaining one's faithfulness as a sick person. One person said, "One of the important things about disease is patience, rather, the suffering of patience." Another added, "If I get sick, I pray that I may be given patience to suffer through the sickness."

> [*So, if we get sick, we must be patient, and accepting of our illness, and trust in God.*] Always. Even in the worst times. Always make sure you are together with Christ. Try to not to become hopeless.

Then, when one is healed, it is a sign that we have been washed clean of our sins. "Jesus said that when we get well it is because we have been cleaned of our sins. Because Jesus has forgiven us for our sins," one woman said.

One can experience forgiveness and turn to God either through the prayers of the faithful or through the ritual of confession to a priest, and both are linked to healing. One woman said,

> [*Why is it important for the priest to go and hear the confession of those who are sick?*] The Lord made it very clear that it is important to confess to a priest to be freed of those sins. [*Does that help them get well?*] Yes. If the person is guilty of something, it's important for the person to know that they have sinned and that they give that over to the Lord.

Then the woman told the story of her sister who was sick.

> She wasn't married but she was living with a man. She wanted the priest to come to her house. [But when he got there] the priest said that her boyfriend had to be outside. Since her boyfriend didn't want to be outside, he said that he would marry her so that he could be there with her. And the priest married them. And even though she was nearly dead, he married them so that she could die in peace, so her boyfriend could be by her side. The next day, she drank water. [A sign that she was getting well.] Before that she wasn't eating or drinking anything and then the next day she was drinking. That was 22 years ago. She's alive today.

The woman got well because she repented of her sin of living with a man to whom she was not married. She left her state of guilt, and then she was healed.

Here there is a blurring of boundaries between body and soul, a wholeness of the human person. The moral state of the soul is linked to bodily well-being. Furthermore, this link renders illness meaningful, useful, to good purpose, something beyond sheer absurdity. This belief-practice weaves illness into the fabric of a meaningful life. It puts illness into a narrative where God's redeeming power is stronger than illness' power to maim and destroy. This belief-practice is way of claiming that nothing can separate us from the love of God in Christ Jesus, that even this illness is harnessed in service of God's redeeming purposes. Illness is transformed from that which destroys to that which heals one's very soul. It has past and present reverberations: it is an opportunity to make amends for past misdeeds and to move into the future unencumbered by them.

This is, of course, a highly individualized view of health. The only sin is personal sin. Social sin is ignored. Such a heavy emphasis on personal responsibility can be empowering. It rests on the belief that individuals do have the power to choose a new way of living, of turning from what was self-destructive to what is life-giving. However, the gift of purifying us of our sins is a conditional one: we must accept our illness without rebellion or despair. We must be patient, not lose hope, and not become angry. God's good gift of purifying our lives of sin is not freely given, but is dependent on our righteousness. God is not completely free to purify us. The risk of idolatry here is that either the illness or we ourselves are the agent of purification, and not God.

CHRIST IS CLOSEST DURING ILLNESS

Not only can our faithful endurance of illness purify us of our sins, but our suffering can bring us closer to the crucified Christ.

> I have always thought that pain, that when we receive it with patience, we are the closest we can be to Christ, because we can associate with the cross of Christ. The suffering we are going through is nothing compared to what he experienced on the cross.

A caregiver said, "Our mission is to allow them to understand that in that moment [when they are sick] is when Christ is closest." Another added, "It is an encounter that we have with Jesus, because when we are sick, we are on the path to find Christ."

This is another instance of giving meaning to the suffering in illness: it brings us close to none other than God incarnate, Jesus Christ, the Savior of the World. Therefore, not only does illness redeem us of our sins, but, even apart from sin, illness also redeems our suffering, transforming it to a good end. Again, illness is knit into a narrative of redemption. Illness is an opportunity to draw close to the centerpiece of our faith. It is a means of "sanctifying to us our deepest distress." The belief that we are closest to Christ when we are sick captures a profound truth of the Christian faith, that when we are closest to the edge of human power, we are more able to see where the power of God begins. The power of this belief is that it is the opposite of the Gospel of Health or the Gospel of Wealth, which would claim that in our robust health or our ever-increasing wealth we are closest to God. The belief that one is closest to Christ in illness is a way for the sick to affirm that, far from our illness being a sign of our depravity or failure, it is rather a time of being drawn into the very presence of the divine.

Pope John Paul II himself extended this belief in his *Address to the Sick and Health Care Workers.*

> Beloved brothers and sisters, I would like to entrust myself to your prayers. . . . Just as the crucified Christ is powerful, so are you too powerful despite your physical state . . . your strength lies in your likeness to him. Use this force for the good of the Church, for your families, neighbors, countries, and the entire humanity. Use it also for the good of the Pope's ministry, who in a certain sense is also very weak.

The risk is that illness would become a good in itself. Rather than celebrating the power of God in Christ to transform illness from a time of loneliness and despair to a time of communion with none other than the Creator and Redeemer of the universe, the illness itself could become the object of celebration in a glorification of martyrdom. When the object of awe shifts from God to the suffering in the illness experience, then the dynamics of idolatry are at play. This is the risk of the close association of God with suffering. When the suffering is valorized instead of God, the sufferer and those around her are not mobilized to address sources of suffering, such as social injustice.

PEOPLE GET SICK FOR A VARIETY OF REASONS

The Lifestyle of an Immigrant to the U.S. Contributes to Illness

Several people emphasized the stress of being an immigrant. "Sometimes as immigrants, Hispanics, we come to this country and we get worked up about something we can't do anything about." Life in America is more stressful than their home countries.

> Because most of us come from different countries where the style of life isn't so hard as far as being a slave of work. Here you do have to become a slave of work. You have to pay the bills, pay the rent, etc. So this is a big change.

An American-style diet can also lead to illness.

> [In America there are] changes with our diet, what we eat. There, [in our home country,] everything is natural. Here everything is processed, has chemicals, and we eat a lot of canned food. So it changes how you eat. Before, you used to eat eggs with tortillas and refried beans. Here you have to have coffee with water and meat. Just like that, on the go.

When one young man said, "We exploit our bodies too much," I wondered whether he was referring to long hours of physical labor. I also wondered, "Just who is exploiting your bodies: you or people making money off your labor?" Another person added other factors and did include excessive hard work as a cause of illness.

> Sometimes I believe somebody gets sick because they abuse their own body. Sometimes because you eat too much or when it is cold you don't protect yourself. Too much work. Not going to bed on time. Many worries or stress.

The respondents paint a picture of a difficult life with a lot of hard work and stress. They describe being unable to live at a slower pace and eat healthy food as they had in their home countries. They recognize the toll immigrant life is taking on their health.

They are aware that many of the people to whom they give care are alone in this country. "Sometimes there are sick people who come from other cities who are alone and we try to give them this [pause] love. They feel alone and we try to give them that family." They are aware that some of the health difficulties are because they are separate from their families who would normally provide a base of accountability. One man said, "They come to this country and they don't have solidarity with a family and then they fall into alcoholism and drugs or other circumstances."

Spirits and Demons Sometimes Cause Illness

Even as the world is a place where material things can mediate the mystery of the transcendent God, so can the material body be afflicted by spirits and demons that cause bad health. Bad health cannot only be explained through biomedical models, but also through the activity of mysterious suprahuman beings. One man who could not read or write gave a multifactorial account of the incidence of illness.

> For me illness is something very natural. One can see that everything gets sick. Even the plants get sick. Sometimes we get sick because we get too angry and our heart can't handle that. Or too sad. In my branch [part of the country] we also know ghosts, bad spirits. And there are many other illnesses that only God could know the reason.

He lists natural reasons, God, emotions, ghosts, and sheer mystery as explanations for illness, all with equal status. Here we see the crossing of multiple dualisms: natural vs. supernatural, body vs. mind, human world vs. spirit world. For him each explanation was equally possible, affirming the possibility that one factor did not preclude the possibility of another. For example, to claim the possibility of ghosts causing illness does not rule out the possibility that there might be natural causes.

Another young woman described an experience in the hospital as an experience of dealing with "black shadows that spoke to me."

> I cried a lot to God and to the Virgin. "Don't take me, I have two children. . . ." I cried and I kept asking him, "Don't take me

because my children are 3 and 4 years old." . . . I felt as if I had died. . . . I saw something black, black, black. Everything, black shadows that spoke to me. I didn't feel [physically] bad, but the anguish of thinking of my children was weighing on me. All I saw was black, black, black and then somebody spoke to me: "You are strong. You are strong. You will not leave [die]." And then I felt like somebody grasped my hands . . . [*Where was God when that was happening? What did God do?*] The faith that one has in God gives us strength to continue forward. . . . An important thing that they teach us since we are very young is to have faith in God and in the saints. They teach us that they are always accompanying us and always helping us.

Her struggle was between the "black, black, black" and "God and the saints" who would help her, who are "always accompanying" her.

An older woman said, "I believe in demons. We say there are demons when you don't have the love of God. But if you have the love of God, demons don't exist." Then she gave the example of a person who avoids going to church because she is angry with someone she will see there. Her anger is caused by a demon, and if she had the love of God in her heart then this demon would not exist.

The demon is that everybody is bothering her, and that is the demon's pleasure. But if you have the love of God, bad people can't exist for you. You eyes are the eyes of God, your heart is the heart of God.

In another statement, she referred to illness as a result of "things that don't exist in the world."

If we don't have faith, pay attention, look out. When we don't have a big faith, in the love of God, and the love of Mary, then things go bad. *Because sometimes also sickness is part of the things that don't exist in the world.* Not in the world. Rather, there are things that we do bad, and then depression comes to us, sickness comes to us, because we had done bad things.

In this one statement, many Western dualisms are crossed: internal world of faith and external world of the body; this world and things that don't exist in this world; mental health and physical health.

Illness Can Be a Test of Faith

Though everyone interviewed roundly rejected the notion that God makes people sick as a punishment, some offered the belief that God sends illness as "a little test."

> I think sometimes we get better because when we get sick we are brought to remember God. Perhaps it is God that is giving us a little test to see if this will make us remember God. So when we are sick, or a son or daughter or mother is sick, and we remember God, we say, "Oh God." And when we are too well, and everything is working too well, then we don't remember God, and that is why we believe that God gives us a little test.

Illness, then, is a humbling experience, a reminder that humans depend on God and not the self for well-being.

The wide-ranging reasons for illness include stress, anger, sadness, hard work, bad diet, eating too much, getting too cold, drugs and alcohol, bad spirits, demons, ghosts, self-exploitation, and testing from God. As described earlier (162ff.), the whole creation can be the site of God's self-revelation, God's activity, as well as the human body. The body is subject to varieties of means of damage as well, such as emotions and invisible malevolent forces, in addition to the failure to avoid excessive work, harmful ingestions, and the cold. The porosity of the body, the blurred boundaries between the body, feeling, and the otherworldly, is in stark contrast to the separate, bounded body of the Cartesian world, disconnected from mind and transcendence. One is reminded of the Psalmist's invocation of the mysteries and marvels of the human body and soul that is "fearfully and wonderfully made" (Psalm 139), interconnected in untold and wondrous ways to the created world and beyond.

If there were any risk of idolatry here, it would be that the power of God is relegated to merely one power among others. If this belief did slide into an idolatrous form, the world and its resident demons would have equal authority in its construal of the body and its relation to the varieties of entities that act on it. Should one live in a world where the goodness and love of God are affirmed, but where they are a goodness and love that are impotent in the face of all that can do us harm? Then this is a world where other gods are given fearful homage, and the Lord of All is shuttled to the side as ineffectual and irrelevant. Such is an existence in bondage, filled with desperate attempts to appease the more powerful gods that would hurt us, rather than a life lived in trust in the One God whose goodness and love are both real and the most powerful force in the universe.

People Get Well for a Variety of Reasons

God Gives Us Medicine and Doctors

There was no hesitation in affirming God's activity through modern medicine. "God gave us earthly doctors and medicine." But the activity of the doctors is sanctified by the receiver of their care.

> God put doctors here on earth and we take the medicine in the name of God. [*Do you, literally, say something? What are the exact words?*] I say, "I was prescribed this medicine for my pain, in the name of Jesus may it be for my health." Always.

There was no suggestion that seeking medical care was in any way a sign of a lack of faith in God's healing power. God works through medicine, doctors, hospitals, and the whole biomedical establishment. One woman affirmed, however, that medical care without faith is not efficacious.

> If you are going through a time of sickness, and you feel sick like you have a headache, you say I'm going to take a pill. If you don't have faith in God the pill isn't going to cure you. What will cure you is the faith that you have in the Lord.

Prayer Brings God's Healing

The most often cited reason for a person's restoration to health is prayer by the individual or their community. There was great confidence in prayer as a means to healing.

> That is where we have actually seen the healing of others. Through the faith of the people and through the people opening their hearts. Both their own faith and the faith of others.

The prayers of the community were equally efficacious. Healing does not depend on the faith or the prayers of the individual who is sick.

> So when we get sick and we get better, it is because there are others who are praying for us. Even though we don't pray there are other brothers that are always praying for the sick. [*Even if we don't pray ourselves, if there are others praying for us, will we get well?*] Yes! Of course!

However, it was acknowledged that it is "easier" if the community's prayers are joined by the prayers of the sick person.

> It would be easier if the person who is ill has faith that through the prayers of others they will get well, then it is easier.

One description of a hospital visit shows how prayer is not simply a magical incantation, but is embedded in other practices that are relational, reassuring, and connected to Scripture.

> Sometimes we visit somebody with a lot of stress, and they are very sad, with a very depressed face. We see that after we talk about God, tell them to have faith in God and that God is the one who has brought doctors to us, we see in them a reaction and we see how they start changing. So, we notice that after we pray we start seeing this change. The facial expression starts to change. This makes us feel that what we are doing is worth it and that the presence of God is there. And there we start seeing the healing.

One Prays to Jesus and Mary for Healing

The sick and their community pray to both Jesus and his mother Mary. Some believe only Jesus heals, not Mary. It is he who has the power to work miracles. If one prays to Mary, it is because she is Jesus' mother, and he will listen to his mother. She is a mediator, like a "lawyer" as one woman said.

> The Virgin Mary is the mother of Christ. If she hadn't said yes to the Father, Jesus wouldn't have come to us. She is the mediator between the Father and the Son and us. She is the heavenly lawyer for us.

Parents with a sick child go to Mary to urge her to appeal to her son, Jesus, on their behalf.

> We ask Mary, "Señora, heal my son because he is sick. Because I have no other remedy for him. Help me Señora, Mary." So then Mary goes and says to the Lord, "*Ándale, hijo,*[25] listen to your daughter [the petitioner], listen to her who is requesting help for her son." And so Mary asks it of the Lord, and the Lord gives us love, and he sends relief. So if we have a problem we ask him, and we ask Mary, so that she will intercede. It is Jesus through Mary.

But others believe Mary herself performs miracles.

> We have faith in her and she gives miracles. I have faith in her and she accompanies me by the grace of God.

Some revere Mary as a member of the family, a mother. They expressed an intimacy, a deep love for her. One woman said with reverence and affection, "She is the mother of Jesus, but she also is the mother of all of us." She continued with a description of her prayers, which started with a petition to "Father, Lord God, my God" and then to the "Holy Virgin of Guadalupe."

> When we go to make a prayer, and we talk to the Lord, we say, "Father, Lord God, *Dios mío*, have mercy, have mercy on us, it is you who is always with us. We ask you Holy Virgin of

Guadalupe, mother, mother, of Guadalupe, who is the mother of God, we ask you Señora, that you intercede for us. To you, your son Jesus, you are the mother of Jesus and our mother, we ask you to intercede for us to the Lord. We ask that you plead for us." And she pleads for us.

Promesas Can Play a Part in Restoring Health

A *promesa* is a promise made to God. Petitioners promise to perform an act of sacrifice as a thanksgiving if God fulfills their petition. The promise is meant to persuade God to act as petitioned, and it is the promise that is persuasive, not the sometimes grueling sacrifice afterward. The sacrifice is not offered before God acts in order to convince God to act; it is rather offered as a form of gratitude after God acts. One woman explained, "I had an accident and I was in a wheelchair for a year. Science told me I wasn't going to walk again. My mother and my husband made a *promesa*, and then I am walking. It is through faith."

Yet another woman's explanation suggested that the sacrifice itself might convince "the Virgin or Jesus" to act.

> *Promesas* have to do with the sick. When a doctor tells you their child is sick and that medicine can't help it, and the person goes to the Virgin or to Jesus and offers a sacrifice, maybe carrying their child for two or three hours in the procession, or another person walking on their knees, that suffering they offer is to ask for healing, for help that the doctors can't find. With God nothing is impossible.

There is no consensus about which is efficacious: the sacrifice itself or the promise to make a future sacrifice.

Promesas most often do not involve a priest. Though I heard of many *promesas* in interviews, the priest devoted to the Latino community in this church is only occasionally called upon in the making of one. He did, however, tell a story of a woman in ill health who made a promise to cut her hair.

> When I first heard the woman's request to allow her to walk on her knees to the statue of the Virgin and then have me to cut

her hair, I was going to simply say, "No." I thought, why would the Virgin of Guadalupe need the woman's beautiful hair? Certainly, I would not want to take an active part in this strange ritual. Thank God, however, that I paused and then asked her to explain to me why she was doing it. Having learned that she was going to donate her hair for children who suffer from cancer, I was touched and humbled by her faith.

This priest very often, at least twice a week, sees something similar to a *promesa*, a *juramento*, an oath, almost always involving a pledge to control alcohol or drug use. Typically, a man will come to the priest after Sunday morning worship and say that he would like to make a *juramento*. The priest will give him a pledge card to fill in, which commits the person to refrain from drinking alcohol or taking drugs for a certain period of time. They both sign and date it, and the priest suggests that the man go to pray at the altar of Our Lady of Guadalupe, with friends and family if they are there. The man leaves carrying the card with them. For many of the Latinos who come to make a *juramento*, the card "acts as a cover or shield" from peer pressure. When such a person finds himself in a situation where his friends or neighbors try to talk him into drinking or using drugs, he can show them the *juramento* card as a proof that he had made a promise to the Virgin of Guadalupe. Generally, his friends, out of their respect for the Virgin of Guadalupe, would then leave that person alone. While the priest is "dubious about its effectiveness," he would prefer that some of the people attend Alcoholics Anonymous or Narcotics Anonymous, he believes it is important from a pastoral perspective "to meet them where they are" and to use that opportunity "to offer them some guidance, pray with them and remind them that God loves them and wants for them and their families a wonderful future."

Sometimes the priest, while maintaining respect for *promesas* and *juramentos*, intervenes to modify them. He told of a woman who had promised to "go back to Mexico to a sanctuary in the town where she grew up and visit the sanctuary on its feast day." She and her family had already been living in the U.S. for several years. Recognizing that it would be difficult and dangerous for this woman to cross the border back into the U.S. from Mexico, he said, "Forget about it. I really do not think that the Virgin of Guadalupe would like what you were planning to do. Do something else." So, the priest modified for that woman what she needed to do to fulfill her promise: "Come to the feast of Our Lady of Guadalupe, and bring her some flowers." Father Jorge's improvised pastoral response made the woman's promise more manageable, and "it avoided putting the poor woman in unnecessary danger." His pastoral authority was sufficient to modify the woman's *promesa*.

In matters of healing, both seeking medical care and praying are part of the repertoire of the faithful. There was no hesitation to affirm the fruits of human knowledge in biomedicine, nor any lack of confidence in appeals to God, Jesus, and Mary, nor any suggestion that there might be any conflict in such a worldview. The entire world is under the control of a merciful God whose desire is to heal.

As in all human efforts to see the divine in the created order, the risk is that the finite would be identified with the infinite. Therefore a slavish adherence to the terms of a *promesa*, or reliance on widespread, frequent, and ardent prayers, or exclusively depending on medical care can all be forms of idolatry. The focus on the finite as the means to the infinite can slide into a merging of the human with the divine, which is, of course, the very definition of idolatry.

THE SICK NEED TO HEAR THE WORD OF GOD

As noted above, the group that visits the sick is heavily influenced by the charismatic movement in the Catholic church, as are 54 percent of American Hispanic Catholics.[26] Probably for that reason there is greater emphasis on biblical literacy and uses of Scripture in personal piety than in other parts of the church. In addition to prayer, reading Scripture is the central act of the hospital visits. "We try to go in groups to pray for the sick, and we give the Word to the hospitalized." In describing what the group did for her in her illness, one woman reported, "They taught me how to read the Bible. And to find in it what God wants us to read. And to find in it what God wants us to do. And to search in my heart to do what God has asked me to do."

God gives internal prompts through Scripture ("the Word of God") as well as the institution of the church. They are lead to care for the sick because "*we have heard inside of us* the Word of God, and of the church. We need also to help to let others experience this because it is something that *God puts in our hearts*."

> We go to them and we talk to them about the Word of God. And if that person listens and opens their heart to the Lord you see a very fast change, a good change, and you can see through our contact that there is a big change in them. And then that is when we really believed that God did the work in that person.

There is concern not only for comfort, but also spiritual and moral upbuilding. "We try to give them something a little bit more and to motivate them a little bit more to be with God." Another person added, "Above all we try to motivate him when he is fallen." A member of the group told of visiting a young man in the hospital who also had "fallen."

> Last month we came across a youth, sixteen years old, who had a pain in his heart. Sometimes as immigrants, Hispanics, we come to this country and we get worked up about something we can't do anything about it. We exploit our bodies too much, and this boy, he fell! He told me he had a disordered life: alcohol, drugs, sex. How can you get involved in so many things?

In addition to reading the Scripture, there is also the offering of fellowship, money, and devotional aids.

> We don't leave him lonely. We give them what we can, we give them our little grain of sand, like God has given us. We give them something monetary or motivational in the faith, like a rosary or an inspirational pamphlet.

The group goes week after week to visit all the Latino patients in the hospital. And week after week they pray, read Scripture, and offer words of support as well as material objects such as a rosary, a pamphlet, or a picture of *la Virgen de Guadalupe*. The Word of God functions like a window, or a touchstone to realms of divine mercy and power. They rarely quoted Scripture, but their frequent references to it suggest that, while biblical content was important, that it also played an iconic role, functioning as a portal to the holy. One wonders if the well-developed imaginal and symbolic sensibility of Latino Catholicism has been expanded from images of saints, *la Virgen*, and the Crucified Christ to include the Bible. If so, it allows Scripture to be read in both cognitive and devotional realms, both as propositional content and as symbolic reference to a realm beyond the propositional. This way of reading Scripture through which they hear God "speaking in their hearts," coupled with charismatic corporate worship, prayer, and song, fuels their ministry with the sick.

As is in all forms of Christianity, the vulnerability to idolatry in a piety focused on "the Word of God" is that God's Word is conflated with the words of the Bible. In these more literalist readings of the Bible, the believer can become overly confident in their knowledge of the mind and will and ways of God. Such an inflated confidence can result from an overidentification of the Scripture and God's Word. The risk is that there would be a failure to recognize the historical nature of biblical texts and the historically situated nature of all acts of reading. Without a consciousness of the inevitable interpretive lenses we bring, for good or ill, the reader loses an appropriate humility about the possibility of direct access to the mind of God.

Care for the Sick Is a Testimony to What God Has Already Done for Us When We Were Sick

Most of the members of the group that visit the hospital are former recipients of the group's care. When they spoke of their ministry, it was with a passion to pass on a great gift that they had themselves received. They spoke with humility of when they had been weak and in need and how they had been encouraged and sustained by the group. It is a ministry sustained by deep gratitude for what they had already received. "[We visit the sick] as a testimony to what the Lord has given us." One group member who had received the care of the group previously, told the story of what they had done and concluded,

> If we all understood what God provides to us, then we would be visiting the sick with a cup of milk and a piece of bread. The sick need the love of God and to be able to find the trust and confidence in the Lord.

After her story a man added, "Experiences like hers, each one of us has a story like that. And it motivates us to be on this path." Faith demonstrated during illness "manifests God" and is a "testimony" to others who are sick that it is possible to maintain faith in God even during the hardship of illness.

> When we are the sick person, and we are testifying, God is manifest through us, because I can talk about my suffering. If I [only] talk about the sickness of my brother, I'm not feeling the illness. But if I talk about *my* pain, and I try to give praise to Jesus, it is because Jesus has allowed me. Otherwise, I would be crying and angry. And how can I help anyone else? I can't help anyone else. I have to tell my brother that I trusted, and I'm not feeling well and I still trust.

In the final analysis, ministry to the sick also heals the caregiver. Both the caregiver and the care receiver are enriched by the ministry.

> When I brought the Word of God to the sick, I would say that I was going to bring them that strength. But I actually experienced the opposite, to my own surprise, which was that I was the one that would be healed at the end. Because God has granted the opportunity to hear and to see the testimony of those who have been healed. And that has made me stronger in my faith. So that is why I say what I do is nothing compared to what God has given to me.

When discussing their motivation to care for the sick, the members of the group did not speak of Christian duty, the mandates of Scripture, or the moral responsibility of the strong to care for the weak. Rather the primary motivation was their own experiences of weakness when they experienced the mercy and grace of God. They ministered out of experiences of human weakness and divine power.

The risk of idolatry in this belief-practice is that visiting the sick would be repayment for God's grace, which corrupts the notion of grace as a gift freely given. If the actions were a form of payment for a debt to God, it would then be seen as a necessary step in the completion of the correct God-human interaction, and thus impinge on the sovereign freedom of God to grant mercy when and where God pleases, independently of human responses of acts of recompense.

CONCLUSION

I pulled up to a small, one-story house and heard Mexican *ranchera* music coming from a nearby car. I was there to interview a woman that Father Jorge had recommended to me as a person who had received the care of the group that cares for the sick. She had not known of the group until she was hospitalized during a difficult pregnancy. During her long stay in the hospital, she met several members of the group who gave her a rosary and visited her regularly. At one point she made a *promesa*, promising to give her son a particular name if he was born healthy. When he was born a healthy eleven pound boy, she fulfilled that promise. She then joined the caregiving group. She told me, "They did so much for me, and I want to do the same for others: to help them, raise their self esteem, and make them so they are not feeling down."

As she told me her story, her now three-year-old son was happily playing, showing me photos of his family. The story has a happy ending, but life remains difficult for this family. Her husband works very hard. He would not return home until 10 p.m. that night from his restaurant job. She spoke of his stress while supporting their family. He was also sending money to Mexico regularly, to both her family and his. As I looked at her and saw how pregnant she was now, it seemed that life was only going to grow more difficult when their infant girl arrived in a month. Up on the mantle were a couple of *veladoras* that she lights regularly. As I left, I wondered if this woman would soon be in a new phase in the cycle of giving and receiving. She began her history with the group as a receiver, then in gratitude became a giver, and perhaps now she would return to a season of receiving their care. Her life seemed to be a vivid expression of the mutuality and interdependence of the body of Christ as it is meant to be manifest.

CONCLUSION

A PRACTICAL THEOLOGY OF CARE
FOR THE SICK

INTRODUCTION

*J*ohn Swinton's helpful book on the uses of qualitative
research in practical theology begins his practical theological inquiries with a description of the "situation."[27] If I were to
describe the situation where this inquiry begins, it would be this:
churches caring for the sick in this diverse and changing small
city. To this situation I bring several questions. What are the
varieties of beliefs and practices regarding illness and the care
of people who are ill? What do they do and believe in relation to
the reality of human frailty? Most important, what do they have
to learn from one another?

To study these churches, I have employed the ethnographic methods of individual interview, focus group, participant observation, and the collection of material objects in
order to answer these questions. From this material, I identified
"belief-practices," units of assumptions and behaviors that characterize these churches. These belief-practices cannot be fully
understood "flatly," simply as they are manifest in the present,
no matter how "thick" the description is. They are manifesta-
tions of a deep past. Therefore this study includes a history of
the individual congregation, its denominational history, and

185

converging theological threads from the past. Finally, each congregation is situated within the power structures of this city, state, and nation, particularly as they are designated by race. Therefore a description of the belief-practices in relation to local and national distributions of power, particularly regarding health, is included.

The central fruits of this study, the identified belief-practices, are presented in three moments. First, an "empathetic description" in which they are presented on their own terms, with judgment withheld as much as possible. Second, they are given an "appreciative interpretation" when I offer a reading of them from my particular theological perspective. Finally, I offer a "cautionary warning" regarding ways they might be vulnerable to universal human impulses toward idolatry. The last two moments are unapologetically from a particular theological stance. At this point, I will articulate the theological stance shaping these questions and the fruits of this research.

FINITUDE: CENTRAL THEOLOGICAL ISSUE

The theological category most relevant to this study is finitude. Each of the belief-practices can be understood as connected in some way to questions of human finitude.

Trials of Human Finitude

Each congregation has developed belief-practices to deal with the *trials of bodily finitude*. Toward that end, they all provide such practical help as meals and transportation. They also all provide presence in visits to the sick at home and in the hospital. They all pray for people who are sick. Yet each specializes in what they believe is the primary form of God's presence to the sick and how they, as a church, mediate it. At Healing Waters Church, healing is the primary way they mediate God's presence to people facing the trials of human finitude. Through the prayers of the faithful, the strength of the belief, and the channel of particular healers, "God is going to move"; God will heal the sick.

It is also firmly believed that the prayers of the faithful can heal the sick in the Latino ministry with the sick at Our Lady of Durham, and there were accounts of such healings. But this ministry, influenced by the Catholic charismatic movement, is focused on the dual activity of prayer and bringing the Word of God to the sick, particularly when they are in the hospital. The Word includes both comfort and enjoinders to be faithful in piety and lifestyle. Scripture, prayer, and words of encouragement are the primary ways that the group at Our Lady of Durham seeks to mediate the presence of God to people struggling with the trials of bodily finitude.

First Downtown Church seeks to mediate God's presence through the support of "the community." The interpersonal bonds of sustaining presence, care, and ongoing commitment are described as the primary way God is present during the trials of bodily fini- tude. Again, both practical help and words of prayer and Scripture are also part of First Downtown Church. The most emphasized way of mediating God is, however, in the realm of the intersubjective.

God's Relation to the Finite

Each congregation's belief-practices also deal with the question of *God's relationship to the finite*, God's relationship to the created order. In the case of illness, it is a matter of God's relation to the sick body and to material objects that mediate God's presence to the sick body.

At Healing Waters Church the sick body is the site of God's healing power. God intervenes directly and heals the sick body. God invokes praise in the people who respond with fully embodied prayer as they engage in a holy dance. The moving, active bodies in worship serve as icons to the God who moves and who acts in healing, transforming ways. Material objects, such as healing oil, prayer handkerchiefs, salt, and herbs, as well as the body of the healer, are channels for God's power.

At Our Lady of Durham, God uses the sick body as an occa- sion for growth in one's faith. Illness calls us back to our faith and cleanses us of our sin. The pain and suffering of the body bring us closer to the crucified Christ. Material objects such as rosary beads and statues and pictures of Jesus and the Virgin of Guadalupe are viewed as holy objects that aid in that process.

At First Downtown Church, the body is only indirectly the site of God's healing power. God's healing power is manifest primarily through modern medicine, though the emphasis on the mystery and unknowability of God leaves claims about the mode of God's healing action somewhat open ended. Because of the strong Protestant, iconoclastic Reformed tradition, members have a spare historical corpus of material objects to call upon in times of illness. However, they have improvised with cards and letters and created such "sacred objects" as prayer shawls, paper hands, quilts, flowers, and customized T-shirts to communicate divine sustaining presence.

Relative Access to Finite Goods

Each congregation's belief-practices reflect a negotiation of *relative access to finite goods* accessible through social power—such goods as health care, housing, jobs, and status. At Healing Waters, where relative access to finite goods has historically been limited, particularly access to medical care, there is greater confidence in extra-biomedical forms of healing. Furthermore, in African American communities there is greater suspicion of the reliability of biomedicine in the wake of such injustices as the Tuskegee Syphilis study.[28] The church and its healers are the locus of trust and confidence.

At Our Lady of Durham, where many are in the U.S. without legal papers, there is great effort to meet the material needs of the sick. Calling cards and financial contributions are part of their ministry. In addition, many of the Latino members of Our Lady of Durham have been driven by poverty to leave their families and come to the U.S. in order to earn money to send back home. When they become sick, they are isolated from loved ones—border crossings are difficult and expensive and prevent family members from traveling to the U.S., as well as preventing the sick from returning home to convalesce. The visitation ministry is acutely aware of this particularly painful consequence of being an undocumented worker, and they provide their bodily presence to the sick as a way to address the need for comfort and nurture during illness.

At First Downtown Church, where there is greater relative access to material goods, such as the offerings of biomedicine, there is greater confidence in the effectiveness and trustworthiness of medical care. Unlike Healing Waters, there is little talk of invoking God's power to heal the sick. Unlike Our Lady of Durham, there is little talk of offering financial assistance, though when there is a need for financial support for an individual or family, members quietly come forth with donations. While most First Downtown members are not in financial stress, their relatively greater access to the finite goods of society renders them vulnerable to the isolating effects of wealth. These effects are meliorated by the congregation's emphasis on interpersonal support during illness. The American "pursuit of loneliness" is disrupted by this community (Slater). The support is in the form of affirming communal bonds and expressions of sympathy rather than material offerings.

Because illness is a vivid instantiation of the reality of human finitude, the theology that drove these questions and gave shape to my interpretation of them is one that gives ample weight to a consideration of human finitude. Below is a theological account of illness as an instantiation of finitude, as a time when human finite existence comes to the fore. This account is heavily influenced by the work of Edward Farley.

A Theological Account of Illness

Finitude. Illness highlights human finitude. In the experience of illness our finitude is experientially in the foreground, not in the Freudian sense of fear of death at some future time, but in the sense of experiencing the body as fragile and finite in the present. The sick come face to face with vulnerability to injury, bacteria, and faulty DNA, with the reality that bones break with impact, and our flesh tears when penetrated. One who saw the devastating effects of her chemotherapy says, "I looked near death." She continues, "To have such a thing happen to your body, even briefly, is to see your own mortality rising up to greet you, like one of those gaudily dressed skeletons in a medieval dance of death" (Hooper, 118). Illness underscores finitude.

Finitude refers not only to bodily mortality and fragility but also to limited emotional capacity, limited abilities to understand or predict, limited powers to cure, limited control over what is most precious, limited capacity to adjust to new circumstances, limited power to protect the beloved. When healthy, these ever-present limits often recede in the jumble of areas where there is some degree of control. But when illness descends, these limits are thrown into relief. Illness strips any illusion of unlimited human power to control or predict the future.

Goodness. Though finite, vulnerability and fragility are no indicators of an inherent lack of goodness. Human beings are created good in our finitude. There is nothing inherently sinful about our fragility as finite creatures, nothing inherently sinful about our vulnerability to illness. The measure of our fragility is no measure of our sin. The materiality of our bodies and of the rest of creation is in no way tainted, bad, or sinful. In fact, for some, illness is the occasion for affirming the goodness of our bodies because they recognize that *bodies matter*; they are not a regrettable aspect of human life but a good and necessary one. Illness can be the occasion for affirming the plenitude and blessedness of the body and a rejection of the notion that the body is an unfortunate vessel for what is the true essence of humanity, the spirit. During ill health the body comes to the fore and its necessity and pleasures become apparent in their absence.

Not only is the body good but the rest of material creation is good as well, which brings the sick a multitude of sources of healing and palliation. Those who are ill know the goodness of material creation in its offerings that are both "useful and pleasurable" (Farley, 1990, 149). The created order offers the fruits of human medical and technical knowledge. The senses reveal the exquisite beauty of the world, its creatures, life forms, and widely varied landscapes. Human beings see, hear, touch, and perform bodily symbols of God's love and transforming power in the visual arts, music, dance, ritual, and myriad sacred material objects. In the touch of a loved one or a healer, in the affection and compassion given and received through bodies, the goodness of the material world unfolds.

Desire for Safety. During an illness, many deep human desires come to the fore. First and foremost, there is the desire for safety, a desire to survive and be restored to full health and vitality.[29] Beyond mere survival, there is also the desire to be safe from pain, from mutilation, from permanent damage. There is a desire for not only bodily safety, but also emotional safety, safety from humiliation, abuse, and dehumanization. Many report the indignity of illness, the embarrassment of dependency, the lack of control of bodily functions that violates social etiquette, the unpredictability of the body's needs, the unwelcome eruption of evidence of the body's demise. People in pain report feeling humiliated when the reality of their pain is called into question. A physician writes of his patients' embarrassment over describing pain:

> The patient believes that any attempted description is necessarily unhelpful, or an acclamation of weakness and petulance. *She senses that her pain is always doubted, partially disbelieved*: if the pain is invisible, it must be trivial or imaginary or evidence of hysteria. Speaking of pain makes patients feel sullen and *embarrassed*. (Stein, 30, emphasis added)

In Margaret Edson's play *Wit*, the main character is an accomplished English professor who discovers she has advanced ovarian cancer. During the beginning stages of her aggressive treatment, she retains her verbal facility and cognitive agility as she holds forth eloquently from her hospital bed. Suddenly, midsentence, she lurches forward and vomits. Her infirmity erupts onto the scene, from some place impervious to any intellectual powers. It is humiliating to the distinguished professor. Her illness was beyond any control by her "wit." Under conditions of a lack of control, the sick person is especially vulnerable to abuse, humiliation, and manipulation.

During illness, the desire to be safe from both physical demise and emotional injury runs deep, and this desire is not always fulfilled.

Desire for Relationship. Illness also frustrates the deep desire to stay connected to one another. Close relationships are challenged by illness for many reasons. Illness is a season of nonreciprocal relation when the person who is sick is often not able to return empathy or acts of kindness or to do daily chores. The capacity to fulfill requirements of parenting or the chores of a household is diminished. Furthermore, illness strains one's internal resources of tolerance, patience, flexibility, and forgiveness that are so necessary for the interpersonal domain. Time to attend to one's illness can mean the sick person is experienced as self-absorbed and self-centered, which can be trying on relationships. Yet this is often when the nurture, unconditional attention, and practical aid of a relationship are most required. A deferral of their own desires is often required from loved ones. These interpersonal stresses are exacerbated when financial resources are limited.

Arthur Frank describes a particular deformation of relationships, where both the sick and their family and friends labor to fulfill the social expectation that good cheer is a moral norm for being a "good patient."

> Society praises ill persons with words such as *courageous, optimistic,* and *cheerful.* Family and friends speak approvingly of the patient who jokes or just smiles, making them, the visitors, feel good. . . . No matter what the actual odds, an attitude of "You're going to be fine" dominates the sickroom. Everyone works to sustain it. But how much work does the ill person have to do to make others feel good? (1991, 64, emphasis in original)

Frank describes a bargain, a deal, forced on the sick.

> To be ill is to be dependent on medical staff, family, and friends. Since all these people value cheerfulness, the ill must summon up their energies to be cheerful. Denial may not be what they want or need, but it is what they perceive those around them wanting and needing. This is not the ill person's own denial, but rather his accommodation to the denial of others. . . . We have to decide what support we need and what we must give others to get that support. Then we make our "best deal" of behavior to get what we need. (1991, 68)

Beyond interpersonal stresses and deformations is the essential loneliness of illness, the inaccessibility, the unshareability of the experience of the sick person no matter how great the empathic powers of another. There is something essentially isolating about "the kingdom of the sick" (Sontag, 3). Again, Stein describes the experience of illness.

> There is a particular alienation that illness brings. I have come to understand that the ill person's distance from others is the most profound experience of illness, and that this sense of otherness—of loneliness—is more common in illness than any other emotion, and more dangerous and disturbing. (Stein, 11)

Stein describes the poignancy of hospital visits to a patient named Charlie.

> He read worry and fatigue on the faces of friends and family members and realized that his pre-illness relationships with these visitors had shifted. In their attempts to care by being overly sweet, the well made him feel separate and different, exacerbating the feeling he'd had when his body deserted him. He wanted to be the same; they treated him differently. Visitors bring flowers and look around for a place to hide their concern. Charlie had suddenly understood the term "visiting": living apart, he was in one place, visitors arrived from another, and in the brief interlude of "visiting hours," they could not know where he had come from. (186)

Illness is often a season of heightened awareness of the limits of all human relationships, the deep knowledge that our desire for full intimacy, our need to be fully known, and our need for complete emotional availability from the other will never be met by another human being.

Desire for Truth. In addition to the frustration of the desires for safety and relationship, illness also frustrates the deep desire for the truth, for explanations for illness: Why me and why at this time? There is a strong need to have the answers, for the complete truth of self, other, the world, and God. There is often a desperation to render intelligible the incomprehensible: the threat of decay and death. There is a desire for an underlying logic or predictability to the universe that renders suffering and threat controllable and predictable.

Patients search for medical explanations. One woman had been to four doctors who each interpreted her severe pain differently.

> "I wanted to put all of these professionals in one room and listen to them argue with one another," she said. ". . . Even if the answer at the end of the argument is, '*Your pain will never go away,*' it'll be a relief." (Stein, 43, emphasis added)

The desire for the truth is not only for medical explanations, but also for theological and spiritual ones, not only *what* is happening to my body, but *why* is it happening? What kind of a world do we live in such that this makes sense? What is the ultimate landscape of the universe such that this experience is consistent with the greatest power that is the power of love? Yet the desire for full disclosure of the truth of life's mysteries is never fulfilled, and the illness experience emphasizes that fact.

Illness frustrates these God-given passions for safety, for relationship, and for truth. During illness it becomes clear that, though they may be satisfied to a degree, none of them will ever be completely fulfilled. Humans experience "desire that ever exceeds its fulfillment" (Farley, 1990, 123). During illness, it is clear that no one will ever be perfectly secured from harm; no love will ever completely fulfill the need for intimate connection; no human knowledge will disclose the complete truth of things. During illness, we know a certain degree of safety, relationship, and truth, but the world is still experienced as "an offering and a withholding" of these objects of our passions (123). We know the world as a "mixture of satisfactions and sufferings" (121). A gulf always remains between our passions and their fulfillment.

Tragedy. This gulf between our deep desires and their actual fulfillment is the definition of tragedy. We are given the good gift of life with its exquisite offerings of love, goodness, and beauty, yet we fall sick, grow old, and die. We are created with a passion for connection and intimacy, yet our loved ones die, or, through no one's fault, relationships grow cold and wither. In relationships that do survive, our limited time, energies, and emotional capacities mean our loved ones never receive all they need from us. We are created with a thirst for truth, for an understanding of ourselves, one another, the world, yet the full truth will never be disclosed; we will always live with partial truths, hazy sight, and a degree of distortion. Tragedy is an integral part of human life, and the human experience of illness is an expression of it.

But tragedy is not a result of sin. Nor does tragedy cause sin. There is a strong element of tragedy in illness, an element that is neither the result of sin nor the cause of it.[30] Like all complex, lived human experience, illness is never only tragedy. Sin, whether individual or corporate, is always present in the experience and the response to illness. But adding the category of tragedy offers the ill a way to talk about what is broken in the world, what is awry, what is not God's will, *without calling upon the category of sin to interpret their illness.*

Christian biblical and theological tradition has linked sin and sickness, offering individual sin as an explanation for individual illness.[31] Tragedy is an extremely important addition to the repertoire of interpretive categories for understanding illness. To claim the tragic elements of illness challenges the traditional and simplistic direct association of sickness and sin. Many who suffer from illness not only suffer from the illness symptoms, as well as its fear, loneliness, and humiliations, but they also suffer from *the belief that this state of things is their own fault.*[32] They believe they deserve it. They live with a punishing and disempowering guilt. Tragedy as a "meaning scheme" for illness decouples the centuries-old, tight theological connection of moral failure and illness.[33]

Awareness of Tragedy. While tragedy is not the occasion for sin, human anxiety created by our *awareness* of our vulnerability to tragedy *is* its occasion. At all times, at some level, we are *aware* that nothing in all creation will ever completely satisfy our desires for safety, for relationship, and for the truth. During illness, consciously or unconsciously, we *know* that nothing can guarantee our healing. We know that our relationships are under greater pressure during illness and that the essential loneliness of illness can never be removed. We know that we will never have the full truth of our illness, its cause and course, or what will reliably heal and palliate.

In short, we are capable of recognizing our "unavoidably imperiled future" (Farley, 1990, 124).

Anxiety. This awareness gives rise to a core human anxiety, a "timbre of discontent" with which we live at all times, and it is intolerable (Farley, 1990, 123). It is excruciating. This anxiety is not the same as clinically defined anxiety; rather, it is a deep existential dread. This existential anxiety is the occasion for sin. Mere fragility is not the occasion of sin, nor is the tragic gulf between our passions and their fulfillment its occasion. Rather it is the intolerable anxiety created by our *awareness* of this gulf that is the condition for sin. During illness, this deep anxiety surfaces to a greater extent than during times of health. Though existential anxiety cannot be collapsed into the sort of fear experienced by the sick, nevertheless a deep dread of the void, of nonexistence, can fuel the felt fear of people who are ill. Stein tells us of the varieties of sources of this fear.

> For many patients, there is the fear of the unknown, the fear of making wrong turns and bad choices, of being separated from companions and of traveling alone, of humiliation, of getting into something they can't escape. (71)

He describes the experiences of two of his patients, Luke and Mrs. R.

> Luke possessed nothing but terror; he was experiencing nothing beyond a mere sense of existing. He couldn't pin down his terror, and it preoccupied and troubled him: it was pinning him down and isolating him. (86)

> Terror has a physical aspect. Some mornings [Mrs. R.] woke up shaking. Other mornings she ground her teeth to get through to noon. Her swallowing sounded loud and distinct. She reported the smell of sweat, the scent of terror, was vaguely repellent during the week she waited for her heart operation. (88)

The combination of vulnerability and a lack of control is a particularly potent for generating anxiety. Luke, the patient described above, discovered his terror was rooted in a fear of the anesthesia required for surgery. Stein reminds us, "Anesthesia depends on the competence of others: the patient must completely give over control. Going under signals the end of vigilance and self-protection, the fundamentals of patienthood. Patients must agree to trust blindly, to let others take over this concern of theirs." People who are sick often experience this anxiety-producing combination of fragility and powerlessness.

Again, the fears experienced by the ill are not identical to the excruciating existential anxiety that is the occasion for human sin. But the fear associated with illness and the underlying dread within human finitude can coalesce during illness with the possibility that each might intensify the experience of the other.

Idolatry. In the presence of this dread, the temptation for the ill is to turn to a piece of the finite creation for ultimate security. They experience the strong lure of idolatry. When one is sick there are many candidates for idols: the medical regimen, diet and exercise, or medication can all function as idols, that which will secure us from the contingencies of finite human existence. Arthur Frank writes about "the disciplined body," one of several ways to live as a sick body.

> The disciplined body-self defines itself primarily in actions of
> *self-regimentation*; its most important action problems are those
> of control. The disciplined body experiences its gravest crisis in
> loss of control. The response of such a body-self is to reassert
> *predictability* through therapeutic regimens, which can be ortho-
> dox medical compliance or alternative treatment. In these regi-
> mens the body seeks to compensate for contingencies it cannot
> accept. (1995, 41, emphasis in original)

The desperate attempt to restore control and predictability through regimentation is one form of idolatry when it displaces love of God and love of neighbor. The partial truth of modern medicine can be worshipped as the whole truth, its relativity and limitation unrecognized.

There are religious candidates for idolatry as well: correct performance of religious ritual, prodigious Bible study, and acts of righteousness and self-sacrifice. "The healing power of prayer" can become a particularly seductive form of idolatry. Rather than worshipping God who is the recipient of prayers, claims about the power of prayer to heal can unintentionally lure the believer to trust in the exercise of human capacities to believe and to pray rather than in the power of God who is beyond all human knowledge and control. A particular person in the form of a healer, a shaman, a guru, can be also be worshipped as the source of salvation. Religious icons as windows to the God beyond the created order can slip into a place of devotion that only the divine should occupy. Relationships once recognized as imperfect yet very good and full of love can be transformed to idols that are expected to erase all traces of the loneliness of pain and suffering.

Illness is the occasion for claiming many of the goods of the creation as more than good, rather as gods, as sources of ultimate security, as idols. Each of these pieces of the finite world that are part of God's good creation can be transformed from a good to a god.

What is the nature of idolatry? What does it do to us? *Is it more than simply a waste of time?* Is it more than worshipping something inert that cannot offer health, love, or the whole truth? The Psalmist claims that idolatry is more than just a waste of time, something that does not work. The idolater becomes like the idol.

> [5]They have mouths, but *do not speak*;
> eyes, but *do not see.*
> [6]They have ears, but *do not hear*;
> noses, but *do not smell.*
> [7]They have hands, but *do not feel*;
> feet, but *do not walk*;
> they *make no sound* in their throats.
> [8]*Those who make them are like them;*
> *so are all who trust in them.*[34] (Psalm 115)

Beyond simply rendering us dull, wooden, and lifeless, the traditional Christian view of sin adds the element of bondage. In order to stem the dread successfully, to address our excruciating anxiety, our idols require "unqualified loyalty" (Farley, 1975, 143). For the idol to work, it "must be invested with perfection, powers, and marvelous attributes," and we must "preserve these perfections from relativity and criticisms" (143). Therefore, self-deception is an element of idolatry. We lie to ourselves and to others about any evidence of the idol's limits, about its inability to save us. The impulse to protect the idol, serve the idol, is strong because great things are at stake: *we believe the idol is what will save us.* Therefore, the contingent, only partially fulfilling nature of all relationships, all biomedical knowledge, all religious beliefs and practices, all churches and their leaders, is denied when they are rendered idols. We are thus closed to the mysterious, surprising God who is both in *and beyond* the finite and "who is able to do more than we ask or hope for" because our allegiance, focus, and powers of self-deception are harnessed in servitude to our idols.

Furthermore, idols require that obligation to the neighbor be of secondary importance. Our enslavement to the idol means that all other loyalties, obligations, and loves become of less importance than service to the idol. With idolatry, "insecurity is compounded and is transformed into fanaticism and fear and the willingness to do anything to oneself, the other, or to the world" (Farley, 1975, 145).

Not only does service to the idol require that we renounce the neighbor, but our relationship to the finite that we have idolized is deformed. We turn from loving the earth in its finitude and goodness to attempting to wrench salvation from it, and this distorts and damages our relationship to it. The loved one, the friend, the fellow church member is transformed from the fellow fragile creature, a cotraveler, to the object who will save us, a thing whose purpose is to secure us from harm, to alleviate our anxiety. Idolatry not only means that we ignore or renounce the other, it can also mean that we make fellow human beings into idols whose purpose is to save us. Our fellow creatures become a means to an end, a potential source of redemption from the pain and vicissitudes of human finitude. During illness, an unhealthy dependence on caregivers can develop. When these loved ones do not offer salvation or redemption (i.e., when they fail as gods), the person struggling with illness can be enraged with them for their failure to save. The idolatrous relationship between a person and the piece of the finite world that they worship as god is unhealthy for both.

Redemption. Given this construal of the human predicament as it is displayed in illness, what then is redemption? Redemption is *freedom from* bondage to idolatry and *freedom for* the neighbor. Whatever language is used—a relationship with God, dependence on God, saved, born again, knowing Jesus, letting go and letting God, being founded—in redemption there is a primordial transformation that addresses anxiety's grip, anxiety's drive to self secure through idolatry. It is only God who can break the bonds of idolatry and turn our face in love toward our fellow fragile neighbor. God is the only one who can free us to love passionately the created, finite world without being enslaved to it. God is the only one who can free us to love the neighbor as a person who shares our vulnerability and finitude. God is the only one who can create and sustain a community of the mutually supportive and vulnerable.

Of course we cannot tease out a sequence to the elements of redemption, as though in time, there is first an amelioration of anxiety and then, second, we are able to turn from the idol and turn to the neighbor. Judith Hooper, a breast cancer survivor, describes a sacred moment in which release from the fear of finitude and the embrace of the stranger are coupled. She remembers sitting in a surgeon's waiting room where "the atmosphere was thick with fear, it seemed to me, and I was too terrified to read."

> To transform my fear into something else, I tried mentally sending love to the other patients in the room. I especially focused on one incredibly ancient woman slumped in a wheelchair in the corner. . . . Her craggy face, the hollows of her cheeks, the deep solitude of her eyes, seemed to contain all the beauty and pain of the universe. Meditating on her, my heart seemed to open in the midst of hell and fill with an overwhelming love for my fellow creatures. I was, for a brief moment, in what Native Americans call the "sacred hoop," and my fear was gone. (Hooper, 137)

In this excerpt, we see that the release from anxiety is not always the prerequisite for the turn to the neighbor, but that the opening to the neighbor as beloved cocreature, a beloved sister in finitude, gave rise to the release from the bondage of fear. To behold in the face of the other a cherished fellow traveler on this limited journey on earth can usher in the central act of redemption: a loosening of the anxiety that drives us to turn from neighbor and turn to idols for salvation. What she calls the "sacred hoop" we might call an instance of redemptive existence, whose impact is far beyond "a brief moment" but can have lasting import for the living of the rest of our days.

Courage. With redemption comes the gift of courage: the capacity to love the world in full knowledge that it is fragile and cannot save us (Farley, 1990, 146). Redemption transforms our relationship with the finite world. We are able to love the world passionately and all that dwells therein without demanding that it save us. It involves living with the truth that the whole creation is vulnerable and limited, including our bodies and the bodies of those we love, yet giving ourselves in deep love to the creation. It involves recognizing the futility of trying to save oneself, of self-securing, through a piece of the finite world, recognizing that nothing in this world will fully satisfy our deepest desires. At the same time, courage means *risking loving that world anyway.* Courage means a willingness to risk venturing into the world, relationships, love, always aware that they cannot save us, *and* in full knowledge that their fragility means they can be lost at any time. It is a willingness to engage the world fully aware that it is good and beautiful, but fragile in its goodness and beauty. It is a willingness to seek to know and to understand without ever fully knowing or understanding anything. A life without courage is one where we "withhold commitments, avoid decisions, and restrict our activities to environments that are confirming, predictable, and safe" (150).

Courage is displayed in illness when one strives toward finite forms of safety, relationship, and truth all the while recognizing their relativity, their fragility, their partial nature. When one vigorously seeks health by the means of biomedicine, diet, exercise, meditation, yoga, massage, while recognizing them as part of the created order and therefore limited and not sources of ultimate salvation, then one is exercising courage. In the giving and receiving of deep love for friends and family, for fellow creatures who are one with us in their limits, knowing that they can never redeem us ultimately, we see courage. In the exercise of ritual, individual and group prayer, communal worship, meditation on Scripture while knowing full well that none of these religious practices guarantees access to the divine, one sees courage. In the continued pursuit of one's vocation, the persistent dedication to following one's God-given call in spite of being hampered by illness, we see courage. In the willingness for one's illness to be transformed into an avenue of connection to others who are suffering, in the openness to the solidarity possible through shared pain and debility that opens one to the eternal Thou, we see courage.

Judith Hooper displays deep courage within finite existence in the love and celebration for her limited time on earth.

> When you walk this earth on borrowed time, each day on the calendar is a beloved friend you know for only a short time. You know that a year is 365 days, twelve months, four seasons, two equinoxes, two solstices, thirteen full moons, thirteen new moons—each of them a celebration. (136)

Finitude, vulnerability, tragedy, and fragility will not go away in relationship to God, but we find the courage to live and love within finitude, and the ability to reach out with love for our fellow, fragile creatures. This courage is a form of power to live in a world where there is much we cannot control, where we do not really know the future, where our deepest passions will never be totally fulfilled, and where those that we love will die. Yet we have the ability to continue to live with openness to God and to one another. The first moment in redemption is the courage to live in a tragic world without self-securing idols. It is not submission, belief, obedience, or accepting the acquittal for our guilt. It is courage.

People who have suffered illness discover that courage is not only a capacity or a virtue that one stores away to be brought out of the closet and put to use when illness strikes. But it is also something that illness occasions; illness can give birth to courage. And thus, illness is the occasion for a great gift.

> Of course, no one would willingly choose cancer. But healthy people can never really know what we cancer patients have. We have a gift beyond measure, the daily bliss of being alive. Forced by our illness to walk through the valley of the shadow of death, like any woman who gives birth, we get to experience the sacredness of life. (Hooper, 137)

Finally, courage culminates in solidarity with others who are suffering. Frank describes this kind of courage as "communicative body-self" (Frank 1995, 48). This self "sees reflections of its own suffering in the bodies of others . . . , wants and needs to relieve the suffering of others . . . , [and] never belongs to itself alone but constructs its humanity in relation to other bodies" (49).

Even strangers who suffer are included in the community of suffering humanity with whom the courageous are in solidarity.

> [O]ne side effect of cancer is an instant, indelible, searing empathy for victims of misfortune everywhere in the world. Flood victims in Bangladesh are truly your brothers and sisters; their pain reaches out to you across the continents. (Hooper, 115)

A CHURCH THAT EVOKES COURAGE

The above is an articulation of the theology in my discernment and discussion of the three churches' belief-practices. Given this theological account of illness, what is the church that fosters courage in the experience of illness? This church will have the following features.

A church where human finitude is regularly and mutually acknowledged.

Some consider the "denial of death" to be a universal human impulse: Death is so unthinkable, so irrational, that human beings refuse to accept mortality (Becker). One writer, limiting his

comments to Western culture, goes as far as saying that the modern denial of death is so extreme that it is considered "forbidden"
(Aries, 85). Arnold J. Toynbee focused the denial of death in one
particular Western country, the U.S., when he famously wrote,
"Death is un-American, an affront to every citizen's inalienable
right to life, liberty, and the pursuit of happiness" (Toynbee, 131).
Multiple social and cultural realities reinforce the denial of death
in America. Death is hidden, sequestered in institutions away from
the home; traditional exposure to cycles of birth and death in farm
life is limited to less than 10 percent of the population; attendance
at funerals is down significantly in the last twenty years (Leming
and Dickinson, 169). "Is it any wonder that Americans find it difficult to cope with death when it is experienced infrequently, is
highly impersonal, and viewed as virtually abnormal?" (169).

A church that is faithful in its care for the sick makes the
acknowledgment of human finitude a regular part of church life.
It is a place where evidence of human finitude can be openly discussed without fear of criticism or even exclusion. The church will
recognize that we all die, that we all are physically limited, and
that we share vulnerability as creatures. The pains, dependencies,
and limitations of illness can be brought into the accepting arms,
the compassionate heart, of the community. Not only will physical limits be recognized, but also emotional limits and the limits
of knowledge and skill are acknowledged. Furthermore, there is a
mutual recognition of need for care, an understanding that caregiving is reciprocal, that no one group is chronically the receiver of
care, and that no one group is the invincible, invulnerable, permanent giver of care.

In this church it is safe to be physically imperfect. It is not a
place where youth, fitness, and beauty are idealized as moral goods.
To have cancer, to be disabled, to live with a mental illness, and to
die are not denied, un-American, forbidden, or in any way stigmatized. Cancer's baldness, wheelchair logistics, dulled sight and
hearing, celiac dietary requirements, autism's social particularities,
the strictures of a life with chronic fatigue syndrome, the requirements of life with a colostomy, the specific circumstances needed

to control chronic pain, all of these can be openly shared and discussed without shame, embarrassment, or fear of exclusion.

More than ever, the American view of death is challenged from several directions, including the publication of Elisabeth Kubler-Ross' *On Death and Dying*, the rise of the hospice movement, and a spreading concern for end-of-life care in medical circles. Additional challenges to the denial of death come from nondominant cultures in the U.S. It is being recognized that these generalizations about the fear of death that supposedly characterizes all of humanity, or the West, or American culture, are in fact the dominant Western culture writ large and do not apply to all sectors of the American polyglot.

Mainstream Protestant churches have a great deal to learn from churches that have historically been forced to confront the reality of death. Historically, African American churches have had to respond to premature deaths secondary to poverty, such as hunger and inadequate health care. They have had to respond to violent deaths at the hands of slavemasters, lynch mobs, and those seeking to drive them away from their land through terror. Gang deaths, drug deaths, drive-by shootings, and stray bullets claim the lives of proportionally more members of the African American community. Similarly, Latin Americans have historically suffered from conquest, wars, backbreaking labor, hunger, lack of health care, and high infant mortality. Death as a part of life has historically been thrust upon these populations, and their religious communities have incorporated a well-developed repertoire of responses. Churches in these cultures speak more freely of the fragility of human life. There is greater acknowledgment that all are vulnerable, that we all depend upon God for every breath we take. In the sermon, prayers, announcement, iconography, and open shedding of tears there is regular recognition of our mortality, our finitude, our limitations of health, time, and energy. What Aries generalizes about "Western attitudes toward death" applies to the dominant culture and does not reflect these subcultures, and mainstream churches have much to learn from churches in more marginal cultures.

One effect of the regular acknowledgment of finitude is a well-developed biblical/theological/liturgical vocabulary for speaking of illness, frailty, death, and suffering, *along with* God's faithful, redeeming presence within them. These churches have a map, a narrative, a landscape, a drama, metaphors that embrace both human finitude and God's redeeming power. When members speak of their pain, spoken or unspoken is the understanding that it is a valley of shadow of death *where they need fear no evil for God is with them, and the rod and staff of God will comfort them.* When they speak of their suffering, spoken or unspoken is the connection to the wilderness *and the promised land is ahead, and even now manna awaits them.* When they speak of abandonment, speaker and listener hear Jesus' words from the cross *as well as Easter hope.*

Healing Waters and Our Lady of Durham spoke openly of God's acts in the midst of illness. They spoke of God's healing, forgiving, calling, comforting, and judging among the sick. Through specific acts of healing, through prayers for forgiveness, through specific ritual actions, God acts. At First Downtown Church, references to God's actions among the sick were more oblique, possibly a reflection of the Reformed churches' reticence about claiming to know the mind of God and possibly a desire to avoid appearing to operate out of a premodern worldview. Again and again, at First Downtown people referred to God in diffuse terms, "in the community," for example. A clarity and confidence about the knowledge of precisely how God's redeeming power is related to illness was less evident. Language for God's relation to illness was not wholly absent, however, and compelling images came from the pulpit. The theology, images, and narratives of God's transforming power in relation to illness were present, but more subtle, and congregational members referred to them less frequently.

A church that recognizes that the body is in the realm of God's redeeming power.

Arthur Frank speaks of the "colonization" of the body by medical discourse (1995, 10). Rather than the ill telling their own illness stories that include hopes and fears, loves and losses, healing and brokenness, feelings and family connections, their stories are told from the perspective of biomedicine, the unfolding of particular treatment regimen and the responses of invading bacteria, malignant cells, and blood chemistry. Many mainstream Protestant churches' illness accounts have similarly been colonized by biomedical discourse. In many churches announcements regarding the welfare of a person who is sick may include blood counts, surgical procedures, and drug doses, for example. The story of a person's illness is a medical story. As discussed earlier, the body has become the province of the doctor and the hospital, while the spirit is the responsibility of the pastor and the church, a development that impoverishes both medical and spiritual care.

For many in mainstream churches, the realm of God's redeeming power is limited to the spirit, mind, emotions, attitudes, and outlook, and God's power to transform, heal, redeem is excluded from the materiality of the body. Such a bifurcation of the body and spirit is mitigated in churches from nondominant cultures. Mainstream Protestant churches can learn from their neighbors that the body is not only responsive to the interventions of the doctor, but is also the site of divine action. God calms, soothes, palliates, nourishes, and heals the body. God may be present in chemotherapy and the surgeon's knife, but also in the anointing oil and the healing hands of the minister. Jesus healed the sick and the church has engaged in healing practices from its earliest days. In remembering that healing is not confined to cure, and that healing can also be the gift of learning to live, love, and serve faithfully while remaining ill, the encounter with other churches brings a call to recover the body as the realm of God's redeeming power.

At Healing Waters Church, healing practices were a regular part of the church's ministry, both from the pastor and lay leaders. In Our Lady of Durham, there were multiple references to God's direct healing of the sick, because they had asked for it in prayer, because the group had prayed for them, or because they had repented and returned to God. At First Downtown, there were occasional references to a person who lived longer than expected, who got well unexpectedly, or who "beat the odds"—references delivered with a raised eyebrow that suggested something more was going on. Healing was understood in terms of restored relationships, finding meaning or purpose in illness, or the strength to go on.

A church that knows that any part of finite creation can mediate
God's presence.

Protestant iconoclasm has left its churches vulnerable to a flattening of the material world that hints at a form of Docetism where physicality is incompatible with God. We are cautious about associating the finite with the divine, worried that something might capture our loyalties and lure us into idolatrous attachments that turn something finite and partial into something infinite and absolute. We therefore have a spare material culture and few habits that continually open the world as a place "shimmering with the divine." We are a form of religion that provokes no infusions of the Holy Spirit to move our bodies into ecstasies of tongues and dance; we live with no home altars with profusions of flowers, lights, foods, ribbons, pictures of loved ones, and images of saints and the very Mother of God that might move us to core connections with the divine, a place that the cognitive and rational does not access. Certainly the cognitive and the rational are realms where God can be revealed, but they do not exhaust the multiple faculties of the human being; there are other dimensions of our humanness that can be brought to the "temple of the most high."

Biblical scholar Marcus Borg has criticized the dominance of a "supernatural theism, [which] emphasizes only God's transcendence and essentially denies the immanence of God. God is other than the world and separate from the world. God is 'out there' and not here" (26). Is this a result of the Barthian thought that arose to prominence in the wake of the devastation of the Second World War, a reaction to nineteenth-century liberalism's confidence in progress toward the kingdom of God here on earth? Did the emphasis on the transcendence of God in neo-orthodoxy that shaped so many clergy educated in the mid-twentieth century strip mainstream Protestantism of modes of connecting intimately with God through sacred objects, images, and rituals of healing that call upon sight, hearing, touch emotion, and body? Farley, asking why worship has lost mystery, frames the question like this: "Is it the outcome of a long historical process in which the Protestant movement failed to discover how to relate proclamation to *sacramentality*, how to retain both *iconography* and *iconoclasm*?" (emphasis added).

Whatever the historical origins, can the feel and taste of the materiality of the bread and wine of communion and the water of baptism bear the weight of the human desire to commune with God with heart and soul, mind and body, ear and eye, hand and foot? Referring to distinctions between the analogical imagination and the dialectical imagination drawn by David Tracy, theologian Mary McClintock Fulkerson says,

> It is not that Presbyterians don't believe that God has entered the world in a profound and transformative way. Indeed, we attach God's presence to some worldly things. The Biblical text and the preached Word are the places we insist that we will find God. . . . However, our sacramentalism seems shrunken in comparison to that of the analogical imagination, with its marvelous capacity to perceive similarities with the divine everywhere. . . . The dialectical imagination must rush quickly in to negate what it affirms, always on the lookout for self-promotion and false idol making. Calvin's *finitum non capax infinitis* is a deeply felt sensibility. (2006, 3–4)

Fulkerson refers to a "thin, austere religiousness" (4). The question of how to retain both iconography and iconoclasm is important as Protestants seek to care for the sick in a way that enables courage in the face of finitude.

An important question for Protestants, particularly in the Reformed tradition, is this: How do we affirm God's presence in and through the created order without making idols of it? We have been too cautious, too reticent in our attempts to identify the sacred, the holy, the divine in our midst. As a result we have become inured, dulled to knowledge of the world that is "charged with the grandeur of God."[35] Our correct suspicion of any identification of the finite with God has led us to an unfortunate embrace of a post-Enlightenment "disenchantment" of the world.

Disenchantment has been described as

> a concept preeminently introduced to social scientific discourse by Max Weber to describe the character of modern, secularized society. Such literal renderings as "de-magi-fication" or "de-mysteri-zation" probably more accurately render the meaning in current American usage. At one point, Weber described the condition as a world "robbed of gods." Disenchantment does not mean simply that the world is no longer seen as filled with angels and demons, but that the category "mystery" is negatively valued: Mysteries are to be solved by science, technology, or other this-worldly efforts. Modern people do not wish to "enter into" mysteries but to conquer them; moderns similarly are pleased when they can say, for example, that a particular event or condition is "no longer mysterious." (Swatos)

One effect of the disenchantment of the finite has been a separation of ill health from the redeeming power of God. Before the modern era, believers had no problem holding together the reality of their illness with the reality of God. They may have believed God had caused their illness for pedagogical or punitive purposes, and they may have believed that God would cure them in due time, or choose not to. Whatever the case, there was no question that the state of their health was intimately connected to God's actions in the world. Yet with the modern era and the notion that the mind and body are separate entities, the mind, or spirit, became the province of the church while the body and its well-being came under the care of science or medicine. Many have claimed that this split between mind and body has had unfortunate consequences, among them, dehumanizing medical paradigms of care for the sick and the divorce of faith from illness.

We see various efforts to bring back together the reality of God with the reality of illness. Popular culture has offered various options. One scholar speaks of "alternative spiritualities" and "new religions" as signs that the West is searching for ways to reenchant the world. Included in his examples is the recognition that there is also a lunge for ways to reenchant the care for the sick.

> [A]n example of what I would understand to be "reenchant-ment" (i.e., alternative forms of spirituality which evolve, cease to remain purely private concerns, and start to "reenchant" the wider culture) is the way a typically modern, science-based pro-fession such as medicine is now witnessing a rise of interest in what used to be called "New Age healing." (Partridge, 50)

There is great interest in the work of Harold Koenig who researches the correlation between religiosity and health (2001). Others, such as Larry Dossey, attempt to use the scientific method to show that "distance prayer" has positive health effects on the sick (1993). There are multiple New Age gurus, such as Deepak Chopra, who provide a mixture of pseudo-Eastern philosophy, pseudo-science, and personal anecdote to establish a healing con-nection between mind and body (1990). The traditional congrega-tion has also adopted programs that bring faith and health together. Nurses trained in modern methods of medical care are showing on church payrolls, having established themselves as parish nurses (Sybil Smith). Some larger churches have diet and fitness pro-grams for their members. Particularly within African American churches, there are Health Sundays when there are blood pressure and diabetes checks and tests for prostate cancer. Other churches have focused on charismatic healing ministries. These widely var-ied approaches can all be understood as strategies for knitting back together the human body and the mystery of God, or human flesh and God's spirit, or corporeality and God.

In the nonwhite, non-Anglo churches I studied, there was a deep awareness of mystery that imbues the finite, not only bodies, but also material objects of all sorts. Many pieces of the material world can be avenues to communion with God. Of course, this includes a deep awareness of the mystery of God's power to heal the body, heal relationships, and give strength, peace, courage, fortitude; God's power is not just accessible through medicine, therapy, and intellectual efforts. There was also an awareness that there is much that is good that we cannot control, predict, or understand, that is of a different order than the rational. Experiencing this mystery in all its goodness and power has to do with letting go, with loosening our grip, and receiving it. Grasping, reasoning, explaining, and planning have their place in the life of faith, but not in the encounter with mystery.

The multiple sacramentals of the Catholic church, the splashing of a new truck with holy water, an image of Our Lady of Guadalupe pulled from a wallet to be blessed by the priest, and a home altar where the sacred and the mundane mingle are all examples of the plenitude of sacred objects in the Latino Catholic tradition. These objects are evident in the Holiness church as well: the foot washing, herbs, oil, water, and prayer handkerchiefs all formed links with the sacred. At the Protestant church there were many improvised objects that served as touchstones to the divine. Certainly the multiple cards and letters functioned sacramentally. Also the T-shirts, quilts, prayer shawls, cutout hands, and flower bouquets comprising flowers from many members' gardens are examples of a congregation creating sacred objects when in a tradition that is suspicious of icons.

A church that abounds in grace so that members are free
to acknowledge their sin.

Illness is often the occasion of intense guilt and self-blame, not only for the cause of the illness but also for difficulties imposed on loved ones. The centuries of association of sin and sickness coupled with a newer "lifestyle correctness" can intensify feelings of guilt. "For many Americans, especially the more affluent, [health] symbolizes *a secular state of grace.* As such, good health constitutes affirmation of a life lived virtuously" (Leichter, 359, emphasis added). In such circumstances, whether or not a person is personally responsible for his or her illness, a congregation where there is an abundance of grace and the mutual acknowledgment of the universal human need for God's grace is a place where the sting of appropriate or inappropriate self-blame is ameliorated. In a church where grace flows freely, the common self-blame of the sick is met with grace.

Therefore, not only does the faithful church have language for the tragic and God's redeeming presence within tragic existence, but it also has facility in the rich language of sin and grace along with the concomitant practices. This is a church that refuses the idolatry of health, or healers, or healing prayer, and there is the freedom to acknowledge and confess such idolatry in a community where grace is abundant. In this church there is the freedom to name sin, moral failure, and selfishness, and the idolatry that is at their core. As with the freedom to acknowledge our finite time, energy, and emotional and physical fortitude, in this church there is the freedom to acknowledge sin without fear of ostracism, rejection, shaming, or humiliation. This is a church where one can be not only physically imperfect, but morally and spiritually imperfect as well. This is a church abounding in grace, second chances, and the mutual recognition of vulnerability to the lure of the idol.

All of the congregations in this study rejected the notion that illness was God's punishment for sin. Both First Downtown Church and Our Lady of Durham were particularly robust in their rejection.

*A church whose worship and personal piety involve fullness
of the human being.*

Bodies. If illness is often an experience of the body's betrayal, then worship that involves the whole body is a way of reclaiming the body for the glory of God. When the body is an instrument of worship and praise then it is no longer simply a traitor. There are ample biblical precedents for bodies in motion praising God: Miriam's unfettered dancing before God after crossing the Red Sea, David before the ark of the Lord, and the psalmic descriptions of praising God with timbral and dance. The bodies of the sick become, then, not only that which is in decay and pain, but also instruments of praise, testimony, and communion with the saints gathered before God. When the body is both "ritual subject and object," as discussed earlier, it is recognized that we both *are* and *have* bodies:

We are bodies, as subjects our bodies praise God, and, we use them as objects that invoke the praise of our fellow worshippers.

Feelings. Our traditions of worship and prayer include not only praise and gratitude, but also lament. Worship and communal prayer in classes, groups, and homes can be a place for the free expression of despair, pain, anguish, abandonment, rage, and fear. Whether in Sunday morning worship or where two or three are gathered, prayer is a place where it is safe to bring the full range of feelings and doubts and places of loneliness and alienation before God and God's beloved community. People in pain can bring all of who they are with the confidence that they will not be abandoned, criticized or, worst of all, ignored. Tears in worship will not be a source of embarrassment or shame but an invitation to the prayers and compassion of others. Expressions of grief will not be stigmatized; nor will there be a silencing, stifling rush to premature comfort. Expressions of anger in worship and prayer will not be judged as sin, lack of faith, or psychological fragility, but as a sign of trust in God's invitation to come just as we are.

Patrick Miller reminds us that "laments are the voice of human existence before God." He tells us that lament holds together both "fearfulness in the face of the contingency of life" and "trust in the ground of our being" (20).

> [So] to recover the language of lament is to learn to pray as if there is no God around anywhere who can or will do anything about our situation—except possibly to make it worse—*and* it is to pray as if God is always listening and can be trusted to help. (20, emphasis added)

Miller includes a christological interpretation of the psalmic laments. For the Christian, the laments are not only expressions of our deepest fear and deepest trust, but they are always prayers that Jesus also prayed. They are prayers that we share with the crucified and risen Christ. Miller tells us that "as the lament becomes the voice of Christ," three things happen (22). One, our prayers that are of both god-forsakenness and trust in God are authorized by none less than Christ himself. ". . . if our Lord can pray that way, so can we" (22–23). Second, to pray the laments "in the voice of Christ" is to remember that we are not alone in our suffering and that our suffering is connected to Christ's. "So our human suffering is terrible and our cries still roar, but neither the suffering nor the cries are the last word" (23). Finally, to hear in our own lament the voice of Christ, we are also able to hear the cries of lament of the other. "So finally Christ teaches us a new mode of crying out, a crying out in behalf of others" (23).

This not simply a description of worship with human emotion, such as tears, exuberance, and rage, though it certainly includes that, but a description of something deeper even than emotion. This is rather a description of worship where deep calls to deep, a place where the depths of the human heart and soul call to the depths of the mercy of God, a place for the worshipper to be ready to receive the voice of God calling to the lost, lonely, and suffering. It is a place for the knowledge that is beyond emotion and cognition, that place beyond earthquake, wind, and fire where the still, small voice is heard, and the place of profound assurance that nothing can separate us from the love of God in Christ Jesus our Lord.

Praise and Adoration. The faithful church also fosters corporate worship and private prayer that includes expressions of deep gratitude for all that has been received. The human being as recipient of God's gifts, including the gifts of life and health, and the human being as giver of thanks, has been challenged by modern notions of human beings as being responsible for their own self-making, as discussed above. Goizueta described the modern *homo faber*, the human as maker:

> Like a sculptor in the presence of a block of marble, the modern subject looks upon the world, and indeed, upon his or her own life, as raw material to be chiseled and molded into a shape in accord with his or her designs. (1990, 87)

Conceiving of the human being as *homo faber* in the instance of illness places the sick person in a painful position. Not only are they failures because they are unable to be productive members of society, a primary source of value, but they are also placed in the position of being responsible for "making" their body well. The pressure is to "make" a healthy body.

Goizueta has spoken to us of a contrasting view of human beings as *homo ludens*, the one who receives and gives thanks. In a congregation where the self is defined first and foremost as the one who receives God's good gifts and responds in gratitude, a subject position the ill can always occupy, they will not be judged as a failure or as inadequate by virtue of their illness. In Healing Waters Church especially, the human as one who praises is particularly emphasized.

Congregations that emphasize mission, service, and liberation can lose the primacy of a celebrative expression of praise and gratitude in worship and personal prayer. The notion of *homo faber* can co-opt the core Christian habits of mission and liberation by severing these activities from their rightful grounding in gratitude for what God has already done. The human being as "maker" can merge with the Christian call to "make" the world a better place to the detriment of the primacy of a stance of gratitude. Goizueta warns of an "identification of *religious* action with ethical behavior, 'doing good' [emphasis in original]" in churches with strong outreach sensibilities (87). He speaks of the risk in service-oriented churches of losing a sense of "religious action [as] aesthetic or affective behavior, 'feeling' at one with God, others, one's self, the environment, the cosmos, and so on" (87).

> If *doing good* requires commitment, engagement, struggle, self-sacrifice, and suffering, *feeling at one with the cosmos* calls for celebration, enjoyment, pleasure, recreation, "being" rather than "doing," and so forth. (87, emphasis added)

The stillness and richness of the "commas," the transitions between elements of worship, in mainstream Protestant worship offer space for the mystery of God to be heard. The majesty of the organ and classical music bespeak the transcendence and grandeur of God. The vulnerability of mainstream Protestant worship, especially in the Reformed tradition, however, is that the emphasis on the Word of God in Scripture and sermon is extended to an emphasis on the structured, read, and spoken Word throughout the service, at the expense of symbol, image, ritual movement, song, color, and candle, as well as variety in posture, light, and voice.

A church that recognizes social sin in the origins of many illness.

The best predictor of ill health in America is poverty (Kahn, 1311). One researcher wrote, "Until the end of life, at each age every downward movement in income is associated with being in poorer health" (James, 108). He summarized current research on the association of lower socioeconomic status with poor health: "the evidence that this association is *large* and *pervasive* across time and space is *abundant*" (108, emphasis added). In order to undo the accusatory message that individuals deserve their maladies because they have sinned, the faithful church will recognize the link between social sin and illness. The effects of racism on access to health care, the links between social powerlessness and obesity, and the negative health effects of air pollution are examples of the connection between social sin and individual ill health. A shared acknowledgment of the link between ill health and social sin ameliorates inappropriate individual guilt. Furthermore, this connection can mobilize efforts to redress social injustice.

The churches in this study all had language for powers beyond the individual that were associated with illness. They all had medical accounts of illness, but some in the African American church also spoke of illness as the devil's work, and some in the Latino group spoke of demons and evil spirits, categories for evil from beyond the individual that are connected to illness. While it could not be claimed that these churches explicitly linked social sin and the devil, demons, or evil spirits, they nevertheless recognized that sole individuals are not completely responsible for their ill health. A few in the Euroamerican church spoke of social sin, but it was not predominant. For most, medical accounts were the prevailing explanation for illness.

A church in solidarity with the sick beyond the church.

The faithful church will recognize that we are also called to care for the sick outside the church doors. The boundaries delineating inside and outside the church are permeable. The stranger is welcomed, and if the stranger chooses to remain outside the walls of the church, he or she remains in the purview of the neighbor. This church will recognize that a core dynamic of the Christian faith is moving into the world. Of course we care for one another, but it is always in order to equip the saints to go out into the world to liberate and serve all God's children. Included in the very definition of wholeness is engagement in the world. Neither a person nor a congregation is whole until their gaze is turned to the other outside the boundaries of self, family, church, race, ethnicity, and nationality.

Like First Downtown Church, intrinsic to the church's identity will be service to the world. This congregation has engaged in care teams for people with AIDS and financially supported ministries with health care components. The hospital visitation group at Our Lady of Durham visited every Latino patient in the hospital, not limiting their care to members of their church. Healing Waters Church offered care to individuals who sought it, and members offered sustained care to nonmembers as a part of their ministry. Each of these congregations showed evidence of permeable boundaries and consciousness of the stranger as neighbor.

A church accepting of difference.

The faithful church is accepting of difference, open to the varieties of ways of being human. It freely includes as full members of the body of Christ those who would be considered "other:" the transsexual, the person with Down syndrome, the undocumented Latino worker, the prisoner on weekend leave. In this context, it is safe to be different. This safety benefits everyone because everyone, including people considered "normal," or "conventional," has some aspect of their lives that would be defined as "different," in some way. Otherness touches everyone: an alcoholic parent, a brother who committed suicide, abuse as a child, the scars of rape, and most people try desperately to keep this otherness a secret. However, in the church where the obvious "others" of the world are embraced, then everyone can feel freer to bring out in the open their secret places of otherness, or difference. In this church, it is safe for the older, traditional woman to grieve openly the death of her grandson with AIDS. The wife can bring her drooling husband with Alzheimer's to Sunday morning worship, and grieve the gradual loss of her presence.

At Healing Waters Church, the stranger who was an addict was surrounded by prayer and praise by the women of the church during the service. Our Lady of Durham Church is a multicultural congregation with people from all over the globe, including Africa, Latin America, Central America, South America, India, and Southeast Asia. At First Downtown Church lesbian and gay members are embraced as full members of the body of Christ. Like all human institutions, each congregation has its blind spots and places of exclusion. Yet each also has its places of subverting the line between insider and outsider, normal and abnormal, friend and stranger.

A congregation that fosters courage among the sick is a place where the regular acknowledgment of finitude means it is safe to share one's bodily frailties with other members. It is a place that affirms the reality that the material, finite body is the site of God's transforming power. Furthermore, not only the material, human body is the site of God's acts, but the whole material world can provide links to God. In this congregation, not only is physical frailty acknowledged, but also the human tendency to turn to the finite world as a source of salvation, the human tendency toward idolatry. In this church, grace flows freely, and members can confess and renounce idolatry without fear of criticism or abandonment. In the worship life of the church, the worshipper worships with the fullness of the human being, body, feeling, and intellect. In so doing, the sick body is redeemed from being only that which is in pain and decay to being an instrument of praise. This congregation will be a place where powers beyond the individual are acknowledged as sources of illness, powers such as social sin. Finally, it will be a place that welcomes the stranger into the circle of care and that recognizes that faithful care for the sick is not confined to the church family, but to all whom Christ loves, the world.

NOTES

Introduction

1   "Little Bit of Light," Carol Johnson, Noeldner Music.
2   Chhatrapati Shivaji Terminus, formerly Victoria Terminus, was built over ten years' time, starting in 1878, when British colonial presence held sway in India. My appreciation of this architecture is in no way an endorsement of a western, engulfing colonialism that gives an obligatory nod to local styles. Rather it is meant to be an example of how one style can retain its identity while being transformed by another.
3   Elaine Scarry speaks of the "translation" of the body's pain into "insignia of power" and "an emblem of the regime's strength."
4   See Ralph Ellison's *The Invisible Man* (New York: Random House, 1947).

Chapter 1

5   All the names of the pastors, caregivers, and care receivers have been changed.
6   Dr. Willie Jennings, personal communications.
7   It was Howard Thurman who first observed slaves' affirmative answer to this question. *Deep River: Reflection on the Religious Insight of Certain of the Negro Spirituals* (New York: Harper, 1955).
8   Raleigh, N.C.: Protestant Episcopal Church in the Confederate States, 1862.

9   I am grateful to Tammy Williams for this insight.
10 "Contract" language is from Wacker, 2001.
11 Wacker quotes G.B.S. [Studd], in *Upper Room*, November 1910, p. 134.
12 Wacker quotes John G. Lake, "Transcription of John Lake's Diary," November 29, 1910, typed, p. 11, Flower Pentecostal Heritage Center, Assemblies of God, Springfield, Mo.
13 First formulated by William A. Clebsch and Charles R. Jaekle, *Pastoral Care in Historical Perspective* 4 (Northvale, N.J.: Jason Aronson, 1975) 8–9.
14 Tammy Williams (2002) defines three understandings of healing in African American churches: care, cure, and holism. Healing Waters Church largely emphasizes healing as cure, but at times speaks of healing in terms of both care and holism.

Chapter 2

15 The scholar is Glenn Hinson, who wrote about the Hanford family in *Fire in My Bones: Transcendence and the Holy Spirit in African American Gospel* (Philadelphia: University of Pennsylvania Press, 2000).
16 Further description of African American women's historical commitment to health work in churches and in clubs often associated with churches can be found in Susan L. Smith's *Sick and Tired of Being Sick and Tired: Black Women's Health Activism in America, 1890–1950* (Philadelphia: University of Pennsylvania Press, 1995).

Chapter 3

17 Northern and Southern Presbyterians remained alienated longer than other denominations. Though the Methodists and Baptists also split at the time of the Civil War, the Southern Presbyterian Church was the only one to remain a regional, southern denomination at the time of the Civil Rights movement. The Methodists had reunited in 1939 and the Southern Baptists had moved beyond the boundaries of the south to become a national denomination (Alvis, 6).
18 This long, complex, yet still grammatically correct sentence is also an indication of the way Presbyterians articulate their ideas carefully and according to precise rules of grammar.

Chapter 4

19 Intuition and personal conversations hint at gender differences in the desire to maintain distance during illness. One can speculate that men do not want to appear weak and women do not want to appear

unattractive. Men fear being seen as frail; women fear being seen as ugly.

20 This, of course, begs the question of a parallel history of damage at the hands of much received tradition. It could also be argued that women, lesbian and gay people, and the Jewish people are some groups whose suffering has been intensified because of Christian tradition.

21 Robert Wuthnow lists various motivations for caring offered by interviewees. They include biblical tradition, compassionate feelings, self-interest, and obligation to serve others. The First Downtown Church people emphasized a subset of biblical tradition: Jesus' example. (*Acts of Compassion: Caring for Others and Helping Ourselves* [Princeton: Princeton University Press, 1991], 49ff.)

Chapter 5

22 This was explained to me by Teresa Berger.

23 *Pollero* is another word for *coyote*, a person hired to transport illegal immigrants across the U.S. border.

24 Cora Bass, *Sampson County Yearbook, 1956–57* (Clinton, N.C.: Bass, 1957), 84. On the Confederate memorial, see S. L. Smith for the United Daughters of the Confederacy, North Carolina Division, *North Carolina's Confederate Monuments and Memorials* (Raleigh, N.C.: Edwards & Broughton, 1941) 117–18; Joseph Abram Ryan, "The March of the Deathless Dead," *Poems: Patriotic, Religious, Miscellaneous* (New York: P. J. Kennedy, 1898), 76–77.

Chapter 6

25 *Andale, hijo* is an informal imperative that a mother would give to a child, somewhat like "come on, get moving."

26 See "Changing Faiths: Latinos and the Transformation of American Religion," Pew Hispanic Center and Pew Forum on Religion and Public Life.

Conclusion

27 Proposed earlier by Edward Farley. See his "Interpreting Situations: An Inquiry into the Nature of Practical Theology" published in *The Blackwell Reader in Pastoral and Practical Theology*, edited by James Woodward and Stephen Pattison (Oxford: Blackwell, 1999).

28 For a discussion of the effects of this experiment where African American men died of untreated syphilis, see Emilie Townes' chapter, "'The Doctor Ain't Takin' No Sticks': The Tuskegee Syphilis Study," *Breaking the Fine Rain of Death: African American Health*

Issues and a Womanist Ethic of Care (New York: Continuum, 1998).

29 My discussion of the desire for safety, relationship, and truth is based on Farley's notion of "passions" subjectivity, of the interhuman, and for reality. See Farley, 1990, 101–3.

30 Illness is never one thing. Like all things human, illness can be interpreted as a muddled mixture of sin, redemption, tragedy, and many others. Tragedy is one term among others in our theological anthropology that includes finitude, sin, tragedy, redemption, and others.

31 See especially *Morality and Health*, edited by Allan Brandt and Paul Rozen; and *The Wages of Sin* by Peter Lewis Allen.

32 I am indebted to Duke University Medical Center psychologist Susan Hazlett for the insight that the primary form of suffering she sees in her practice is from patients' belief that their suffering is their fault.

33 "Meaning scheme" is a category from Aaron Beck's writings on cognitive therapy.

34 I am grateful to William Sloane Coffin's work for pointing out the relevance of this particular Psalm. *Letters to a Young Doubter* (Louisville: Westminster John Knox, 2005), 13.

35 Gerard Manley Hopkins, "God's Grandeur," from his *Poems* (London: Humphrey Milford, 1918).

BIBLIOGRAPHY

Albrecht, Daniel E. 1992. "Pentecostal Spirituality: Looking Through the Lens of Ritual." *Journal of the Society for Pentecostal Studies* 14. 107–25.

Alexander, Bobby C. 1989. "Pentecostal Ritual Reconsidered: Anti-Structural Dimensions of Possession." *Journal of Ritual Studies* 3. 109–28.

———. 1991. "Correcting Misinterpretations of Turner's Theory: An African American Pentecostal Illustration." *Journal for the Scientific Study of Religion* 30. 26–44.

Allen, Peter Lewis. 2002. *The Wages of Sin: Sex and Disease, Past and Present.* Chicago: University of Chicago Press.

Alvis, Joel. 1994. *Religion and Race: Southern Presbyterians 1946–1983.* Tuscaloosa: University of Alabama Press.

Ammerman, Nancy. 1997. "Golden Rule Christianity: Lived Religion in the American Mainstream." In *Lived Religion: Toward a History of Practice,* edited by David H. Hall. Princeton: Princeton University Press. 196–216.

Andrews, Dale P. 2002. *Practical Theology for Black Churches: Bridging Black Theology and African American Folk Religion.* Louisville, Ky.: Westminster John Knox.

Anzaldúa, Gloria. 1991. *Borderlands: The New Mestiza = La Frontera.* San Francisco: Aunt Lute Books.

Aries, Philippe. 1974. *Western Attitudes Toward Death: From the Middle Ages to the Present*, translated by Patricia M. Ranum. Baltimore: Johns Hopkins University Press.

Ashby, Homer U., Jr. 2003. *Our Home Is Over Jordan: A Black Pastoral Theology*. St. Louis, Mo.: Chalice Press.

Baer, Hans A., and Merrill Singer. 2002. *African American Religion: Varieties of Protest and Accommodation*. Knoxville: University of Tennessee Press.

Becker, Ernest. 1973. *Denial of Death*. New York: Free Press.

Borg, Marcus. 1997. *The God We Never Knew: Beyond Dogmatic Religion to a More Authentic Contemporary Faith*. San Francisco: HarperSanFrancisco.

Brandes, Stanley. 2003. "Is There a Mexican View of Death?" *Ethos* 31. 127–44.

Brandt, Allan, and Paul Rozin, eds. 1997. *Morality and Health*. New York: Routledge.

Butler, Lee H. 2000. *A Loving Home: Caring for African American Marriage and Families*. Cleveland, Ohio: Pilgrim Press.

Capossela, Cappy, and Sheila Warnock. 2004. *Share the Care: How to Organize a Group for Someone Who Is Seriously Ill*. New York: Fireside.

Capps, Donald. 1993. *The Depleted Self: Sin in a Narcissistic Age*. Philadelphia: Fortress.

———. 1995. *Agents of Hope: A Pastoral Psychology*. Minneapolis: Augsburg Fortress.

Carroll, Jackson W., and David A. Roozen. 1990. "Congregational Identities in the Presbyterian Church." *Hartford Seminary Review of Religious Research* 31. 351–65.

Castillo, Ana, ed. 1997. *Goddess of the Americas: Writings on the Virgin of Guadalupe*. New York: Riverhead Books.

Chafe, William J., Raymond Gavins, and Robert Korstad, eds. *Remembering Jim Crow: African Americans Tell About Life in the Segregated South*. New York: The New Press, 2001.

Chopra, Deepak. 1990. *Quantum Healing: Exploring the Frontiers of Mind/Body Connection*. New York: Bantam Books.

Clebsch, William A., and Charles R. Jaekle. 1975. *Pastoral Care in Historical Perspective.* Northvale, N.J.: Jason Aronson.

Coffin, William Sloane. 2005. *Letters to a Young Doubter.* Louisville, Ky.: Westminster John Knox.

Couture, Pamela. 2003. "The Effect of the Postmodern on Pastoral/Practical Theology and Care and Counseling." *Journal of Pastoral Theology* 13. 85–104.

Dixon, Barbara M. 1994. *Good Health for African Americans.* New York: Crown.

Dossey, Larry. 1993. *Healing Words: The Power of Prayer and the Practice of Medicine.* New York: HarperCollins.

Dupré, Louis. 1993. *Passage to Modernity: An Essay in the Hermeneutics of Nature and Culture.* New Haven: Yale University Press.

Durham Health Partners, Inc. *A Report to the Major Stakeholders on the Health Status of Durham County.* Synopsis by Andrew Wallace, January 22, 2004.

Edson, Margaret. 1999. *Wit: A Play.* New York: Faber & Faber.

Elizondo, Virgilio. 1980. *La Morenita: Evangelizer of the Americas.* San Antonio: Mexican American Cultural Center.

———. 1994. "Popular Religion as the Core of Cultural Identity in the Mexican American Experience." In *An Enduring Flame: Studies on Latino Popular Religiosity,* edited by Anthony M. Stevens-Arroyo and Ana María Díaz-Stevens. Notre Dame: University of Notre Dame Press. 113–32.

Espín, Orlando. 1994. "Popular Catholicism: A Brief History." In *Hispanic Catholic Culture in the U.S.: Issues and Concerns,* edited by Jay P. Dolan and Allan Figueroa Deck. Notre Dame: University of Notre Dame Press. 308–59.

Farley, Edward. 1975. *Ecclesial Man: A Social Phenomenology of Faith and Reality.* Philadelphia: Fortress.

———. 1990. *Good and Evil: Interpreting a Human Condition.* Minneapolis: Fortress.

———. 1996. *Divine Empathy: A Theology of God.* Minneapolis: Fortress.

————. 1998. "A Missing Presence." *The Christian Century*, 18–25 March. 276–77.

————. 1999. "Interpreting Situations: An Inquiry into the Nature of Practical Theology." In *The Blackwell Reader in Pastoral and Practical Theology*, edited by James Woodward and Stephen Pattison. Oxford: Blackwell, 118–27.

Fett, Sharla. 2007. *Working Cures: Healing, Health, and Power on Southern Slave Plantations*. Chapel Hill: University of North Carolina Press.

Fox-Genovese, Elizabeth, and Eugene Genovese. 1987. "The Divine Sanction of Social Order: Religious Foundations of the Southern Slaveholders' World View." *Journal of the American Academy of Religion* 55, no. 2. 211–33.

Frank, Arthur. 1991. *At the Will of the Body: Reflections on Illness*. New York: Houghton-Mifflin.

————. 1995. *The Wounded Storyteller: Body, Illness, and Ethics*. Chicago: University of Chicago Press.

Frazier, E. Franklin. 1963. *The Negro Church In America*. New York: Schocken Books.

Frederick, Marla. 2003. *Between Sundays: Black Women and Everyday Struggles of Faith*. Berkeley: University of California Press.

Fruth, William H. *Where the Money Is: America's Strongest Local Economies,* 2d ed. (Jupiter, Fla: Policom Corp., 1997).

Fulkerson, Mary McClintock. 2006. "Narrative of a Southern White Girl," Words and Knowledges Otherwise. In *The Poetics of the Sacred and the Politics of Scholarship*, vol. 1, dossier 2. http://www.jhfc.duke.edu/wko/dossiers/1.2/contents.php.

————. 2007. *Places of Redemption: Theology for a Worldly Church*. New York: Oxford University Press.

Gilkes, Cheryl Townsend. 1986. "The Role of Women in the Sanctified Church." *Journal of Religious Thought* 43. 124–41.

Gill, Hannah. 2006. *Going to Carolina del Norte: Narrating Mexican Migrant Experiences*. Chapel Hill: University Center for International Studies at the University of North Carolina at Chapel Hill.

Goizueta, Roberto. 1998. " 'Why are you Frightened?' U.S. Hispanic Theology and Late Modernity." In *El Cuerpo de Cristo: The Hispanic Presence in the U.S. Catholic Church*, edited by Peter Casarella and Raúl Gomez. New York: Crossroad. 49–65.

———. 1999. "Fiesta: Life in the Subjunctive." In *From the Heart of Our People*, edited by Orlando O. Espín and Miguel H. Díaz. Maryknoll, N.Y.: Orbis. 84–99.

———. 2002. "The Symbolic World of Mexican American Religion." In *Horizons of the Sacred: Mexican Traditions in U.S. Catholicism*, edited by Timothy Matovina and Gary Riebe Estrella. Ithaca: Cornell University Press. 119–38.

———. 2003. "Our Lady of Guadalupe: The Heart of Mexican Identity." In *Religion and the Creation of Race and Ethnicity*, edited by Craig Prentiss New York: New York University Press. 140–51.

———. 2004. "The Symbolic Realism of U.S. Latino/a Popular Catholicism." *Theological Studies* 65. 255–74.

Griffith, R. Marie. 2004. "Maintaining Empathy." *Harvard Divinity Review* 32. 18.

———. "Material Devotion—Pentecostal Prayer Cloths." http://www.materialreligion.org.

Harrell Jr., David Edwin. 1975. *All Things Are Possible: The Healing and Charismatic Revivals in Modern America*. Bloomington: Indiana University Press.

Hinson, Glenn. 2000. *Fire in My Bones: Transcendence and the Holy Spirit in African American Gospel*. Philadelphia: University of Pennsylvania Press.

Hoge, Dean R., Benton Johnson, and Donald Luidens. 1994. *Vanishing Boundaries: The Religion of Mainline Protestant Baby Boomers*. Louisville, Ky.: Westminster John Knox.

Holloway, Karla. 2002. *Passed On: African American Mourning Stories*. Durham: Duke University Press.

Hooper, Judith. 1994. "Beauty Tips for the Dead." In *Minding the Body: Women Writers on Body and Soul*, edited by Patricia Foster. New York: Doubleday. 107–37.

Hopkins, Gerard Manley. *Poems*. London: Humphrey Milford, 1918; Bartleby com, 1999. www.bartleby.com/122/ (accessed February 24, 2009).

Hunter, Rodney, et al. 1990. *Dictionary of Pastoral Care and Counseling*. Nashville: Abingdon.

Hurston, Zora Neale. 1983. *The Sanctified Church*. Berkeley: Turtle Island.

John Paul II. 1978. Address to the Sick and Health Care Workers, on occasion of his first visit to "Gemelli" General Hospital, 18 October; *L'Osservatore Romano* (Italian Edit.), Thursday 19 October. 1–2.

———. 1999. "Ecclesia In America." January 22. Mexico City. http://www.vatican.va/holy_father/john_paul_ii/apost_exhortations/documents/hfjp-ii_exh_22011999_ecclesia-in-america_en.html (accessed January 25, 2008).

Jones, Dorothy Phelps. 2001. *The End of an Era*. Durham: Brown Enterprises.

Jones, Serene. 2002. "Graced Practices: Excellence and Freedom in the Christian Life." In *Practicing Theology: Beliefs and Practices in Christian Life*. Dorothy Bass and Miroslav Volf, eds. Grand Rapids, Mich.: Eerdmans. 51–77.

Kahn Robert S., Paul H. Wise, Bruce P. Kennedy, and Ichiro Kawachi. 2000. "State Income Inequality, Household Income, and Maternal Mental and Physcial Health: Cross Sectional National Survey." *British Medical Journal* 321. 1311–15.

Kidder, Tracy. 2004. *Mountains Beyond Mountains: The Quest of Dr. Paul Farmer, A Man Who Would Cure the World*. New York: Random House.

Kleinman, Arthur. 1988. *The Illness Narratives: Suffering, Healing, and the Human Condition*. New York: Basic.

Koenig, Harold. 2001. *The Healing Power of Faith: How Belief and Prayer Can Help You Triumph Over Disease*. New York: Simon & Schuster.

Kubler-Ross, Elisabeth. 1969. *On Death and Dying*. New York: Macmillan.

Leichter, Howard M. 1997. "Lifestyle Correctness and the New Secular Morality." In *Morality and Health*, edited by Allan M. Brandt and Paul Rozin. New York: Routledge. 359–78.

Leming, Michael R., and George E. Dickinson. 1997. "The American Ways of Death." In *The Unknown Country: Death in Australia, Britain and the USA*, edited by Kathy Charmaz, Glennys Howarth, and Allan Kellehear. London: Macmillan. 169–83.

León, Luis D. 1999. "Metaphor and Place: The U.S.-Mexican Border as Center and Periphery in the Interpretation of Religion." *Journal of the American Academy of Religion* 67. 541–72.

———. 2002. "Soy una Curandera y Soy una Católica: The Poetics of a Mexican Healing Tradition." In *Horizons of the Sacred: Mexican Traditions in U.S. Catholicism*, edited by Timothy Matovina, Gary Riebe-Estrella. Ithaca: Cornell University Press.

Leyburn, James G. 1989. *The Scotch-Irish: A Social History*. Chapel Hill: University of North Carolina Press.

Lippy, Charles. 1977. "Sympathy Cards and Death." *Theology Today* 34, no. 2. 167–77.

Madsen, William. 1967. "Religious Syncretism." In *Social Anthropology*, edited by Manning Nash. Vol. 6, *Handbook of Middle American Indians*. Austin: University of Texas Press. 369–91.

Mallard, R. Q. 1892. *Plantation Life Before Emancipation*. Richmond, Va.: Whittet & Shepperson.

Miller, Patrick. 2005. "Heavens Prisoners: Lament as Christian Prayer." In *Lament: Reclaiming Practices in Pulpit, Pew, and Public Square*, edited by Sally A. Brown and Patrick D. Miller. Louisville, Ky.: Westminster John Knox..

Morris, David. 2000. "How to Speak Postmodern: Medicine, Illness, and Cultural Change." *Hastings Center Report* 30, issue 6. 7.

Moschella, Mary Clark. 2008. *Living Devotions: Reflections on Immigration, Identity, and Religious Imagination*. Eugene, Ore.: Pickwick Publications.

———. 2008. *Ethnography as a Pastoral Practice: An Introduction*. Cleveland, OH: Pilgrim Press.

O'Connell, Marvin R. 1984. "The Roman Catholic Tradition Since 1545." In *Caring and Curing: Health and Medicine in the Western Religions Traditions*, edited by Ronald L. Numbers and Darrel W. Amundsen. Baltimore: The Johns Hopkins University Press. 108–44.

Orsi, Robert. 1997. "She Came, She Saw, She Conquered." *Commonweal* 124. 24–25.

———. 2003. "Is the Study of Lived Religion Irrelevant to the World We Live In? Special Presidential Plenary Address, Society for the Scientific Study of Religion, Salt Lake City, November 2, 2002." *Journal for the Scientific Study of Religion* 42.2. 169–74.

Paris, Arthur E. 1982. *Black Pentecostalism: Southern Religion in an Urban World*. Amherst: University of Massachusetts Press.

Partridge, Christopher. 2004. "Alternative Spiritualities, New Religions, and the Reenchantment of the West." In *The Oxford Handbook of New Religious Movements*, edited by James R. Lewis. New York: Oxford University Press. 39–67.

Patton, John. 1993. *Pastoral Care in Context: An Introduction to Pastoral Care*. Louisville, Ky.: Westminster John Knox.

Pérez, Arturo. 1994. "The History of Hispanic Liturgy since 1965." In *Hispanic Catholic Culture in the U.S.,* edited by Jay P. Dolan and Allan Figueroa Deck. Notre Dame: University of Notre Dame Press. 360–408.

Pew Hispanic Center and Pew Forum on Religion and Public Life. 2007. "Changing Faiths: Latinos and the Transformation of American Religion." http://pewhispanic.org (accessed March 10, 2009).

Pinn, Anthony. 2003. *Terror and Triumph: The Nature of Black Religion*. Minneapolis: Fortress.

Prothero, Stephen. 2004. "Belief Unbracketed: A Case for the Religion Scholar To Reveal More of Where He or She Is Coming From." *Harvard Divinity Review* 32. 10–11.

Raboteau, Albert. 1978. *Slave Religion: The "Invisible Institution" in the Antebellum South*. Oxford: Oxford University Press.

————. 1986. "The Afro-American Traditions." In *Caring and Curing: Health and Medicine in the Western Religious Traditions*, edited by Ronald L. Numbers and Darrel W. Amundsen. Baltimore: Johns Hopkins University Press. 539–62.

Riebe-Estrella, Gary. 1997. "Latino Religiosity or Latino Catholicism?" *Theology Today* 54. 512–15.

Rieff, David. 2006. "Nuevo Catholics." *The New York Time Magazine*. December 24. 40–45, 85–87.

Rodriguez, Jeanette. 1994. *Our Lady of Guadalupe: Faith and Empowerment among Mexican-American Women*. Austin: University of Texas Press.

Said, Edward W. 1979. *Orientalism*. New York: Random House.

————. 1994. *Culture and Imperialism*. New York: Random House.

Sanders, Cheryl J. 1996. *Saints in Exile: The Holiness Pentecostal Experience in African American Religion and Culture*. Oxford: Oxford University Press.

Seamone, Donna Lynne. 1998. "Body as Ritual Actor and Instrument of Praise: Verna Maynard's Experience as Praise Leader in the Kitchener Church of God." *Journal of Ritual Studies* 12. 17–26.

Slater, Phillip. 1970. *The Pursuit of Loneliness: American Culture at the Breaking Point*. Boston: Beacon Press.

Smith, James P. 2004. "Unravel the SES-Health Connection." In *Population and Development Review* 30, suppl.: Aging, Health, and Public Policy. 108–32.

Smith, Sybil. 2003. *Parish Nursing: A Handbook for the New Millenium*. Birmingham, Ala.: Haworth.

Smylie, James. 1986. "The Reformed Tradition." In *Caring and Curing: Health and Medicine in the Western Religious Traditions*, edited by Ronald L. Numbers and Darrel W. Amundsen. Baltimore: Johns Hopkins University Press. 204–39.

Sontag, Susan. 1978. *Illness as Metaphor and AIDS and Its Metaphors*. New York: Doubleday.

Stein, Michael. 2007. *The Lonely Patient: How We Experience Illness*. New York: HarperCollins.

Swatos, William H., ed. 1998. *The Encyclopedia of Religion and Society*. Walnut Creek, Calif.: AltaMira Press. http://hirr.hartsem.edu/ency (accessed March 29, 2008).

Swinton, John, and Harriet Mowat. 2006. *Practical Theology and Qualitative Research*. London, SCM Press.

Synan, Vinson. 1971. *The Holiness-Pentecostal Movement in the United States*. Grand Rapids: Eerdmans.

Townes, Emilie. 2001. *Breaking the Fine Rain of Death*. New York: Continuum.

Toynbee, Arnold J., et al., eds. 1969. *Man's Concern with Death*. New York: McGraw-Hill.

Tracy, David. 1987. *The Analogical Imagination: Christian Theology and the Culture of Pluralism*. New York: Crossroad.

Turner, Victor. 1967. *The Forest of Symbols*. Ithaca: Cornell University Press.

Tweed, Thomas A. 2002. "Our Lady of Guadeloupe Visits the Confederate Memorial." *Southern Cultures* 8.2. 72–93.

Vidal, Jaime. 1994. "Synthesis in Iberian and Hispanic American Popular Religiosity." In *An Enduring Flame: Studies on Latino Popular Religiosity*, edited by Anthony M. Stevens-Arroyo and Ana Maria Díaz-Stevens. New York: Bildner Center for Western Hemisphere Studies. 69–95.

Wacker, Grant. 1986. "The Pentecostal Tradition." In *Caring and Curing: Health and Medicine in the Western Religious Traditions*, edited by Ronald L. Numbers and Darrel W. Amundsen. Baltimore: Johns Hopkins University Press. 514–38.

———. 2001. *Heaven Below: Early Pentecostals and American Culture*. Cambridge, Mass.: Harvard University Press.

Watson, Julie. 2006. "Women Risk Rape, Death in U.S. Journey." *Washington Post*, April 27. http://www.washingtonpost.com/wp-dyn/content/article/2006/04/27/AR2006042701169.html (accessed January 8, 2008).

Weaver, Michael S. 1991. "Makers and Redeemers: The Theatricality of the Black Church." *Black American Literature Forum* 25. 53–61.

Weeks, Louis. 1998. "The Incorporation of American Religion: The Case of the Presbyterians." *Religion and American Culture* 1. 101–18.

West, Cornel. 2001. *Race Matters*. New York: Random House.

Williams, Melvin D. 1974. *Community in a Black Pentecostal Church: An Anthropological Study*. Pittsburgh: University of Pittsburgh Press.

Williams, Tammy. 2002. "Is There a Doctor in the House?" In *Practicing Theology: Beliefs and Practices in Christian Life*, edited by Miroslav Volf and Dorothy Bass. Grand Rapids: Eerdmans. 94–120.

Wilson, Joseph R. 1861. "Mutual Relations of Masters and Slaves as Taught in the Bible. A Discourse Preached in the First Presbyterian Church, August, Georgia, On Sabbath Morning, Jan., 6, 1861." Augusta, Ga.: Steam Press of Chronicle and Sentinel.

Wimberly, Edward P. 1999. *Moving From Shame to Self-Worth: Preaching and Pastoral Care*. Nashville, Tenn.: Abingdon.

Wuthnow, Robert. 1991. *Acts of Compassion: Caring for Others and Helping Ourselves*. Princeton: Princeton University Press.

INDEX